Mountain Flowers

Sean Wright

Edited by Paul J. Cumbo

Co-edited by Meghan M. Wright

ISBN: 0615837344
ISBN 13: 978-0615837345

Library of Congress Control Number: 2013912722
Purple Cap Publications: Dillsburg, Pennsylvania
www.purplecappublications.com

First Edition. August 2013

Cover photo provided courtesy of Luna Amelingmeier
Cover design by Molly Wright
This book is also available in e-book format.

For Amber

Editor's Note

I had the pleasure of meeting Bob and Jana Amelingmeier for the first time in January of 2002. I was a twenty-two-year-old, first year teacher at a Jesuit prep school in the DC area. I was on a scouting trip with two colleagues, preparing to lead a group of students on an international service program called *Somos Amigos*. The Amelingmeier family and the Crossroads organization embraced me just as they have so many travelers, teachers, students and soul-searchers.

Twelve years and more than twenty trips to the country later, Jana's wry humor, Marcus' low key smile and Bob's welcoming hugs have become as familiar to me as the pastel Dominican sunsets visible from their kitchen. I've led nearly one hundred students through three to six week immersive service-learning experiences in the central D.R., all of which have concluded with a few days at Crossroads working with their regular outreach programs. Without exception, these few days in the company of such dynamic people—and the poor whom they serve—change my students' lives forever, going a long way toward making them, as the Jesuits are fond of saying, "ruined for life." To walk alongside the poor with the Crossroads family is to take a few steps closer to understanding the plight of global poverty, the intrinsic goodness of the heart amidst struggle, and, indeed, the world we all share—in all its tragic beauty.

You are about to delve into a challenging, engaging story of a young man's personal pilgrimage. Sean Wright's story tells of his journey toward one of life's biggest decisions. It is told with clarity, honesty, and without affectations. That Sean's path took him through a landscape of incomprehensible human suffering makes it only more stark and revealing. His experiences in this wounded part of the world have made an indelible mark upon him. He has galvanized his commitment to organizations that work daily to provide sustenance, hope, and dignity to the poorest population in our hemisphere. One hundred percent of profits from the sale of *Mountain Flowers* will be donated to Crossroads and other charitable programs that alleviate the suffering of the Haitian poor.

It has been an honor to work closely with Sean on the editing of his fascinating story; moreover, it is with genuine gratitude that I thank Jana, Bob, Marcus, and the rest of the Crossroads family for twelve years of friendship and partnership in mission. There are few in this world who do so much for so many—with so little expected in return.

Paul J. Cumbo, Editor
June 11, 2013
Buffalo, New York
Freelance Editing by PJC Services, LLC dba One Lane Bridge Publications
On the web at www.paulcumbo.com

Prologue

On January 12th, 2010, a 7.0 magnitude earthquake struck Haiti. Centered just sixteen miles west of Port-au-Prince, it caused catastrophic damage to the capital. In a matter of minutes, thousands of personal, business, government, and service structures collapsed, leaving many of the region's 700,000 inhabitants in a state of emergency. The newly displaced populace faced injury, sickness, panic, and death while trying to find loved ones, establish new homes, and find enough food and water to survive the brunt of the earthquake's successive impacts.

Hundreds of support groups from around the world responded to the disaster by providing aid in the form of food, water, supplies, medical care, and on-site volunteering. Crossroads, an outreach mission based in Puerto Plata in the neighboring Dominican Republic, was only one of many groups that formed a team and entered Port-au-Prince to assist the injured and provide essential supplies to those in dire need.

This is the story of that experience told through the eyes of one of its volunteers. Some of the names have been changed; however, the events portrayed in the main storyline are the author's recollections of factual events. The story of Lucas and his mother is a combination of fact and fiction, assembled by the author based on the boy's account leading up to the time of their encounter.

One hundred percent of the profits the author makes from book sales will be donated directly to outreach groups like Crossroads to further their ability to help those most in need of it in Haiti and the Dominican Republic.

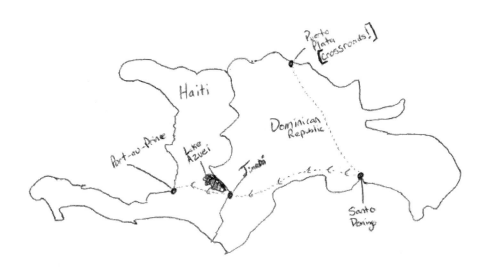

Puerto
Plata
[crossroads.]

Haiti

Port-au-Prine

Lake
Azuei

Jimani

Dominican
Republic

Santo
Doming

Friday, January 15th 2010

2:53am

Jimani, Dominican Republic

"Hold her down!" the doctor yelled as he cut into her. "Keep her calm." Adrenaline pumped at full speed, and the veins jutted from my skin as if screaming to escape. Each movement stirred pain and stiffness in my joints, as if they were made from bunches of dried straw that cracked under each twist and turn. It had been hours. Much more of this and I'd fall apart. I hadn't slept in two days, kept busy with the rigors of the outpost constantly outpacing the team. My mind pushed on through the days fueled by adrenaline and caffeine. I felt drugged and sickly, as if stuck in a dream that persisted throughout the night. My perception of reality blurred and my stomach hardened as I prepared to assist in the surgery room.

I looked down at the patient. She wasn't more than seven or eight. She wore a sky blue dress decorated with pictures of flowers, but it had mutated into something else—a thing soaked in blood from the waist up, caked in red clay and sand. Her skin shone coal black and oily under the lights. It contrasted with her white eyes, which were saturated with bloodshot capillaries in a way that leapt out among the chaos in the room. They darted back and forth as if searching for something they couldn't find, her brown pupils giving pause for moments before hiding behind clenched eyelids. Only fragments of her hair remained. Once it had been neatly braided and decorated with beads, but much was taken forcefully by a chunk of concrete during the first quake and subsequent collapse. Jagged, deep gashes littered her scalp and sizable lacerations revealed parts of her skull.

The outpost had depleted its small supply of anesthetics for pain and pins to set broken bones, but the surgeon's mission at hand remained. He would try to save her life regardless of cost or the path there.

I only knew vague details about how she'd made her way to the outpost. Two days earlier, a piece of metal debris had trapped her arm under its weight as she played in her bedroom. I glanced at it when she first arrived; it was evident that to free her from the lifeless jailer someone had cut her arm hastily just above the elbow with whatever sharp object they found first. Tendons, muscle, and bone tangled with each other at the open end to create a mess of human flesh that crusted over with blood, dirt, and rags. A tattered leather belt had been wrapped tightly around the stump several times in an attempt to hold back the rush of blood that begged to pour out. In the two days it had taken her to reach the outpost, bacteria had sprouted in the opening and transformed everything to shades of yellow and brown. The surgeon needed to remove the rest of her arm to stop the infection. Waiting for anesthetics presented a deadly option.

I found out the next day that the space we stood in had once been a family physician's examining room for routine checkups. In just a few hours, it had been transformed into a fully functioning surgery station. Equipment brought in from other parts of the Dominican Republic was plugged into every outlet. The floor, once a checkered blue and white tile mosaic, held pools of blood and heaps of red bandages that sat in wet clumps. Mountains of clean gauze, racks of tools, and boxes of supplies hid walls covered in paintings of cartoon elephants, giraffes, and gorillas. Toy mobiles sat in a tangled pile in a corner on the floor, their hooks in the ceiling now used to hoist bags of saline, extension cords, and lights.

The girl lay strapped to a table that now only vaguely resembled examining beds at home. The brown leather top and metal foot extensions peered through endless modifications. Welders had tacked hard steel to the painted metal frame to hold arms that balanced tools, lights, mirrors, and straps. The legs creaked under the weight of the modifications. It now resembled an overweight man with legs too small to carry him. The work of doctors, nurses, and patients rocked it back and forth and bent some of the welds, leaving it leaning precariously to one side.

The room itself opened up like a mother offering a hug for a scared child. The once lighthearted atmosphere, designed to set children at ease, was now gone. It had been perverted from its original vision, yet held onto its spirit to help others. It felt surreal to stand there in my blood soaked New Balance sneakers and designer Nike sports socks while dire, Civil War era procedures took place. As one does in a dream, I felt for signs that I could control the situation, perhaps morph it into something I could handle. Suddenly, the cloud lifted and the room grew cold again as the doctor yelled and snapped me back to the present. My mind kept wandering; exhaustion soaked my brain. But I needed to focus.

The doctor gave only a brief signal before starting. As he cut into her arm she tensed into a board and frantically tried to knock away the team by flailing her free limbs. I leaned forward and put all my weight on her hips to keep her still while a muscular man and a young, thin woman held her legs firmly. The other doctor in the room kept her healthy arm still while taking used tools from the surgeon. The mother held her daughter's neck in place and they locked eyes. I watched as they looked at each other, the child noticeably stiller. The mother spoke in Creole as she repeated the same phrase over and over again to express her love: *"Mwen renmen ou,"* all while placing kisses on the patient's forehead as her tears streamed down onto the girl's cheeks. She placed her chin against her child's brow and closed her eyes. Then she remained still and quiet for a brief moment that hung in the air for eternity.

Then, out of nowhere, the child's mother began to sing.

It began with just a few words and grew only slightly in volume from a whisper. As she sang, tears fell from her eyes. Though overwhelmed with pain and fear, the daughter maintained a glassy stare toward the ceiling. The surgeon successfully managed to ignore the moment as he put all his focus and strength into finishing his work. I couldn't take my eyes off the two Haitians.

Then something happened that I did not expect. The girl started to sing, too. She uttered only a few words, but hummed with her mother even against the relentless and indescribable pain she endured. I kept still, my body positioned on the girl's hips. I didn't dare shift my weight and risk allowing her to jerk around. Though the mother's voice was ragged, raw, and strained from her cries and screams over the past few days, the sound she produced created a calming effect that blanketed the room like a warm quilt. The girl struggled much less as her muscles relaxed into a constant yet subtle vibration, and she closed her eyes as she sang. I picked up my head and looked at the rest of her body. She stopped struggling and lay almost completely still.

The doctor removed the tissue and muscle first but left the bone for last. For a moment he moved out of view and I saw her bare shoulder. He had cut the flesh cleanly and only a few fragments of bone remained. He grabbed a saw with extremely small teeth and used it to cut the bone deeper than where he'd worked on the flesh and muscle. His arms were soaked in blood and sweat as if he had dipped them in a bath of swill, and with each movement his muscles flexed under his thin, vein-webbed skin. I barely knew the man and had forgotten his name moments after he'd introduced himself, but it seemed to me that I could tell his life story based on what I saw and heard.

The doctor had arrived at the outpost only a few hours before we did, yet he looked much more exhausted—clearly spent after a day of non-stop surgery in brutal conditions. He was a white man in his late fifties with pale grey eyes sunk deep within the sockets. Above the bloodstains that covered his mask, black circles undercut his eyes and left deep marks on his grey face. Brown hair stained with streaks of white and gray clung to his aging scalp. His face bared deep wrinkles along the forehead and cheekbones, no doubt the battle scars of many years of surgery in much more proper facilities. He wasn't toned, but his thin arms seemed more powerful than a bodybuilder's as he twisted and turned to fix the awful damage. As one of the first to arrive, he had become a leader. He took responsibility not only for surgery, but also for logistics and security.

Before I had met him, I'd heard him yell at one of the coordinators, "This is insane! We can't hope to succeed like this, and I can't save any of these people with the supplies we have. We need them now!" The outpost had nearly run out of medical gear, but dozens of new patients arrived by the hour. The math told a dire tale—there wasn't enough inventory to help everyone.

He found me in the surgery room with a mop and bucket but recruited me for his team, willing to take whatever help he could get. To be honest, I didn't want to assist at all—I much preferred to clean the room in quiet. Looking at the gore and then trying to clean it up seemed hard enough; I didn't want to see how it was made. Our meeting seemed almost too simple. He'd walked up to me and asked, "Son, do you have any medical training?"

I told him I about my history as a Boy Scout, but that no, I had no formal training. The answer made me feel useless and dumb. I didn't want to lie, and part of me just wanted to be left alone. His reply surprised me.

"That's going to have to be enough. I need you in surgery to help hold a girl down. Can you handle that?"

I didn't even know how to answer, so I stammered and nodded. At home I always felt confident. I only really came to Hispaniola to prove just how great I was to my girlfriend's parents. Suddenly I felt like pissing my pants. Before I could think it through, I nodded a sheepish yes to the doctor.

"Good. Let's get her in."

The doctor dragged me through half a dozen surgeries throughout the night. Time became a sadist that passed slowly during procedures but quickly between them. Three days before I had been working at a candy factory in Virginia.

The doctor finished and closed up the girl's arm. She lay back and stared at the stump, speechless but whimpering as her mother sobbed with arms wrapped around her baby's chest. The doctor wiped his face with his forearm and left a stain of blood and dirt across his forehead. He took off his gloves and mask and threw them on the floor. His legs trembled from exhaustion and stress. No one said a word, but he shook the hand of the other surgeon and just walked toward the door as he used a bloody hand to pull a pack of cigarettes from his pants pocket. He lit up right in the doorway of the room, still in the hospital, and pulled a long, deep drag that consumed more than half the length of the cigarette. He exhaled through his nose and sucked the smoke back in through his mouth. He pulled out another, lit it with the first, and held it in between his index and thumb as he killed the first. He left the room, disappearing down the hallway.

A man carried the girl out of the room in his arms. Her mother followed close behind, keeping a hand on her daughter all the time. Then the room was empty. A miracle had occurred and ended just as suddenly, and I couldn't seem to keep up.

In the hallway the glow from cheap fluorescent light reflected off my mint green scrubs in a way that tricked the eyes. The few clean parts left on my clothes glowed with a green tint and made the blood appear black. Green paint covered the walls too, and white tile floors complemented them to create a sterile glow. Only blood and dirt broke up the unending sea of green and white in streaks on the walls and small dried pools on the floor. People sat packed as tightly as they could as they fought over a place to rest their backs. Most sat on the floor in the middle of the aisle or stood in small groups near doorways.

The extreme nature of each injury in the crowd bewildered me. At my feet was a man covered in third degree burns that peeled back his flesh. He sat next to a woman whose left hand had been severed midway up the palm. Down the hallway the same amount of gore repeated over and over again. Just to be allowed inside this building the injuries needed to be "critical." Everyone else lay on the ground outside on sheets, thin mattresses, and the bare earth. Those inside waited at least a few hours until a doctor could see them.

To my right and against one of the surgery room doors sat a man with his four-year-old son asleep on his lap. Severe lacerations covered the boy's face and chest and oozed a steady flow of blood through loose bandages. Jagged skin replaced the pointer and middle finger on his right hand. I marveled at how he slept through such pain. The father looked at me and asked me a question, *"Tanpri, ede mwen,"* yet I did not understand his Creole. Four years of French did nothing for me, and I cursed myself for never taking the time to truly learn the language. I never paid attention in school. *"Parlez-vous Anglais?"* I asked the man in a horrible accent forced from watching French movies. Sadly, he shook his head to say, "No."

A woman behind me spoke up. "The boy won't wake up." I turned to see her. A large piece of her shin had been sheared away cleanly to reveal fat tissue and bone. "Can you ask him how long he's been asleep?" She spoke to the man and replied, "Hours."

I looked down both ends of the hallway for anyone to help, yet the search proved fruitless. The entire outpost was staffed by perhaps four doctors and a dozen nurses, who were all completely overwhelmed. The injured vastly outnumbered the volunteers.

I jogged down the hallway and turned the corner before locating a nurse at the end of the next corridor. I moved quickly but carefully as I stepped over countless people lying haphazardly on the floor. I made my way to her as she walked away carrying a pile of supplies stacked to her neck. She held a few things in place with her chin and strained to look at me when I caught up with her.

"Nurse, there is a boy at the..."

She cut me off. "End of the other hallway, won't wake up? I know, I know. He has sepsis, and we don't have the supplies to help him. His back opened up and he's pretty far gone. I'm sorry." She turned her head back and continued down the hallway.

Stunned, I stood for a moment alone. I didn't want to return to the man without anyone to help. I didn't have the slightest clue what to do for the boy.

I wanted to go back and talk to the man, maybe offer some words of encouragement, but it felt like lying. Truthfully, I didn't want to go back anyway. I just wanted to erase the image from my mind. The main entrance to the building lured me like light lures a mosquito. I could just leave and go outside. I'd never see the man again. I didn't know how to help anyway. In a moment of cowardice I faltered and left the building. I moved into the night air and sat on a ledge overlooking the caskets piled behind the building.

Sitting there, I began to cry. At first my tears came slowly and I felt them push through the dirt and blood on my face one by one. I allowed them to fall slowly into the dark. I couldn't decide if I was experiencing shock from surgery, exhaustion from the trip, or guilt for leaving the man inside. I pulled my Ravens hat out from between my bare back and shorts. Just a few days ago I'd sat in a sports bar at home with some buddies. I've never cared about football so they told me to root for the Ravens as they chose all the other "Northeast" teams. I'd purchased the hat right before the trip as a good luck charm. I looked at it now, intently, as tears streamed more rapidly. Its purple color had faded during the trip. I wiped my face with the back of the cap. The motion left a thick layer of grime on it and provided a gruesome reminder of my surroundings. I cared for my friends and thought about what they'd think about my situation. I knew they wouldn't believe any of my stories from the trip. I always felt like a boring guy. Truth is, I *was* a boring guy. This place existed way out of my element.

I sobbed heavily but attempted to keep my voice down. I wasn't a doctor—not even anything close to it. But to these victims I represented hope, and I had just bailed on someone. Just my being here meant something to them. I wasn't strong enough to keep helping—I needed a moment to disengage.

I suddenly had an urge for a beer. I had an urge for anything I could get my hands on. I needed something to escape, to *evaporate*—even for a minute of solitude. But no such sanctuary existed. Only a few days ago I had lived in a different world, a different reality, and a different time. The first night at the outpost had crept to a close, and the morning sun was just beginning to rise as a faint purple glow illuminated the east sky.

As I looked at the stars a peace took over my body. I thought about how I had gotten here just a few days ago, with what I thought at the time was such an easy plan to win the blessing of my girlfriend's parents for her hand in marriage.

Tuesday, January 12th 2010

5:30am

Stuarts Draft, VA

My alarm shrieked in the darkness on a nearby desk. The cell phone vibrated across the surface with flashing lights in a seizure stricken fashion. My eyes failed to focus in the blackened room so I reached out in desperation to quiet the siren. I rolled my legs out of bed and sat still while blood warmed and softened my limbs like oil for the rusty Tin Man.

I was a few weeks into a project at a Hershey candy factory in central Virginia. As a chemical engineer for The Hershey Company, I often worked with teams at our facilities to improve efficiency, eliminate waste, and change anything that could make the products better. This was another open-ended assignment with the same goal: higher output, lower cost. After only a few days, the mission felt hopeless, and my morale hit rock bottom. The goals they wanted us to reach seemed unattainable. I was away from my home, my girlfriend, my family, and my friends. It felt like a prison sentence, as though my destiny were to do the same thing every day for the rest of eternity. The hotel room I lay in substituted as my second home for the project. I even kept a stash of clothes in it over the weekends and to make my weekly four-hour commute a little easier and give the little room some illusions of home. My life consisted of days at the plant, company paid dinners, and fresh sheets in a king size bed every night as I zoned out with the TV or played video games on my laptop.

Rising from bed in the early morning, I stood by an enormous window in the hotel room. It was an extremely cold January, and

19

the world outside embraced the dark under a blanket of frozen air. The eerie, desolate parking lots of the nearby strip mall hid under a thick residue of spent salt that dyed the blacktop a chalky grey. Trees stood naked with thin branches clinging to their parents against a relentless wind that howled against the walls of the hotel. Beyond the shopping centers, endless fields full of reaped corn stalks appeared razor sharp in the distance. The dark green and brown Shenandoah mountain ranges loomed beyond, like walls blocking out the rest of the world. I felt a sudden chill just looking outside. I loathed the thought of leaving my room to enter the unforgiving landscape that waited outside.

I walked to the breakfast lounge to eat. I ate the same thing every day: cereal, milk, a banana and yogurt. I found Ben and Stu, two senior engineers on the project team. I knew Ben only from this project. At first, he personified only professionalism and a willingness to work and nothing else, but I had cracked a little of his shell early in the month by finding something he liked to talk about: his daughters. He lacked a similar sense of humor but remained easy to work with as long as I did a good job. He'd worked with the company forever and did capital projects and installations all over the country. I respected his experience, but I just didn't want the same career. Working with him helped remind me of that. I constantly thought of finding another job in the company—something different, but my aversion to risk kept me from really looking hard.

Stu didn't possess an engineering degree, but instead had collected years of experience that made him smarter and faster than most of his degree-holding counterparts. He'd worked all over the world and had even met his wife in Brazil while working at another factory owned by the company. Somehow he started every day with a positive outlook, even if at night he sometimes looked like a drained victim attacked by a vicious vampire. He put all his energy working long days full of fixing problems, developing new ways to make production lines more efficient. My batteries didn't recharge nearly as fast.

I said good morning with forced enthusiasm and tried to hide my exhaustion.

"Hey," Stu replied in a cheery voice, a chunk of syrup-soaked waffle floating in front of his mouth. He took a bite and moved his focus back to his paper. Ben didn't reply. He was half asleep with eyes intently focused on the television, eating as he watched the morning news.

The weather played on the television. I tried to draw something out of him, perhaps more as a challenge than an actual desire to communicate. "Looks like it may snow today. What do you think, Ben?"

He took his eyes off the television for a moment, giving a slight nod, "Maybe."

I arrived at the plant just before 7:00 am. Morning passed normally with the typical schedule: a meeting with the plant staff, another meeting with the team, and then I went alone out to the candy factory. The facility creates dozens of product lines including Reese Peanut Butter Cups, Almond Joy, Nutrageous, and Take 5 to name only a few. Sometimes I liked to walk the twenty minute route around the inside perimeter while going over checklists and deliverables in my head. The dull grey and mustard yellow paint scheme and exposed bare metal ceiling made me tired when I looked at it, so I kept my eyes toward the ground.

As one of the youngest engineers at the plant, I often felt out of place among others. It also made it harder to enforce changes, command respect, and even make friends. Hailing from "corporate" compounded the difficulty—most plant employees distrusted me even before they got to know me. Even so, I did find a few friends. Years of working construction helped me connect with people on the plant floor. In some ways, my experience on a construction crew proved more valuable than a chemical engineering degree when dealing with people day-to-day.

I spent the morning analyzing a nut placer in hopes of understanding it better. It places nuts on top of candy bars with pinpoint precision through the use of relays, cylinders, and articulating arms. Watching it operate is like watching skilled dancers: components dodge each other by millimeters at speeds that blur their movement. It hums and whistles as air hoses breathe in and out and give it a personality as it works. I fell into a trance and stared blankly until I heard a voice behind me.

"Sean. Hey, my man, what's up?"

I turned my head and saw Danny, the head operator for the line and one of my few friends in Virginia. He was a short, pudgy black man who wore thick round glasses and coveralls. He created new ways to take observations including data sheets to track down times, routinely found new causes for problems on his line, and kept morale up on his team. My first day at the plant a few years ago he'd played a prank on me in front of some other operators. I didn't know it, but the plant had scheduled a machine to go down for cleaning. He asked me to push a button while he took a reading off the screen. When I did, the machine shut off and he screamed, "Oh my God, the other button, the *other button!*" I almost vomited right there, scared to death of maybe losing my job. Then everyone laughed. I had a choice to make at that moment: be angry, or just laugh along. I chose the second option and he'd proved to be a great friend at the plant ever since.

I asked him how his day was going and how the line performed.

"Good now, but I'm sure it'll break down as soon as you leave."

I chuckled, nodding my head in agreement. "You're probably right. I'd like to get this done, though, so I can go home."

"What? Why would you ever want to go home?" He smiled.

A few hours later I took a break to go to lunch with Nathan, one of the plant engineers and another one of the few friends I kept in Virginia. We always ate at the same Italian restaurant. It felt hard to have a new conversation every day in a place where nothing changed, so we usually talked about variations on the same topics: girls, movies and friends—but never work. If I didn't eat with him, I ate alone. Today I brought up a slightly different subject than normal: marriage proposals.

I'd thought about the idea for some time—asking my girl-friend Amber to marry me. I met her through an online dating site a few years earlier. Never a bar hopper or a strong social bug, I'd found it difficult to meet anyone outside my small circle.

I paired with Amber as my first match. Her curly blonde hair and green eyes mesmerized me when we first met, and the small freckles on her nose complemented her small figure. Born in Haiti to missionary parents, she grew up in the Dominican Republic before moving to my area for a short time to go to college. It amazed me how much different she was from all the other girls I'd met. While I spent time fixing my house, playing video games, and working, she excelled at ultimate Frisbee, rock climbing, hiking, and camping. An avid biology student, she loved animals. She didn't like me right away, but I slowly whittled down her defenses. I found myself doing things I hated just to impress her. I went camping on private property, attended parties with people I didn't like, and danced at clubs that played music I despised.

On our second date she invited me to a reptile convention show an hour north of my home. When we arrived, I quickly learned that the "convention" she spoke about was really just a hundred people crammed into a small warehouse that sat on a dirt road against the highway. People walked out of the building with cages full of rats, snakes, spiders, and other creepy-crawly things that I couldn't even identify. I wasn't interested in touching anything with the potential to kill me, but I acted courageous to try and impress her.

We browsed the vendors inside the darkly lit room, and for a while I believed that I would get out of there without testing my limits in front of her. Then a man with a grey and black pony tail and a grey muscle shirt called us over to his booth covered with very small plastic containers.

"Hey guys, want to hold a scorpion?" he phrased it almost as if the question was as normal as asking someone for the time.

Absolutely not, I thought to myself. But Amber, as I would learn, never turned down an opportunity like this.

"Of course we do," she answered for both of us before looking to me and smiling, "You want to, right?"

I lied and said yes. In seconds she grabbed three of the containers and emptied the black, shiny scorpions on her arm. They danced on her skin and she used her free hand to guide them around. Even the vendor looked concerned about the stingers as she carelessly grabbed them by the tail before putting them on me.

I felt my blood freeze up. I was convinced that one of them would sting me and I'd die. One of them stopped on my hand and inspected my fingers. I tried to straighten out my digits to keep the stingers as far as possible from my skin. Then something happened that I didn't expect—they just kept crawling on me. They didn't sting me. I started to feel calmer about the situation, and I didn't feel so nervous. I looked at Amber. She was smiling at me. She had just gotten me to do something that without her pushing, I never would have done.

"See, they like you." She giggled as she grabbed them and put them back in the container.

"Yeah," I shrugged in an effort to look tough, "they're not so bad after all."

She leaned in and kissed me on the cheek. I felt the skin rush to my face. It was the first time she kissed me, and little pins prickled my cheeks as I felt myself blush. My stomach fluttered slightly like the first moments of a roller coaster's descent.

"Good, can we get a few?" she asked as she hugged my arm. I knew at that moment it would always be hard to say no to her.

Only a few years had passed, but sitting in the restaurant I knew I wanted to get married. I just wasn't sure how. Her parents still lived in the Dominican Republic, and I wanted to ask them for permission in person, without her knowing.

Amber's parents live a very unusual life. They run Crossroads, a mission organization that supports several villages of Haitian refugees along with countless impoverished Dominicans. They spent most of Amber's childhood near Puerto Plata, a coastal town on the north coast of Hispaniola, building the mission. It grew from a single outreach based at the family's home into a full sized organization that works to provide medical assistance for the poor along with food, clothing, and shelter. Several of the villages they've built are now the permanent homes of hundreds of Haitians, and the list of volunteers willing to come and help pushes the wait list to visit out over a year. The short time I spent at their home changed my sense of reality, granting me a shocking awareness of life in developing countries. Once I witnessed the extreme poverty of the Dominican and Haitian people that Crossroads cares for, I never could quite forget it.

Bob and Jana, Amber's parents, have lived abroad for over forty years. Before moving to Puerto Plata in the late 1980's they worked and lived in Columbia, Costa Rica, and Haiti. Bob, a veterinarian, worked as a program manager for a swine flu recovery in Haiti. He also managed Jana's jewelry business before settling as a veterinarian in the Dominican Republic. Jana had run an estate in Costa Rica before taking on an apprenticeship as a jeweler. Her ambition eventually blossomed into a thriving, multi-store business that dotted the Dominican Republic's northern shore. In between raising their seven children and running several businesses, they continually helped the Puerto Plata community by treating AIDS victims, building homes for the poor, and volunteering.

The first time I visited her family I spent most of the week helping with the outreach programs. I did medical work, provided food and clothing for the poor, visited the sick at the hospital, and even brought supplies to those living in the local dump. The trip felt like a whirlwind meant to jostle my sense of reality, and it succeeded in that regard. I spent my short amount of downtime getting to know her parents, eating with her family, and I even got a chance to visit the local beaches.

It's an understatement to say that ever since I'd met Amber and her family, life had not been the same.

Back in the restaurant, Nathan and I talked about it for a while, but didn't come up with any real solutions. How could I possibly visit them in secret? Calling on the phone wouldn't suffice, but doing it any other way guaranteed release of the secret to Amber. The stress ate away at me and lingered in the back of my mind.

After lunch I spent the rest of the day at the plant finishing up my work. After I completed my email and finished the last meeting I clocked out for the day at 5:00 pm. I usually left much later, but today I wanted to go back to the hotel and work out. Outside, the weather had frozen everything, and the cold wind and rain coated my car in a thin sheet of ice. I got into it and turned on the engine as I hugged myself to warm up. The radio played and I sat quietly as I listened to the news.

"Haiti has suffered a massive 7.0 earthquake just outside of Port-au-Prince. Damage is extensive, and recovery efforts are underway."

I sat stunned and freezing as the headline repeated. I thought briefly about Crossroads and hoped it hadn't been damaged. I put my hands over the hot air coming from the ducts to keep the blood flowing to my fingers. I closed my eyes and thought about the hot air at Amber's home in Puerto Plata.

Monday, June 15th, 2009
2:25pm
Puerto Plata, Dominican Republic

The plane landed to loud applause from the Dominican crowd aboard the JetBlue flight from JFK to Puerto Plata, Dominican Republic. The relief brought on by returning safely to solid ground immediately shrunk next to the impending fear that hung so close: meeting Amber's parents for the first time, the summer before the Haitian earthquake of 2010.

Amber and I were traveling together to spend a week at Crossroads. Over a year had passed since we started dating in early 2008, and the time had finally come to see if I fit in with the rest of her family. I'd spoken with several of them a few times over the course of our relationship, but we'd never traded anything more than a few words, or a nicety here or there. Now I prepared myself for a week of staying in their home.

"This way," Amber offered as she grabbed my hand to pull me through the tangled web of Dominicans waiting in the airport. "Don't get lost in here!"

I never fully appreciated her ability to speak Spanish fluently until I felt lost in a sea of people that spoke it. Not understanding anything that anyone says is embarrassing, overwhelming, confusing, and quite frankly, scary. I kept my eyes trained on her and my grip tight on her hand as she led me to passport control and through the exit. I likened myself to a baby as she spoke to others for me, gave out my passport to attendees, and laughed with workers in front of me in Spanish. My confidence lapsed and I stood convinced that everyone was snickering at me. I trusted Amber to protect me through to the other side.

Outside, the pathway fanned out into a welcoming crowd that numbered in the hundreds and waited for passengers arriving on our flight. Suddenly I noticed her family standing just beyond the main crowd. They held a huge handmade paper sign that read, "Welcome Home, Amber and Sean." Butterflies fluttered in my stomach and fled from my mouth as I exhaled a sigh of relief mixed with anticipation for the greeting. Before I could think about what to say, Amber pushed us toward her family.

"Hello," I said sheepishly while putting out my hand to shake Bob's. Before I straightened my arm, Jana walked up and wrapped her arms around my back to hug me. She held my head on her shoulder for a moment, pulled away, and said, "Welcome Sean, we are so glad to finally meet you." She looked over at Amber, "Woah, he is cute, Amber! How'd you get him?"

Amber laughed and shrugged her shoulders before Jana joined her and they hugged as well, leaving me standing alone for only a moment. Amber looked a lot like her mother, except Jana wore loose, long dresses dyed in mixtures of blacks and tropical colors. Her skin was permanently tan from living in the Caribbean most of her life.

Bob stood right in front of me, a literal Santa Claus in doctor's scrubs, and pulled me in for a hug before I could even try to shake his hand, too. He spoke much more softly than Amber or Jana, and said to me in a quieter tone, "We're happy to have you here Sean. Amber has said a lot of very good things about you." He smiled in a way that made his cheek bones tighten around his eyes.

"Thank you for having me," I said politely. "I'm excited to be here."

Amber's entire family had come to greet me at the airport. Marcus, or Uncle Fester as the kids called him, stood alongside Bob and also pulled me into a hug as I got close. His brown and gray curly hair frizzed into the air, and his round frame glasses gave him a very intelligent appearance. He wore scrubs like Bob, but also wore a big safari cap that tried to keep the bulk of his hair in check. He reached out to grab my bags and took them before I could refuse.

Amber's sister, Faith, also stood in the crowd and spent a few minutes with Amber before coming over to give me a hug too. She looked like Amber in many of the ways that sisters often do: similar face, eyes, smile, and build. She stood a little taller than Amber and almost the same height as me, and she looked pretty in a way that didn't require make-up or tons of preparation— just like Amber. Like Amber, she was naturally pretty, her skin light with faint freckles barely visible that dotted her nose and cheekbones. Often in the morning or after a long day, I'd find myself amazed at how pretty Amber looked after sweating or sleeping. Amber's eyes were green; Faith's were blue. The similarities caused me to feel immediately comfortable around Faith.

Next I met Shekena, Amber's adopted Dominican sister. Shortly after, I met Shekena's twin brother, Zion. Shekena stood just over five feet and a few inches tall, was very thin and fit, and wore her hair in a frizzy afro that she held back with a blue and yellow bandana. Her brother was slightly taller. As a surfer, he possessed a very muscular physique that complemented his buzzed haircut. He shook my hand as he said hello and welcomed me to the island. I'd never spoken to him before that moment, so I replied with a sterile "Nice to meet you." He laughed and shook his head, replying, "Relax man, we're happy to meet you. It's not every day Amber brings someone down here to meet us." He looked over at Amber and winked, and she gave him an icy stare. "Stop teasing him, Zion." He giggled and joined Marcus as they packed our bags in the ancient, hobbled Land Cruiser parked a few feet away. Shekena joined Faith, Amber, and Jana in a discussion a few feet away from me.

Finally I met Maya, the oldest of the Amelingmeier children. She was an adopted Haitian that worked as a teacher in one of the local schools. "How are you doing?" she asked, and went on, "Our family is a bit different, but you'll get used to our ways."

I nodded slowly as I feigned confidence in my choice to visit. "Thanks, this is all a bit different than what I'm used to."

"Don't worry, we'll take care of you. I'm sure you won't want to go home at the end of the week." She gave me a small hug before helping me walk toward the Land Cruiser with the rest of the family.

The vehicle parked in front of me looked like a collection of family memories glued together over the years. Pictures pasted to the inside walls, sculptures bolted to the outer body, and paint littered the panels. A large, wooden alligator splayed across the length of the hood and forever pointed its nose towards the path ahead. The entire family piled inside, and Bob got in the driver's seat before driving away to take us to Crossroads.

These were my first moments outside of the United States, other than visits to foreign resorts designed for Americans. The landscape rapidly changed as we neared their compound. Just off the main road the homes devolved into crumbling huts and straw roof dwellings that were nestled near concrete, one-story buildings. The road dwindled into nothing more than smaller rocks held together by patchy mud, and trash littered the gutters. Everyone else in the car continued their conversations, but I felt caught up in the surroundings. I'd never personally seen

① This trip meant the absolute world to me, it showed me who I truly want to become. This trip means that I will now have a life long memory of the joy and compassion I have for all of the inspirational people I met. This oppertunity opened my eyes and made me realize how well I have my life. To some extent I feel selfish for having all that I do. Without this experience I wouldn't be as evolved as I am now. The feelings I experienced are indescribable, there are no words powerful enough to express my emotion

anyone living in a hut before, and I'd never smelled trash rotting so openly in the streets.

We stopped just before reaching an iron gate that seemed to grow out from bushes on either side of it. It didn't really stop people from going down the road, but I bet it would do a decent job keeping a car from pushing through without some serious damage to the front-end.

"Okay Sean and Amber, get out," Bob announced as the rest of the family, including Amber, smirked and giggled. We parked next to a row of beaten homes, and as we opened the doors, a small crowd of Haitian children came out to meet us from inside their homes.

"What are we doing?" I asked, well aware that I gave away my discomfort with the area.

Amber's family wouldn't reply, but instead pushed me out of the back of the vehicle. Then, from behind the largest building, a man walked two horses towards us. I looked at Amber, half stunned and half angry—there was no way I was riding a horse.

In a few moments the rest of Amber's family took the vehicle past the gate and up the hill to what I guessed was the path to her home, leaving me and a very excited Amber next to two tired horses. A crowd of cheering Haitian children that beckoned me to get on the saddle surrounded us.

As it was my first time on a horse, I failed miserably at trying to mount it. I swung my leg over but got it caught in the strap on the other side. The horse tried to move with me still hanging off. The man mumbled something as he helped boost me on top of the animal. Then I joined Amber as she led my horse with a thin rope before we started the trip up the hill to her home.

I'd like to say that I managed to impress Amber with tremendous horse-leading skills, but unfortunately I cannot. Each step up rocked me from side to side as I clung tightly to the horse's mane in an effort to stay stable. I never found a comfortable position, and after a while I whined to get off and walk up myself. But Amber said no, and forced me to remain in the saddle the whole way to the entrance of her home.

Their home is on the summit of a small mountain range that sits diagonally northeast, facing the ocean to the north and the city of Puerto Plata in the west. Over a dozen buildings of various sizes dot the summit and connect with dirt paths, concrete walks, and covered walkways. The main entrance building is the kitchen, and it sits at one of the highest points, providing a 180-degree view from southwest to northeast. It's where the family spends evenings eating dinner and watching the sunset.

In the center of the room a large wooden table sat under stained glass lanterns that cast an orange and blue glow on the tile floor. Countless statues, paintings, pictures, antiques, and memory-laced knick-knacks filled the walls and alluded to hundreds of stories shared by volunteer groups that have visited over the years. Photos of people building homes, digging wells, treating the sick, and feeding the poor formed collages that blended with paintings of Haitian culture, statues of Jesus and Mary, and lots of stained glass, most of which was hand made by Jana.

Amber and I spent part of the afternoon unpacking our bags in one of the rooms given to us for the week. They gave us Zion's old bedroom, a tree house that Bob built on top of one of the other buildings. It seemed unreal to stay in an actual tree house, especially one with running water and electricity. Afterward we ventured back to the kitchen to eat dinner with her family.

Amber and I got to the kitchen last. The entire family stood in a circle, holding hands around the table to pray. I couldn't remember the last time I prayed before dinner, so the ritual felt odd to me at first. Everyone looked at us as we approached and widened the circle to let us in. I held Amber's hand with my right and Bob's with my left.

Then they all started to pray and sing at the same time. I didn't know the words, so I just closed my eyes and bowed my head. Suddenly I felt a squeeze, but not from Amber. I looked to my left to see Bob smiling. "It's okay if you don't know the words yet, you'll learn them."

I smiled back, still unsure of whether I was ready to.

Tuesday, January 12th 2010
4:40pm
Port Au Prince, Haiti

Zac jumped off a cobblestone ledge that traced the outline of a small food market at the base of his neighborhood. He ran down the dusty gravel road toward his friends at the intersection ahead. He was short for fifteen. He wore faded shorts and a t-shirt he'd owned for years but still fit into nicely. The duct tape holding his flip-flops together had turned crusty and gave little adhesion for his broken shoes. Each step threw the thongs out of their sockets and almost caused him to trip and fall, but he learned to flex with each step in order to keep them in place. As he reached his friends he stood as tall as he could to look and see the commotion in the center of the circle.

Lucas, one of Zac's oldest friends, had just bought his first motorbike. It was a very old, rusty white model that wore twisted metal and shattered body panels hanging by tape and rope to the frame. The engine ran, and Lucas sat on the tattered seat proudly and jerked the accelerator as he reveled over the scream of the motor. He practiced letting the rear tire spin in the loose dirt. It dug a deep gash in the gravel, only occasionally letting the bike spit forward a few feet when the bald rubber caught hold.

Zac's friends took turns looking over the bike, poking at the body panels, kicking the tires gently, and slightly caressing the shiny handlebars that Lucas cleaned over and over again with a rag tied to his shorts. The chrome appeared all but worn off, but what remained shimmered in the sun. It reflected Zac's twisted face like a circus mirror when he looked at it closely. Lucas sat like a king on his grand reward and new true love. He seemed even taller than Zac remembered him a few days ago. The local girls hung closer to him now. Each one wanted to take a ride on the bike, and Lucas gave two of them sitting on the ledge nearby a hungry stare as he flexed his arms while twisting the throttle.

Zac had grown up just a few houses from Lucas, but their close friendship had fractured as Lucas' growth spurts outpaced his own. Zac still looked like a child, and didn't yet have a job or girlfriend. Lucas, on the other hand, had been with many girls, had worked for a few years, and now owned a motorbike. Zac couldn't help but feel extreme jealousy. It seemed unfair. Even though he was older than Lucas by a few months, everyone saw him as a child but regarded Lucas as an adult. Zac wanted that bike, even if he knew he wasn't big enough to ride it properly.

The crowd huddled around the bike for a while longer, but eventually dwindled to just a few other boys and Zac.

"It's so nice," he said to Lucas after the noise and commotion subsided. "Can I ride it?"

He felt guilty asking and wondered just how transparent and pathetic he looked in front of the others. Lucas smiled, but not with a gloat or sneer. He was gentle and brotherly, as if he planned to do something nice.

"Sure man, you can ride it back to my house."

The answer stunned Zac but he wasted no time trying to hop on. Lucas held the bike upright and Zac vaulted one foot over the seat and scooted until his butt was centered. The frame swayed back and forth as he shifted his weight. Once he sat square, he felt for the footrests, but couldn't find them. He blushed as he felt Anton, the biggest and strongest of his friends, start to giggle. A little older than Lucas and Zac, Anton sounded slow when spoken to but proved dangerously strong and often broke things by accident when he got angry or hyper. He wore faded jeans and a t-shirt several sizes too big even for him. It draped down almost to his knees and hid his huge chest and arms. Franck, the oldest and smartest of the group, leaned against his younger brother Anton and pointed in a way that made Zac feel even smaller. He stood a few inches taller than Lucas but looked thinner even than Zac, and with his buzzed hair he seemed as light as a feather. Both Anton and Franck made a regular habit of poking fun at Zac's height, but this moment felt especially painful.

Lucas sensed his frustration and leapt to action. "Looks like it's a bit too big for you yet. Those foot rests are broken—they should be a few inches higher."

Everyone knew he'd lied, but Zac swallowed it and played along. "You're right, this thing is broken. You can ride it home after all."

He hopped off and gave the handles back to Lucas, who turned off the ignition and walked beside it.

"I've been riding it all day. Besides, it's only a short walk home."

Franck hit Anton in the chest with his elbow and gestured toward Zac with a diminishing nod, but Zac ignored the move and tried to laugh with the guys.

Once the group arrived at Lucas' house, he set the bike delicately against the front wall of the small, concrete bungalow. The home was crowded on all sides by other equally quaint but worn dwellings. Lucas took a few steps back, turned, and looked at the bike, using his fingers to take a fake photo of it for memory.

"Isn't it beautiful?"

Anton spoke up slowly. "I'm sure you'll get lots of girls." Everyone laughed.

"I hope so! Otherwise, why did I spend so much time saving?"

He grabbed a heavy chain and a lock from below the bike and secured it to the railing on the front of the house. His mother, Tasha, sat on the front porch, quietly watching people walk past on the street.

"Mom, hold onto the keys. I'm going to get some things at the store."

She nodded and put the keys on a plate sitting next to her on a flimsy wooden end table. The table was warped and worn from sun and rain. The boys walked off and left her sitting alone again on the porch. She looked over at the bike and smiled. A friend of hers from the market had owned the bike for years and casually mentioned selling it to buy something newer. It was over twenty years old and barely ran, but she knew that Lucas wanted something just like it. He found another buyer for the old bike right away, but she managed to get him to hold off selling until her son saved enough money to buy it. She did this by fixing the man's pants and shoes in her free time. She'd lied to Lucas about the price. He'd wanted two hundred dollars for it, but Lucas had only saved one hundred-fifty. In the end she'd secretly used some of her savings to pay for the rest. It made her so happy to see her son earn something, to work an honest job. She wouldn't spoil that for him.

The neighborhood streets bustled with activity. Vendors shouted, cars buzzed back and forth, and people walked in all directions. At a major intersection a corner store sat nestled in the alley between a brand new bank and an abandoned two-story office building. It wasn't even a true building, but instead a puzzle of tin and zinc plates propped between the two neighbors. Benches and tables covered with goods lined the walls and center aisle and left very little room to walk. Lucas bought a pack of gum and split it up among his friends. He always liked to share. They left the store and walked up the hill to his home, eager to play with the bike again and maybe even take turns going on joy rides.

Halfway up, Zac, who led the group, fell on the ground suddenly as the earth shook violently and without warning. The rest of the boys ran into the street while looking up in fear at the buildings on both sides. It felt similar to a bomb explosion, except that it lasted for what seemed like an eternity. The crowd panicked in confusion and fear, certain that the end of the world had finally arrived.

Without warning, buildings fell on either side. Where Zac had lain moments earlier, a home fell and crumbled in on itself and created a massive plume of dust and dirt that shot out into the street and covered everyone. The bank's right wall collapsed and fell into the alley, crushing the corner store below it. The office building cracked, and the windows shattered as car alarms sounded in front. A few feet left of Anton, the front wall of another building fell forward into the street and crushed a car as it exploded.

The ground stopped shaking but buildings continued to fall. Lights flickered inside buildings and then went off to leave only the glow from the late afternoon sun. Dust blinded everyone, preventing them from seeing more than a few feet, but they heard things crumbling on all sides. Petrified of being crushed under an unseen collapse, the group kept still in the center of the street for a few minutes until the noise subsided and a deathly quiet blanket wrapped the city in dust and smoke.

Then, the sounds of cries and screams replaced crumbling buildings and exploding cars and came from all sides like an overwhelming shadow too big to escape. The noise filled Lucas's ears until it seemed to be within him. The group walked slowly in a tight formation as they stumbled over each other's feet and felt with their arms to dodge objects in front.

Suddenly Lucas screamed out, "Mom!" and left the group as he ran up the hill toward his home. He disappeared just feet away from Zac has he ran off into the thick dust. Anton moved his body in front of Franck and Zac's to lead the group up the hill. After twenty feet they came across a burning car with a wall slowly crushing it. A scorched man sat in the driver's seat with his head and shoulders pinched between the collapsing wall and the steering wheel. He was dead, but his daughter in the back seat cried loudly. Anton tried to open the door, but it wouldn't budge. Franck pushed the two out of the way and heaved on it. The door was jammed in place from the roof crushing in on it.

Suddenly Zac got an idea. "Put me in the window," he said to Franck, pointing at the shattered glass.

Anton picked up Zac with ease while Franck punched out the rest of the glass with his bare hands. Zac slid in through the opening, his legs and hips held in the air by Anton. Smoke filled the inside of the car and he couldn't see, but the little girl's cries led him to her. He unlatched her seatbelt and moved toward the door. Franck pulled her out and Anton moved backwards to pull Zac. Everyone fell to the ground while coughing up smoke and breathing hard.

"Guess small isn't so bad," Franck said, holding the toddler in his arms.

Zac's eyes watered from irritation, and he moved onto his hands and knees to cough up the spit and smoke from his lungs. When his hands hit the dirt he screamed in pain. Pulling back quickly he turned his palms and realized the reason: burns from the hot metal inside covered his hands. Blood trickled down his forearms between black soot and dirt. He felt a pull as Anton picked him up and grabbed his arms before wrapping them in cloth from his torn shirtsleeves. With Franck holding the girl, the group worked their way to the top of the hill in hopes that the smoke would clear.

At the top Zac saw Lucas by his mother's crumbled house. He crouched on top of the pile and screamed for her as he pulled rocks free from the heap. Anton and Franck stood motionless and watched Lucas franticly dig as the infant cried in Franck's arms. Zac noticed the motorbike under part of the pile, mangled and utterly destroyed. The handlebar had come off and sat by itself on the ground attached to the frame with a brake cable. He ripped it from the bike and tore the remaining wires free from the frame. He joined Lucas at the top of the pile and used it as a lever to pull rocks away. Lucas looked at the handle, and for the briefest moment, paused to realize what Zac held. Then he grabbed it, and using all of his strength, shoved it into the pile to rip out a large rock.

Tuesday, January 12th 2010
5:05pm
Stuarts Draft, VA

I drove back to the hotel in a hurry as the radio broadcast continually updated. Just moments before, an earthquake had struck Port-au-Prince. Readings came in with varying stories but they all agreed the quake registered a massive 7.0 on the Richter scale. I didn't know much about Haiti other than that Amber's parents lived in the Dominican Republic and that they helped several hundred Haitian refugees. To be honest, despite having visited that one time, I couldn't have pointed it out on a map other than knowing it was somewhere south of Florida.

Nonetheless, upon hearing this news, my mind focused entirely on Amber's home.

Crossroads never received an official start date. It slowly grew from the family's small contributions into a full time mission program. In the early years, church groups from the United States camped on their property and worked in the local villages with the guidance and help of the Crossroads family. The number of people requesting to visit increased dramatically through word-of-mouth until Jana and Bob decided to pursue the mission as a full time commitment. As the years progressed they'd sold off the jewelry stores, grew Bob's veterinary clinic, and allowed Crossroads to expand until reservations by volunteer groups extended a year in advance.

Over the years Jana and Bob have bought hundreds of acres in the Dominican countryside and have built expansive villages from their own income and donations. Hundreds of Haitian families have received a concrete home with windows, a solid door, a cement floor, working electricity, plumbing, and a sturdy roof. Volunteer groups continue to visit the compound every week from all over the United States and Canada to build homes, facilitate medical work, and help make the villages stronger.

During that first visit in the summer of 2009, Jana and Faith brought me to their largest village: Ascension Village. They parked the beaten-up mission truck in front of the compound meant to house long-term volunteers, and I stepped into the dirt road. Dozens of Haitian children crowded around me to grab at my shorts and shirt while poking me with their fingers and with small sticks. Some boys kicked a soccer ball to my feet, and I kicked it back. They asked hundreds of questions in Creole, a language I only barely understood.

I looked at my clothes and felt suddenly ashamed. I had packed carefully for a trip—just not the right one. I had anticipated a traditional meet and greet with the parents, and I wanted to look the part of an honest and honorable boyfriend. I didn't understand what Amber had meant when she'd told me to bring clothes I didn't mind ruining or even losing. When I stood among the Haitian children in a perfectly clean and crisp white polo shirt with grey shorts and brand new white sneakers, I finally understood. The children wore dirty, faded pants with tattered shirts. Hardly anyone wore shoes. I thought about how cushy and soft my feet seemed compared to theirs. I stood on an alien planet, but in that moment my heart changed as I witnessed an entirely new way of life that I had never known existed. My simple Honda Civic suddenly felt fancy, my small house looked like a mansion, and my old, boring clothes smelled brand new. By the end of the trip I gave away some of the clothes I came with to others in the village. I wished I had brought more to give. Six months had passed since that trip to Crossroads, but the effects of that week still impacted my daily thoughts and actions. And now this news brought that impact home again.

Back in Virginia, I returned to the hotel and took a hot shower all while thinking of Haiti. The main TV stations broadcasted repeating loops. Collapsed buildings, fires, smoke, and riots flooded the screen.

The phone rang. It was Amber. She sounded shaken on the other end.

"Did you hear what happened?"

I could tell she had cried before calling so I reacted by trying to comfort her.

"How are your parents doing? Are they safe?"

"They're fine. A couple buildings formed cracks, but no real damage. It's a fourteen-hour drive to Port-au-Prince. They could feel it though, even from that far away."

I told her not to worry. I told her you could sometimes feel an earthquake from hundreds of miles away. She paused for a while after that and left me in silence as I kept the phone at my ear with most of my attention on the television and not on her. I didn't excel at talking on the phone; I just couldn't focus without my mind and eyes wandering to something else. Considering how often I traveled for work, I knew I would have to make more efforts to improve in this regard if I wanted to keep the relationship going. But I couldn't help but zone out as images of chaos and gore flashed on the screen.

Amber often played tricks on the phone to keep me paying attention. If she ever thought I was doing something else she'd sometimes start talking about something crazy like our house burning down, or her winning millions of dollars in the lottery. If I replied with "Yeah, uh huh" then she knew I wasn't paying attention. She caught me all the time, but this time the reason was legitimate—the footage from Haiti was hard to not look at.

"...but my mom and dad are going down to help." That caught my attention and ripped me from the TV.

"Wait, what did you say?"

"My mom, dad and uncle are going to Port-au-Prince. Haven't you been listening?"

"Sure I have. So, then, do you want to go?" I asked.

"I just told you that I can't. School won't let me out. But they were wondering if you would want to come."

I paused and let silence hit the phone for a few moments while I processed all the information. Why the hell did they want me to come? I'm not a doctor or nurse. Amber spoke again. "I figured you wouldn't want to. It's okay, Sean." She said it in a way that exposed her disappointment.

Oh, I could detect disappointment, all right. It reminded me of when my dad had told me I'd done a good job at a basketball game when we both knew I stunk. I always felt guilty for being so bad at sports, especially since he'd always volunteered to be the coach. He'd spent every afternoon and weekend with me or my sisters, helping out with sports, school or our cars. He'd always answered our questions, gave amazing advice, and never seemed disappointed. His father died before his eleventh birthday and he'd spent most of his teenage years raising his younger brothers and sister. He'd started a construction company and worked his fingers to the bone six days a week so he could give us everything he never had. He'd sent me to a top-notch university, my first sister to one of the best writing schools in the country, and saved every day to send my youngest sister wherever she wanted when the time finally came.

I'd spent much my childhood trying to make him proud, but as a kid I always sat the bench and never made the game-winning point. He coached every team I ever played on and never made me feel like a "coach's son." Even though my grades always excelled, I often felt sick to my stomach when I let him down at basketball or baseball. I carried an iron lug in my stomach that tried to pull my throat in and made me ill. So yeah, I knew how to disappoint.

The same sickness rose again with Amber. I didn't want to let her down, too.

"No, I want to go." I lied. "I just don't know if work will let me."

"Sean," she persisted. "Don't worry about it. I know this isn't your thing."

When she said this, she challenged me, although I knew she hadn't meant to. I made my mind up out of impulse and defiance.

"No, stop it. I'll find a way to get out of work. Tell your mom I'm coming."

She stuttered on the line, prompting a sudden smug smile to form on my lips.

"You… you sure?"

"Yeah. Love you. Gotta go."

As I hung up the phone, something else replaced the bundle of worry brewing in my stomach. I remembered feeling it only once before, moments after finding out I was to be expelled from college for smoking pot in my dorm room. As a sophomore, I'd gone out one night with buddies and gotten drunk at a few bars that served underage students. Wasted and feeling immortal, I brought a few friends back to my room. We partied too loud, and in our drunken stupor forgot to mask the smell seeping out the doorway. When the RA knocked, I knew I looked at expulsion and thus the end of my entire professional career, before it even started. Luckily it was the first time I'd gotten into trouble, and so I got a one-time chance to change. I never tested the rules at school again afterwards. I laughed silently about the ordeal while tying my shoes in the hotel room before leaving for dinner.

A crowd stood around the central television in the hotel lobby as I entered. CNN played the same clips I'd seen in my room. Already reporters had arrived in the country to do live reports. Some hotel guests stood watching with their hands clasping their mouths while others just shook their heads slowly in disbelief as the shocking images scrolled across the screen. I noticed Stu standing alone by the door still wearing his backpack on one shoulder.

"Those poor people," Stu said without diverting his eyes from the TV.

"Yeah, total nightmare."

"It's going to get worse you know," he continued. "Looting, killing, riots." He paused for a moment, turning to look at me. "You going?" It took a few seconds of silence until I remembered that I'd told him about my mission trip to meet her parents. Why did I always share my life story with everyone? Of course he figured I wanted to go.

The sickness rose again and waved its arrival flag in my gut. If I said yes to Stu then I had to go. Once he knew, the whole team would, too.

"If work will let me, then yeah."

He nodded, obviously thinking for a moment. "They've got to let you go for something like this. I can't imagine them saying no."

"We'll see," was all I could muster.

I planned to eat a juicy steak, drink a few beers, and finish with an oversized dessert. The restaurant sat in the hotel parking lot, which made the visit even more enjoyable when I planned to have more than just a few drinks. A creature of habit, I ate at the same place almost every night and had gotten to the point where they left a seat at the bar open for me.

"Evening Mr. Wright, same thing as usual?" I turned to see Claire tending the bar, her characteristic smile looking right through me. Claire was a short, heavyset woman in her late forties with curly blonde hair and freckles. She wore thick glasses that blurred her eyes. We usually talked about her kids or my dogs. She made me feel at home.

"Sounds good. I'm starving."

My food came immediately. I suspected that on Tuesdays the kitchen prepped my dinner in advance, knowing I always showed. Though convenient, it did tend to depress me. Was I that predictable?

The loop on CNN integrated new clips as the night dragged on. As darkness fell for the first evening in devastated Haiti, firefights and riots broke out, and reports came in of looting and murder. Stu had guessed correctly. The Dominican border patrols reported a massive exodus from Haiti. Even though the news got worse by the minute, no one at the restaurant brought it up. Instead, they kept their eyes on the televisions that played sports as they ate dinner or drank beer.

"Glad I'm not there," said an intoxicated man a few bar stools down. He stammered, visibly drunk. "Looks like it's going to be a bloodbath."

After dinner I returned to the hotel to sleep, but I felt wired from dinner and the day. I flipped through the channels mindlessly as I sat in bed, leaning against the headboard.

Amber had asked me to go to Haiti, but I really didn't know if I wanted anything to do with it. Work seemed boring but it was safe, and I had a decent life going between it, my relationship, and friends. I didn't want to ruin a good thing. In reality, the thought of going mortified me. I replayed the short video clips from the TV in my head. Each time I closed my eyes, I imagined someone robbing, beating, or killing me.

I turned off the TV and plugged in my cell phone as I set the alarm for the next day. Though I was freezing at first, a few minutes of lying wrapped in warm blankets created a safe cocoon to call home for the night.

Then, like a flash of lightning, the idea came to me out of nowhere: I'd ask her parents in Haiti. It sounded perfect.

Tuesday, January 12th 2010
5:35pm
Port Au Prince, Haiti

Lucas dug at the pile furiously, pulling rocks, metal, and glass with his torn, bloodied hands and the mangled handlebar. He called out to his mother Tasha again and again—but she didn't respond. He jammed the handlebar from his bike into a joint and pushed. A rock moved and rolled down the side of the pile to reveal a small crevice. He moved his head and let the sunlight peek through the hole as dust filled the rays and scattered the light under the pile.

At first he thought the glow tricked him. He pulled more rubble away to open the hole and brighten the gap. He peeked over the edge to let as much light in as possible, and then could faintly see it: an arm stuck out from under their wooden kitchen table.

"Mom!" he shouted. She didn't respond. He pulled more rocks from the pile before sticking his arm into the opening, but not far enough to reach her. He screamed again, this time directly in the opening, the shape of the slope making his voice echo. He pulled back to let as much light in as he could and then he noticed it. Her fingers moved.

People crowded around while he screamed, but once he saw her fingers move he shouted in panic and excitement at the same time. "Mom! My mom's alive!" He looked around and waved for some of the men to come closer. "Please help. She's alive! I can't reach her!"

His neighbor Marc, a tall, strong man who worked down at the docks unloading fish, stood closest to him. Lucas didn't know him that well since he worked very late and got up early, but his mother and Marc's wife often hung out together washing clothes or cooking food. Marc held a long, thick iron bar that looked like part of a strong fence.

"Where is she?" he asked as he peeked into the hole as well.

"She's under the table. Her hand is moving."

Marc started digging at the pile with the rod. It was much stronger and longer than the motorbike handlebar. Each thrust pulled out several rocks the same size as the biggest ones Lucas had manage to pry free. Two other men joined Marc and Lucas, each with a pry bar or fulcrum. They dug again and again, working diligently to free her. Once all the big rocks were out of the way only a few boulders sat between them and Tasha.

Marc pulled his beaten car up to the pile and wrapped a heavy metal chain around the biggest chunk of concrete. He floored it and sent the back tires spinning in the dirt as the frame shifted back and forth. The car wheezed heavily under the strain, but the block budged slightly. It only needed to move an inch or so before it crumbled away into smaller pieces.

By the time they reached her, ten people dug at the pile. Lucas pushed to the front of the crowd to pull the table away.

She was alive, but barely. He went to touch her but Marc held him back.

"No boy, don't get too close. Wait for a doctor."

He got on his knees and looked at her. She took in short, staggered breaths as she gasped for air. Thick, deep gashes ran across her chest and face and oozed blood. Her left shin swelled with blood and looked broken. She struggled to stay awake as she looked at him and cried.

"Lu... Lucas."

"Don't talk, mom. Help's on the way." He grabbed her hand and held it tight. She looked away and closed her eyes as pain took hold over the shock.

A nurse who lived in the neighborhood rushed to his side. She just happened to be in the crowd and watched as they pulled the rocks away. She pulled open Tasha's shirt and inspected the gashes and then gently felt the leg. His mother cried out in pain when she touched it.

"Her leg is broken, and those cuts are very deep." She thought for a moment while looking around at the debris in the yard. "Make a splint and straighten it out. Get some clean cloths, soak them with water, and stuff the wounds. Then get her to any hospital you can."

He stopped for a moment, bewildered. "What are you talking about? Aren't you going to fix her?"

She closed her eyes and took a breath. "I can't. I need to help many more. She's not that bad. You have to do this. I'm sorry."

She stood and put her hand on his shoulder. "Just be brave. Make a splint, straighten her leg to set the bone, and bandage the cuts. Then get her to the hospital." She left him and continued down the street to help more people.

He looked around. A broken dresser sprawled haphazardly on the ground with his clothes spilling out. He pulled a drawer from it and grabbed at t-shirts, but only found a few free of any dirt or dust. He tore them into shreds and soaked them at a nearby broken faucet that spewed water on the sidewalk. He balled them into tight ropes and returned to his mom. He gently inserted them into the wounds. The white fabric turned red immediately.

He stood and looked for a splint. His handlebar sat in the rubble with the paint and chrome finish destroyed from relentless digging. It still seemed relatively straight and only a little shorter than her leg. It would work. It had to work.

"Mom, I need to make a splint, but first I need to set the bone." He didn't want to hurt her. The thought of it turned his stomach and forced tears to his eyes. She shook from fear under him as he held the bar. She closed her eyes and looked away. His only training came from watching TV at the store.

Lucas untangled the wires from the motorbike into long strands and slid the metal against her leg. Suddenly and without giving her warning he jerked on her foot and pulled it toward him to set the bone as he sat below her feet. He heard a grind and then a click – then she screamed in pain. Blood poured out, but he thought it looked straight. He wrapped the handlebar with electrical wire while pulling tighter with every revolution. Her skin swelled around the wires as blood rushed to set the bone.

With the splint in place he needed to find a way to get to the hospital. Debris blocked most of the roads, and traffic jammed the few still open. His neighbor had taken his car down the street as soon as they finished. He suddenly remembered that his mother had a small wheelbarrow she used for groceries. Running around the house, he found it against the back wall, undamaged. He sat it behind her and tipped it so that he could drag her onto it. She helped balance with her good leg while he pulled the handles back and upright again. The wheelbarrow held her, but fifteen city blocks stood between them and the closest hospital.

With every step Lucas flexed his arms and shoulders to keep the shaky cart from tipping. Everywhere he walked rubble and debris covered the street and sidewalk and forced him to snake back and forth, which made the distance much longer and slow going. Tasha tensed up in pain every time he ran over a pothole or crack in the street.

Chaos and fear had overtaken the neighborhood. People worked through the night digging out their homes in search of loved ones. Bodies lined the sidewalk covered in sheets and guarded by men. Women knelt over them and wept while beating their chests and rocking back and forth as husbands and friends tried to comfort them. Shops sat destroyed by the earthquake and subsequent looting. Small fires burned everywhere and filled the street with thin smoke. Lucas likened it to what the Egyptians must have felt after Moses brought the plague that killed first-born children. No one had escaped the torment completely unharmed.

His lower back and legs burned from exhaustion and thirst raged in his throat, but he pushed himself to continue moving. He saw the huge hill leading to the entrance of the hospital a few blocks away. He dug deep to get there as his muscles tore and his head throbbed.

He stopped to catch his breath near a busy fork, where the road met a long, steep driveway leading to the hospital. Dust filled his nostrils as he inhaled deeply to catch his breath and slow his heartbeat. His mother seemed barely conscious. She hung loosely from the wheelbarrow with her back arched painfully over the side to keep the broken leg supported.

It took several minutes of desperate pushing up the hill before Lucas realized the truth: He just couldn't make the climb.

"Take a break," she muttered, her eyes now open and looking pitifully on her son. "I'll be okay, just sit and get your strength back." She looked over at the road. "Maybe someone can give us a ride."

He didn't think of that. Cars flew past them in both directions, but many of them went up the hill. A van rushed toward them. He waved, begging them to stop as he stepped into the road. As it neared its horn blared. It didn't slow down but swerved around him at the last moment. It looked packed with people. He tried to flag down a few more, but no one stopped. Everyone rushed to get their own people to the hospital before it filled.

He stopped flagging cars and returned to the wheelbarrow. As he went to lift the handles he heard tires squeal behind him. An old, rusty pick-up truck stopped. Zac peered from the driver's seat and his older brother sat in the front with bloody t-shirts and cloths wrapped around his face. People he knew from the neighborhood filled the bed.

"Lucas!" Zac yelled as he stopped before jumping out of the truck and coming to meet him. "God, let me help you out."

He helped Tasha out of the wheelbarrow while Lucas held her by the shoulders. The truck belonged to one of the other neighbors, an older man sitting in the bed with his wife. He had broken both of his legs under a wall when his home fell. Zac had found him and his wife under the rubble and he let Zac use the truck to get them to the hospital. It filled with people as soon as he turned the engine, and they'd go back for more as soon as they finished the first trip.

With Lucas and his mom in the back, Zac zoomed up the hill while drifting back and forth as rubble spewed under the bald tires. A hundred feet or so from the entrance they hit a clog of vehicles parked on the road and the shoulder, blocking the way in. People unloaded on the street and walked up the hill. The truck emptied, and Zac helped the elderly man's wife get her husband out of the back. Lucas scooted Tasha to the edge of the truck and put her arms around his neck and shoulders. He turned and walked toward the entrance with her hanging from his back like a lead weight. She felt awkward with the leg kept straight and dangling on his side, but he limped forward again and again until he walked through the gates.

Thousands of people clogged the parking lot at the top. Soldiers stood at the front of the entrance with guns drawn and prevented the mob from rushing in. Men and women helped victims with broken bones, missing limbs, severe burns, and blood soaked flesh in every direction. Suddenly, his mother's injuries seemed small in comparison.

An older woman in a white lab coat and a megaphone came out of the hospital and stood on top of a van parked at the front entrance. She raised her hand to quiet the crowd.

"Everyone please calm down. We're trying to figure out how to help everyone. For now you must stay outside."

The crowd screamed in anger, desperate and on the brink of riot.

"We are sending out help to walk through the crowd. If your injuries are serious enough we will bring you inside. If not you will have to wait."

She got off the van and walked through the entrance of the hospital. A few minutes later a dozen employees came out with medical bags slung over their shoulders. Lucas lost sight of them in the mob. He sat down on the curb, his mother almost asleep on the grass beside him. Zac stood nearby with his brother still holding the fabric to his face.

Wednesday, January 13th, 2010

6:30am

Stuarts Draft, VA

I watched the early morning news while still wrapped in covers and propped against the headboard in my Virginia hotel room. I couldn't tear my eyes from the screen. While I'd slept, Haiti had begun tearing itself apart as rioting, looting, fights, and killings spawned all over the capital. Police were quickly overwhelmed, and the military stepped in, attempting to quell the largest of the riots while citizens put out fires and moved rubble from the streets. Disbelief and shock amongst the people transitioned to fear and anger as the mood of the city morphed into a bomb on the verge of detonation.

I turned off the TV and sat in silence as the morning sun peeked through the blinds. My thoughts focused only on the upcoming trip and how terrible it sounded. I took deep breaths to slow my heart as it threatened to beat out of my chest. I really didn't want to go, but it seemed like my only shot of asking Amber's parents my question in person.

I picked up my cell phone to call my boss, Sam. I wanted to get it out of the way. If he said no, then I had a great excuse for Amber. He picked up after the first ring.

"Sean?"

"Hey Sam…" I lost my train of thought and the courage to go any further. A long pause filled the air for an eternity until he spoke up again.

"I guess you're calling about Haiti, right?"

It sort of surprised me that he knew right away. Even though I'd told him in the past about the first mission trip I went on with Crossroads, we never got into the details of my experience. He'd cut to the chase, so I did too.

"Can I go?"

He didn't even pause. I found out later he'd secured permission the day the quake struck in anticipation of my request.

"Sean, we figured you'd ask about this. Normally our policy on these things is no, but this is a pretty unique circumstance and you already have a history with this group. You can go."

He told me I'd have to use vacation days, but I didn't care. I felt so surprised he'd said yes at all. I thanked him and hung up the phone. I sat on the couch in silence and stared at the TV as the clips repeated themselves. I kept it on mute but I knew what they said:

"Stay away, Sean. This is not your thing."

I called Amber and told her the news. After a late night on the phone with her mother, she sounded half asleep, but perked up once I mentioned my talk with Sam. She couldn't believe they'd said yes, and instead had expected me to call and change my plans after being denied.

"I told my mom not to expect you. Neither of us thought your boss would say yes."

"Well, I'm going. I'm coming home today. Can you find me a flight?"

I heard her type on the keyboard, and in a few moments she replied. "2:30 this afternoon."

That evaporated any chance of visiting my parents or friends before leaving.

"Fine. Book it. I'll see you later."

"Megan will be waiting for you in the airport when you arrive. Luke is coming, too."

"Excellent," I replied. "It will be good to know at least a few people in the capital."

Megan lived in Canada but had already completed several long trips to Crossroads over the past few years. She reacted with shock and frustration during her first visit to Puerto Plata. She witnessed how the poor lived less than 700 miles from Miami. Her first visit came with a church group that did the typical ministries in Crossroads: visiting the dump, prison, hospital, and the villages. Unlike most people, she couldn't limit herself to just one experience. Shortly after her group left she returned on her own to help for a longer time. Eventually she made Crossroads a second home. During my first visit I met her at the village while she worked through a several month project to oversee the grounds and to organize building projects.

I'd first met Luke when I visited Amber's family at Crossroads. Luke was dating Faith, Amber's older sister and, like me, tried his best to impress their family, albeit in a different way. While I came to visit, he was in the midst of a multi-month project working in the villages. Every time I heard about him the story revolved around mission work, volunteering, or just helping others. His drive to help others actually frustrated me because it let me know what I had to compete against for Bob and Jana's approval. Even worse, just after spending a little time with him I found him extremely likable. I couldn't help but like him, a fact that only frustrated me more. It would be good to see him again, but I knew I needed to work as hard as I could since we would both be in his element while helping in Port-au-Prince.

"Sean?" Amber interrupted my thought. "I love you so much. I just want you to know that."

"I love you too."

I hung up the phone smiling and happy having made Amber proud. I found that I did a lot of things just to make her happy. I loved her without leaving anything behind for safety, no remnant of reserve that only left me 99% invested. I'd do anything she wanted even if I hated it, but she did the same for me. She often showed up at my home in the early hours of the morning just to wake me up and cuddle, even if she had to drive an hour to do it. She let me play my video games, and even pretended to like them.

I remembered one night where I came back from work just before midnight. Amber and I had planned to go out for dinner together, but an emergency at one of the local plants required me to stay late. I got home and jumped in the shower, fully ready to fall asleep as soon as I hit the bed. When I got out of the bathroom, Amber was at my place and already sleeping in my bed. She had woken up from her dorm at college and driven back to surprise me. When I didn't come home on time, she hung around in secret until I got back a few hours later just so she could surprise me with a sleepover. She always went out of her way to make me feel special.

Back at the hotel in Virginia, I packed my things and went to grab breakfast in the lobby when I ran into Stu watching TV. He looked at me as I rushed through the lobby.

"It's only Wednesday. Where you going?"

"Haiti. Work let me go."

He choked on a mouthful of waffles as he laughed from surprise. He swallowed hard and got up to meet me. I dropped my bags and shook his hand at the door.

"You're really going? Wow, that's awesome. How long will you be there?"

"It's an open-ended ticket, which I may not catch if I don't leave now."

"Well, please be safe. Need you back here when you're done!"

My mind raced as fast as I drove during the four-hour trip. Five-dollar blackjack tables had been my riskiest endeavors to date, yet now I planned to travel to the poorest country in the western hemisphere less than a day after the worst earthquake in its history. I liked to lead a simple and predictable lifestyle and had never veered too far off the course I set in front of me. This existed far outside my comfort zone. Each passing mile felt like falling a few more feet toward a jagged ravine at the bottom of a canyon. That sick feeling in my stomach awoke once more.

At one point I focused more on the scenery around the highway and less on the destination. I'd made my choice. Work had given the green light, Amber had booked the flight, and my house sat less than an hour away. The terrain of Pennsylvania was packed full of farm fields and woods. Interstate 81 cut through the virgin landscape with cold, harsh precision. I felt safe in the aisles of the highway while protected in my car from the winter cold. I felt the warmth of the heater and listened to the sound of the radio mix with the rumble of the engine. Houses along the highway spat smoke from chimneys. Suddenly an awareness of my fortune revealed itself in my mind. I didn't want to leave my home, and I didn't want to go to Haiti.

Forty miles from the exit my cell phone rang. My mother. I answered like a man disarming a bomb.

"Hello?"

"Sean! What the hell are you doing? Amber just called. Were you not going to tell me? Are you seriously going to Haiti? The news is showing people dying all over the place."

Her concern reinforced the fear and doubt lingering in my stomach. I felt terrible about not calling, but perhaps subconsciously I didn't want her to make me more nervous. I grew up as my mother's son and we always remained close, especially through my awkward teenage years where my acne and stringy body kept me from making any other friends. I always confided in her, and I found that she always confided in me. As mothers go, she always felt like the best. She spent my entire childhood as a homemaker and tirelessly worked to raise me and my two younger sisters. I could only remember a few nights over my entire life where she missed making a hot meal for everyone at dinner. She'd made every Halloween costume by hand, tucked us into bed every night when I was young, and kept the secret of Santa alive even when no one else believed. She'd always protected us against the world, and in many ways I felt like this move betrayed the protection she tirelessly maintained for me and my sisters. It wasn't that I'd forgotten to call her. No, I hadn't called because I just didn't know how to tell her what I planned to do. I didn't even know how to explain it to myself.

"I'm sorry mom. I just got the okay from work this morning. I didn't want to worry you until I knew for sure. I should have called a couple hours ago. Are you okay?"

Her tone gave away her fear and tension. I reacted to change just like her.

"It's just so dangerous there. Why are you going?"

This felt like the moment to make her understand. She knew how much I loved Amber and often I joked that she loved her more than I did. After a few failed relationships she couldn't stop fawning over Amber when I finally made the introductions. Perhaps confiding in her once again would make us both feel better.

"I want to ask her parents for permission to marry her and I need to do it in person."

I didn't hear her breathe or even gasp; instead I heard nothing at all. After a few moments passed I could hear her cry.

"Mom, are you okay?"

She spoke up through what I knew was a wall of tears barely held back. "That is the most beautiful thing I've ever heard. I didn't know you wanted to propose."

"Yeah, I do. Do you think it's a good idea?"

I could almost hear her smiling, and imagined her tearing up silently as she softly jumped up and down, keeping the phone to her cheek with one hand while planting the other firmly against her other cheek as if squishing her lips together.

"It's perfect. Oh Sean it's perfect." She repeated the phrase a few times.

"Mom, I'm trusting you—you can't tell anyone. No one knows. Just me and you. Okay?"

I heard my dad cough in the background. She had me on speakerphone. I knew she looked at him with an icy stare when he coughed and she knew I knew the truth. I cleared the air.

"I can hear you dad."

She tried to shoo him away as if it made a difference. I heard him walk closer to grab the receiver, and I knew they argued silently with facial expressions and hand motions like they'd done a million times before over their twenty-six year marriage.

Dad spoke. "Congratulations Sean. We're so proud of you and we love Amber so much."

I felt his pride and happiness through the phone. I tried to keep the talk manly, but I really wanted to gush.

"Dad, you can't tell anyone. And you need to keep mom quiet too."

"Your secret's safe with us."

"What do you think?"

"About Haiti or Amber? Well—both are just as dangerous, I think." He laughed. "I'm sure they'll say yes, but do they know what they're doing? The news looks pretty bad."

"If Amber trusts them then I will too. Come over at 1:30. My plane leaves at 2:30 so I'll have a few minutes to talk."

"We'll be there, Sean. Congratulations again. We love you."

"Thanks, dad. Love you too."

I decided to turn off my phone for the last thirty minutes of the trip. I rolled down the windows and kept the heat on full blast to let the cold air come in and mix with it. The wind felt good on my face and the sun shined brightly against a deep blue canvas of endless sky. I turned off the radio and listened to the wind, taking in the scenes around me.

I wanted to remember as much as I could of home. I knew that the few minutes of peace and quiet would be my last for a while. I didn't know what the future held after that, but I felt ready.

Wednesday, January 13th 2010

11:50am

Hummelstown, Pennsylvania

I turned onto my street just before noon. As I got close to the house I noticed several cars parked in my driveway and along the curb. The air had frozen everything outside, but water still flowed on the hoods. I parked on the street and sat back with my eyes closed as I killed the engine. Worms crawled in my stomach. My lungs felt heavy and half full with water. My head pounded to the point that I sensed the veins in my eyes pulsate with every heartbeat.

The prospect of leaving so soon overwhelmed me with worry. I love to pack at least a day in advance. I always count out my outfits down to the socks I will wear each day as I neatly place them in my bag. I count the days as I pack: "Monday, Tuesday, Wednesday," like some sort of religious ritual. Sometimes I even take an extra day's worth of clothes just in case I lose a day in travel. But this time, Amber had packed for me. No time remained to sleep on the decision to go. I couldn't even shower.

I climbed the steps to the front door and it opened before I grabbed my keys. Gordito, my first dog and best friend, jumped, throwing me back a few steps as I tried to grab hold of him. He was a mutt that I'd brought home after my first mission trip to Crossroads. Dr. Bob rescued him from a landfill and kept him alive long enough for me to see him. Sick and filled with worms, no one believed he could survive more than a few days. Gordito literally means "little fatty," and when we found him his stomach sat distended and he resembled a melon with legs. I'd never grown so attached to something before, so hopelessly in love that all my vulnerabilities came out in one clumsy wave. I spent the first night baby talking with him as I cradled him and fed him yogurt, rice, and scrambled eggs. I brought him back on an empty JetBlue flight on his own seat next to me. The flight attendants brought him dog treats as he slept with his head on my leg. Then he grew into a seventy-pound loaf of fur. He barked all the time and I spoiled him rotten. Yet he still put his head on my leg when I watched TV at night.

After a few moments I pushed past him and met my other dog, Anna, in the doorway. A super shy pit-bull we rescued from the local animal shelter, she crept toward me slowly every time I came home. Anna was a former baiting dog in an illegal dog fighting circuit and had been a victim to brutal abuse. When the humane society rescued her, it took several months before she could be touched without shaking. She only trusted a few select people. She came over slowly with her tongue hanging freely in the air. I patted her head. She moved away after welcoming me home and returned to her spot on the rug.

A big bag sat packed on the couch. Amber, my parents, and grandparents stood in the kitchen waiting for me to finish with the dogs.

"Sean!" Amber yelled and lunged forward. She partly jumped in the air and forced me to catch her. "Are you ready?"

I hesitated. "Yeah, it'll be great."

"Sean, you don't have to go. You know that, right?"

She really meant it, but it felt too late to turn back. "No, no. I'm going."

She knew my mind was racing and my nerves were near the breaking point, so she let the questions stop. She understood how to deal with me—pushing made it worse. I got a big hug instead as she pulled her head onto my shoulder. She always seemed to know the right things to say.

A few months back, Amber and I had been out at dinner when an old friend from college called me. He let me know that someone I knew quite well had died in a car accident the night before. In shock and on the verge of tears, I managed a rattled "thanks for calling" before hanging up the phone.

"Who was that?" she asked, noticeably concerned. I lacked the ability to hide my emotions, especially around her. She knew right away that something was up.

"Someone from school. A buddy of mine died in a car accident."

Most people would start to ask a lot of questions about the person, how it happened, and how I felt about the whole thing. Not Amber. She knew that the only thing keeping me from breaking down in the restaurant was not talking about it, and she knew how much I hated to cry. She just said "I'm sorry," and held my hand as we continued to eat our dinner. I knew it bothered her to not ask more questions, but she understood how my mind worked. She knew I'd tell her everything later when I was ready. I loved her ability to understand me, and always make me comfortable regardless of the situation.

Standing in my family room with Amber in my arms my mind juggled the multiple things that needed to happen before I got to Haiti.

"What time does my plane leave?"

"Two-thirty." She looked at the bags. "I know you like to do it, but I packed for you already." She paused and looked at the luggage before speaking up. "I wish I could come."

"Me too, sweetheart." Amber wanted to help but school had denied the request. If she went on this trip she would have to repeat the semester.

My parents shuffled into the family room along with my mother's parents.

My mom spoke up first, trying to hide a smile. "Are we interrupting?"

I blushed. "No mom, you're good." I walked over and gave her a hug. My dad shook my hand and pulled me in for a hug, all while smirking as his glance passed between me and Amber.

Mom checked the contents of my bag. "I can't believe you're doing this, Sean," she said in a way that made it hard to tell whether she meant the trip to Haiti or my plan to ask Amber's parents for permission. Probably both.

"He'll be fine, Maryrose. Don't freak him out," my dad said.

"Meghan and Molly say good luck and they love you," my mom said, changing the subject. "Molly couldn't get out of school to come over, but she's excited for you. I spoke to Meghan just before coming over here. You should call her before you go."

"I will."

I didn't call either of my sisters about the trip. Molly didn't get out of school for another hour. Molly is my youngest sister and there's a ten-year age gap between us. She's always acted as my biggest fan and greatest ally on all subjects, and I've always tried to do the same for her. She, like many siblings that are much younger than the others, had learned quickly how to speak to and hang out with older people. By the time she reached six I was driving, and when I graduated from college she had only just finished sixth grade. Her time with Meghan and me gave her an ability to relate on a mature level that set her apart from her friends. Her humor seemed more in depth, her dreams more grounded, and her outlook on life very adult. In sixth grade I had feared anyone even a few years older; she, by contrast, preferred their company. She loved Amber and never stopped telling me whenever the opportunity arose. Once my mother told her my plans, I knew she in turn would tell everyone she knew at school.

Only two years separated Meghan and me. For most of our childhood I'd acted often as a bully, instigator, and crook to her. I'd loved to tease her and make her cry, even though she'd rarely done anything to warrant the rough treatment. She'd always spoken sweet words and never stopped requesting hugs from mom or dad. Not until we both went to the same high school did we suddenly start to get along. For me it had begun cautiously, like an elephant trying to navigate a minefield, so I assumed it had seemed an even bigger feat for her. Yet slowly, over time, we'd learned to trust each other, and then, finally, to rely on each other. After college she'd continued to live in Brooklyn, but we spoke almost every day about our jobs, goals, or daily problems. By the time I met Amber, Meghan had grown very protective of me, and selective about whomever I dated. She saw many girls come and go and didn't approve of most, so once she realized how ideally Amber fit with me, she committed to letting her into the family as well.

My grandparents didn't want me to go. The news had gotten even worse than before and they just couldn't understand why I wanted to leave. My grandfather, or 'Poppy' as we called him, looked more solemn than I'd ever seen him before. He usually acted super jolly, a beacon of laughter and a fountain of rusty Irish jokes regardless of the occasion. Right then, however, he was not in a joking mood.

"This is a pretty dangerous thing Sean," was all he said as he wrapped one monstrous arm around me. "But we know you're smart enough to make the right choices. We're very proud of you." As it turned out, my grandfather died a year later, and the way he told a joke is how I remember him the most. They weren't very funny and he told the same ones over and over again, but he committed to telling them so seriously that I couldn't ever help but enjoy them.

My mom finished making tea when I entered the kitchen, and we stood around for a few minutes to talk about my plans. I didn't know much but shared what I did. The fact that Amber's parents ran the mission group and oversaw the trip brought my family some relief, but the concept of entering Haiti pushed the boundaries of normality too far for them to feel safe.

Amber interrupted and reminded me of the time. I hugged my parents and grandparents and they wished me luck before leaving to let me prepare for the trip. Usually they would stay for much longer, and the goodbyes would take almost as long. Our family preferred to talk long into the night, each person speaking louder than the next until the house filled with the chaotic clamor of discussion. Yet they knew I had almost no time, and knew I wanted to spend some of it with Amber. After they left, I exhaled deeply as I settled heavily on the couch. We sat together with the dogs at our feet while the midday winter sun emitted a pale glow through the family room window. I wanted to fall asleep right there with her and never leave the couch again, but we both knew the moment had to be short.

Shortly after, we packed the car and drove to the airport. We unloaded my bags and said goodbye. I kissed her, and she started to cry.

"I'll see you soon honey, I promise," I whispered to her.

"You better! I love you."

Eventually I had to pull away or miss my flight. I watched her drive from the terminal and disappear into traffic. I didn't cry, but I had a lump in my stomach. I couldn't tell if it was sadness over leaving Amber or dread of things to come.

Barely more than a dozen gates sat in the small airport. I showed up minutes before the flight, passed quickly through security, and boarded the plane without much effort. I bought some snacks, bottled water, and a few magazines for the trip. I'd brought my small company flip phone but left my personal one at home.

I sat on an empty plane in a seat near the back. I put up the armrest, stretched my legs out, and put my head against the window. Then I closed my eyes and curled my thighs close to my chest as my mind processed the day so far. It had passed in a whirlwind and it felt in some ways like a dream. Slowly, I drifted off to sleep before the plane left the gate. Soon we took off, headed to Newark where I'd make my connection to Puerto Plata.

I dreamt about my first date with Amber. We went to a McDonald's by Messiah College. We went late at night after a long day at work. I drove over in my Subaru, and I could smell the fresh scent of my red leather seats. The world was trying to emerge from a bitter cold winter into early spring. Flowers had bloomed, but were drowned in frost from the night's cold air. She looked beautiful. On the other hand, my clothes needed washing ir was an unruly mop from wearing a hard hat all day. vve ate fries and drank soda in the parking lot, I in the driver's seat and she on my lap, her legs stretched across the dash. She kissed me in the dream, but we didn't kiss on that date. She acted like a tomboy. She burped louder than me. I acted offended but couldn't help but laugh. I felt so comfortable around her. I went to kiss her again, but then the screech from the plane fractured the dream as I wavered on the delicate line between awake and asleep.

We landed, and I woke as the plane idled on the runway in Newark. By the time I finished stretching my neck, the smell of the fries and my leather seats dissipated as the dream images faded. I looked out the window. A thin layer of snow covered the ground and made the tarmac feel empty, as if the world had ended while in flight.

Although usually packed with people buzzing from one gate to the next, the terminal felt eerie and empty in the mid afternoon. I arrived at my gate six hours before my flight. Above it a large dome of glass encased the hall and formed a globe that allowed me to see up into the afternoon sky.

Thick, gloomy clouds sat heavy in the sky. They produced a dull glow that filled the room with thick light. They seemed ready to burst and pour waves of snow on the airport. I always loved the feeling before a snowstorm; it brought back childhood memories of sledding, building snow forts, and drinking hot cocoa. Cozy under the blanket of clouds, I hugged my pack and curled into my seat in the terminal. I planned to spend the few hours switching between sleeping and reading magazines until the time came to board.

After several hours, my phone rang and I read my sister Meghan's name on the screen. I answered the phone and said hello, immediately apologizing for not calling sooner. I usually performed better with this stuff, especially with her. My mother had told her about my trip right after we spoke, and she'd tried to call me several times already while I slept in flight from Harrisburg to Newark. She asked how long I planned to go, where the team wanted to visit, and what we planned to do while there. Most of my answers turned out to be vague because I didn't know too many specifics myself. After she felt comfortable with the basics, she cut to the chase.

"So, you're planning to ask Bob and Jana about Amber, then?"

Mom had told her, but it didn't surprise me. Keeping a secret within our family meant the rule only applied outside the immediate circle. I replied awkwardly like a kid caught lying, but in truth I really wanted her approval.

"That's the plan. What do you think?"

She paused before responding. To me, her ability to stop for a second and think something through before just mindlessly answering was exactly why I held her opinion above most. She actually cared, and she took the time to think her answers through.

"It's a scary thought, going to Haiti. But it is a perfect opportunity. Are you sure you want to marry her?"

I'd thought it through a million times before. "There's no doubt."

"Then I'm very happy for you. Amber is a great catch."

I felt a small lump build in my throat as she spoke that reaffirmed just how much her input meant to me. An announcement over the loudspeaker in the terminal declared the start of boarding for my flight.

"I'm happy you approve. I love you Meghan."

"I love you too, Sean. Be careful."

"I will, I promise. I'll be back soon."

She hung up the phone and I sat back to look around the room. It had filled considerably while I'd slept and had become packed even further in the last few minutes. I boarded with the crowd. Everyone else on the flight was Dominican, and the Spanish gave me a killer headache and made me feel alien. The seat next to mine was one of the last vacant ones. I hoped it remained that way. Just before I spread out into it, I saw her.

A young woman about twenty-five years old looked at my row and nodded. My heart sank but I tried to smile as I shuffled out into the aisle as she took the window seat. I felt torn between saying hi and closing my eyes. I gambled on the former.

"Hi I'm Sean."

"Tamara."

She looked Dominican and didn't quite fit the clothes she wore, her arms protruding from the undersized shirt like sausage pushed out of a mould. She wore long nails covered in red paint and glitter, dark artificial eyebrows, and tons of makeup. Cheap jewelry covered her fingers, wrists, neckline, and exposed belly button in gold and silver. Her perfume smelled so strong that I needed to catch my breath when it first hit me. She shuffled around in her seat for a few moments and then stared at me. She wanted me to speak. I tried to fill the air.

"So Tamara, where ya going?"

"To see my boyfriend."

I nodded in feigned interest, and she immediately unleashed a wave of information with her baritone, high-velocity voice. I got her life story in a few minutes, but I only soaked up the basics.

When she stopped for a few seconds it left the air clumsily empty again, and I looked over to see her staring back at me. Did I miss a question in the haze, or was she just pausing to take a breath? Neither would surprise me. The plane took off. She closed her eyes and dug both hands into the armrests as she shoved her shoulders into the cheap and stiff seat.

"Don't worry Tamara; you're more likely to die in a car crash than in a plane," I said. She didn't answer, but kept her eyes closed as if opening them would turn her to stone. My comment probably didn't help.

It only took a few moments to get in the air, but the whole plane applauded loudly once we breached the clouds. Every time I've flown to or from the Dominican Republic, the crowd on the plane has celebrated as if taking off wasn't a guarantee and a safe landing was a bonus.

"So, where are you going?" Tamara asked.

"Going to Haiti." I said it casually, and then looked elsewhere as I tried to downplay the comment as much as I could.

She reacted loudly, but not for reason I expected. "What, you a missionary or something? Don't ya know how crazy it is over there right now? It's dangerous, especially for a white boy like you."

"White boy like me? Don't you know I'm half Native American?" I winked, trying to lighten the mood and wanting to phase out of the conversation. She didn't budge. I continued, "I'm on a medical team."

"You a doctor?"

I told her no and gave her a brief idea of why I chose to go and whom I planned to meet.

"My girlfriend's parents run the mission; I'm going to help where I can."

She smiled, "Ahh—trying to get some brownie points with mom and dad? Pretty extreme."

"I guess you could say that."

"Wish my boyfriend did that kind of stuff for me. He won't even fly; I have to come to him."

We spoke for a little while more. It felt nice to get my mind off the trip, but it amazed me how she could go to the same island just a day after the earthquake and not even seem remotely concerned about the turmoil in Haiti. After a while she fell asleep. I slouched back on the seat, tucked my feet under the chair, and drifted off as well.

Wednesday, January 13th 2010
9:10pm
Santo Domingo, Dominican Republic

I awoke abruptly to the sound of cold rubber colliding with hot tarmac as the plane set down in Santo Domingo, the capital of the Dominican Republic. The joyful applause followed as predicted and pulled me from my dreamy state like cold water on the face. The night overwhelmed the city with darkness, but I could see the small airport nestled along the side of the runway, flanked by hundreds of lights.

The mood of the crowd changed as soon as the plane stopped. Everyone wanted to fill the aisle and push their way out. Even Tamara crawled past me from the window seat to squeeze in the waiting line. I stayed in my chair to let everyone else get out first. I've never understood the rush to get into the aisle; people just end up looking silly as they stand still with their butts and crotches in everyone's face. Does it really save any time? I closed my eyes and listened to the cabin grow quiet while the people behind me got their bags and hustled off. The bright lights in the plane tortured my eyes after sleeping for several hours, but my Ravens cap shielded them somewhat from the glow and relieved the strain from my eyelids. Once all the noise subsided I stood and gathered my bags and exited the plane. Near the baggage claim I sat down on the floor by the end, far away from the people hugging the conveyor belt that brought luggage into the terminal.

"Do you know any Spanish?"

Tamara stood just behind me with her head tilted to the side and her hands at her hips. I shook my head, indicating I didn't. She thought for a moment and looked past the baggage claim at the customs aisle that already had formed a long line.

"Want me to help you through customs? I doubt the ones working this late know much English."

I nodded as I stood to meet her eye to eye. "Yea, I'd love the help. Thank you so much." I was truly appreciative. I had a general fear of customs lines and having someone to walk and talk me through relieved all my concerns.

Once my bags arrived I followed her down the hall. Before I reached the customs line an immigration officer stopped me and started to speak. I didn't understand what he said so I kept walking. He threw his hand out and grabbed my shoulder while extending his other as he motioned the international sign for "Give me money." Tamara led a few steps ahead of me but stopped when I called out to her. She turned and gave the man a cold look before storming back to my side.

"I got this Sean. No worries."

She stepped in front and pointed her finger at the man as she lectured him in Spanish. He stared at me in silence as she spoke. Then a second woman joined Tamara. He responded with short nods as he kept his head pointed toward the ground like a boy punished for misbehaving. Then he walked back to the booth.

"You're not paying for a tourist visa. I don't care what the policy is." She looked very proud of herself, and I could tell she'd pulled some strings. I felt honored, but at the same time feared getting on her bad side. If her boyfriend knew what was good for him he'd try to keep her from going into that mode.

"Thanks," I replied sheepishly. "You didn't have to do that, but thanks." I gave a meek smile, and she gave a triumphant nod in reply.

"Like I said, I got your back."

At the entrance to customs the line split and allowed Dominican citizens to take a shortcut, leaving everyone else stand in a long, understaffed line. I thought she planned to split with me there, but she didn't. I tried to convince her to go, already grateful for the visa maneuver, but she resolved to stay. She wanted to help me through.

The line sprawled endlessly though the room, but it moved quickly. The agents gave tourists a hard time by going through their bags and asking lots of questions. My bags overflowed with medicine, clothing, toys, food, and first aid supplies that Jana had asked Amber to pack for our trip. I didn't want to get caught with some tax or fee for my supplies.

When we reached the front, a younger woman waved us to her station. Tamara led the conversation and only stopped momentarily to ask for my passport. As she spoke the agent looked at me and smiled several times, nodding as Tamara answered questions for me. I felt quite useless as I watched from the side. Tamara's presence did comfort me. Usually Amber took care of customs agents. She's traveled to every continent except Antarctica. She speaks Spanish fluently, and I always brags about how she'll flex her international experience when we go somewhere new. I compare it to knowing someone famous, someone who knows the in's and out's of travel and how to go from one place to the next. Traveling seems to be the only time I relinquished all my control-freak tendencies, turning everything over to her. Having her completely in control still makes me feel safe, but up to this point, it had prevented me from learning how to do it myself.

The agent stamped our passports and waved us on, saying *"Buena suerte"* to me as we walked through. I nodded and smiled, not knowing what she said.

"She said good luck, in case you wanted to know."

On the other side of customs we entered a larger hall that led to several exits.

"This is it," she said. "The taxis are down that hallway. Good luck on your trip." She gave me a brief hug and I thanked her for everything she did. I knew that without her help the agents might have checked my bags and could have taken my supplies.

Near the center of the hall a tall Dominican man held up a small bouquet of flowers. When Tamara noticed him, she turned and ran to him. She reached him with her arms outstretched and they embraced with a long and lustful kiss. They seemed blissfully unaware of the people moving all around them. She took his hand and they started toward the exit. She turned one last time and waved goodbye. I held my hand in the air and waved back.

I stood against a wall for a while in the main hall until much of the crowd left. I had arrived on one of the last flights of the night so I knew Megan waited somewhere for me. Once the room cleared enough I spotted her sitting on her luggage on the other side. She waved as I approached, looking equally tired from her trip.

When the earthquake first hit, Megan didn't think she'd take the trip to Haiti. Jana wanted her to go, but her work as a pastor and concern from her family caused doubt. In truth she'd felt much like I did—she didn't want to go and bet on someone telling her she couldn't. Yet everything that stood in her way somehow cleared to leave the decision up to her. Her pastor agreed to cover her sermons, the local church agreed to let her give a talk another weekend, and even her parents and husband, who usually didn't agree with the danger associated with mission work, thought the idea of going to Haiti fit her perfectly. She ended up coming, but had continued to question the decision until she'd reached the Santo Domingo airport.

It made the team much happier and complete that she chose to come. A born leader, Megan possessed the ability to make others feel safe even when she herself doubted the circumstance.

"Hey Meg." I said with half a breath as I slid my bags up to hers. "Been here long?"

"Just an hour or so." She stood and gave me a hug. "It's good to see you again."

We spoke for a short time. She told me all about Jana's plans to hand Crossroads' reins over to her in a few years, and I talked about work, Amber, and my home. I selectively decided to keep the proposal plans quiet. I didn't want Jana or Bob to find out accidently. I had a hard time keeping secrets, but I needed to maintain this one for as long as I could.

"So, who's coming to get us?" I asked as we headed toward the door.

"Jana sent a driver. Should be here already–I've just been waiting on you."

Near the exit we spotted a short man with a ragged piece of paper in his hands. He wore a faded brown hat, a plaid button-down shirt, and a pair of crumpled khakis. On the paper a few letters presented in scribbled and hurried writing read "Meegun" and "Shun."

Megan pointed while walking toward him. "That must be us."

She spoke to him in Spanish. He nodded, and we followed him outside. A compact car transformed into a makeshift taxi sat in the parking lot.

"There's no way we're fitting our stuff in that." I said to Megan while gauging the size of our bags.

The driver didn't seem concerned. He grabbed our luggage and mashed it into the trunk, filling it in moments. He motioned me to sit in the backseat and then piled bags on my lap before I could even get settled. Once nothing else fit on my lap he packed the space between me and the doors and around my feet. He slammed the backdoor shut with a forceful thud to lock me in place. I prayed and hoped for a short trip to Jana. Megan got in the front and set a pack on her lap and on the floor.

She looked back to poke fun. "Comfortable back there, Sean?"

With everything situated the driver hopped in, turned on the car, and sped away.

We drove through the narrow streets at breakneck speeds and with every sharp turn the car groaned from abuse. Each bump caused dozens of things to rattle both inside and out. I worried that a tire could fall off at any moment and send us rolling, even though I'd be cushioned by the mountain of luggage keeping me still. At least I didn't need a seatbelt.

The city streets sat empty late at night, and as we moved through the back alleys to our destination I took note of the area. Santo Domingo was old, very old. Narrow streets twisted and turned through it like spaghetti. Buildings were set so close to widened roads that people walked just inches from traffic. Cars half parked on the curbs and teetered unsteadily, with their roofs angling toward the street. I saw Parque Colon for a second as we passed the old town square. Rich history lined the city like a pillow about to burst. I was disappointed I wouldn't get to explore.

The taxi stopped at a narrow, three-story building huddled between two others on a side street just off Parque Colon. The driver spoke to Megan, and she nodded.

"This is where we get out."

The driver jumped out and opened my door, allowing some of the bags to spill out on the ground. I got out and stretched before looking around. The street was made of cobblestone, and though it looked just wide enough to be a one-way at home, here it served two-way traffic while also accommodating parking. Worn gray cobblestones laced with cracks were packed with sand and trash. A long row of buildings separated by inches sat on one side of the street, each one painted a different bright, tropical color. A light orange soaked the hotel and pink and cream buildings flanked it. Air flowed freely through large openings that replaced windows. White tube lighting covered the front entrance of the hotel and gave the street a calming yellow tint. Large cracks covered the walls like spider webs.

Young Dominicans filled the streets in this part of town, buzzing back and forth to parties and clubs. It felt hot and humid, but the women wore tight jeans that seemed to be painted on while most men wore slacks and button-down shirts. *Bachata, merengue,* and *salsa* music played in the distance and echoed off the streets and buildings, making it impossible to discern the source.

Suddenly Jana appeared out of the hotel entrance. She looked tired but happy to see us as she walked up and gave us both a hug.

"Oh, I'm so glad you came. This'll be an amazing trip. How was your flight?"

We looked at her and nodded slowly. She saw our exhaustion. Jana loved to talk and engage others about every subject, but she let us off for the night.

Two men from the hotel met us outside and helped drag our luggage into the lobby. They threw the bags into an already large pile sitting in the corner. Jana spoke to the owner for a few minutes and paid him for the evening. He nodded and left us alone in the room.

"Guys, only take your personal things to the room. We can keep everything else here in the lobby. Megan, here's a key for the room. Tomorrow we are meeting with Bob and the rest of the group before we head to Haiti. There is an orphanage in the city that will let us stay on the premises. I've known the owner for a very long time and she is expecting us tomorrow night."

Megan grabbed the key and went upstairs. I stood with my pack for a moment until Megan had left and only Jana and I remained. She walked up ahead of me but stopped a few steps up the stairs and turned to speak.

"Sean, I'm so glad you came." She gave me another big hug. I instantly changed my mind about coming; this would be the perfect trip to ask them. Tamara had it right—this would earn some serious brownie points with them. How could they say no?

"Thanks Jana, I just wanted to come and help."

She put her hand on my shoulder. "I know. Amber sure picked a good one with you. We're so glad to have you in our lives."

What a great start. I almost felt like asking her right there and then, but it felt too premature and unearned. I needed to do at least a little helping before I could justify asking them. Plus, I wanted to ask them both together. That was the ideal way to do it.

"Well Sean, get to bed. Luke is already in the room." She gave me another hug and walked up the steps to the room she shared with Megan. I made my way and knocked on our door.

A man answered that I didn't recognize. The Luke I knew kept long brown hair in a ponytail, but this person had completely shaved his head. It took a second to get used to the dim light, but I recognized Luke after my eyes adjusted. He looked buzzed, as if midway through a several day bender with no sleep. I heard the TV in the room and looked over his shoulder to note just how small a room we had. But at least we stayed in a room here; I wondered briefly where we planned to sleep during the days ahead. It didn't resemble my suite in Virginia, but if the roof kept the weather out, it was good enough for me.

"Dude, you made it!" He grabbed and pulled me into a big bear hug that caught me off guard as he squeezed out my breath. I didn't possess the energy to reciprocate. I'm sure I felt like a ragdoll as he pulled me close.

Luke and I shared a lot in common, but I always felt like we competed. I'm sure he didn't see it that way, but I saw it as a silent game of who could impress Bob and Jana more, even if our approaches polarized each other. Bob and Jana admired all the time he spent helping at Crossroads, but I couldn't help but find it odd that he chose mission work over a normal job. I was too risk averse to try and spend time doing anything but advancing my career. I worked full time and made enough to support myself. He worked for free to improve the lives of hundreds in the village. I couldn't tell which path Amber's parents valued more, or if Bob and Jana even cared. Regardless of our differences, I loved hanging out with the guy. His life and political views stood close to mine, and it didn't take a lot to keep him entertained. I smiled when he freed me from the hug and gave my arms back.

"How ya doing, Luke? Been here long?"

"Just today."

"Neat. I heard Faith can't come. Bummer."

I lied. Luke was the only one that didn't know that Faith did, in fact, plan to come. She wanted to surprise him, and up to this point it seemed to be working. More than one person held a secret on this trip. Asking the question presented a gamble for me. My poker face has never won any awards, and I feared his ability to read my expression no matter how hard I tried to suppress it. Thankfully he turned away and went into the room as he answered.

"Yeah, she's busy with school." He replied as he sat back on the only bed. "Amber too, I heard, right?" I nodded. "Guess it's you and me."

I nodded and threw my bag on the floor. I couldn't believe the size of the room, less than eight by six feet with a small bed, end table, a very old television, and a door to a shoebox bathroom. I looked in the bathroom and smiled. Luke caught my expression and countered before I could speak.

"Yeah, no hot water. Only have it in the early morning when they boil it. If you want a cold shower, though, go ahead."

"Damnit. How cold?"

"Frigid."

I grimaced, "Whatever, I'll make it quick. Are there any towels?"

"Nope. Use a clean shirt or something."

I grabbed a shirt and some soap from my duffel bag. I entered the bathroom and looked around at the extremely small setup. At the entrance the toilet pointed toward the shower and blocked the doorway. Its lip even extended into the tub a few inches. The sink and mirror hung over the toilet.

"This is the smallest bathroom I've ever seen."

"It's efficient." Luke laughed again, directing his eyes back to the TV.

"At least we have a shower, I guess. Might be my last one for a long time."

I stepped into the shower and undressed. The water felt so cold that I almost couldn't take it. Goosebumps appeared all over my body, and I lathered up the soap on my chest as fast as I possibly could. I shivered as my teeth chattered. I stopped the water as soon as I could lather myself and stood shaking from the cold as I fought the urge to curl into a ball. I rubbed soap all over my body in a rush. I rinsed, grabbed the undershirt, and dried off. In a moment the shirt was soaked with cold water. I grabbed another and dried the rest of me before jumping back into the main room with my privates in plain view as I rushed to get dressed. I heard him chuckle as I stood shaking.

"Welcome to Santo Domingo, Sean," he said, keeping his eyes on the TV.

Thursday, January 14th, 2010
6:02am
Santo Domingo, Dominican Republic

The loud cry of a rooster rang the drums in my ears in the middle of the night. My eyes opened suddenly, dilating to adjust to the near pitch-blackness of the room. After a few moments a faint glow from the stars allowed me to make out shapes well enough to see my way around. My legs had sweat profusely in the small sleeping bag. I didn't want to get in bed with Luke since it was so small I knew we'd be sleeping on top of each other, so I'd opted to stay on the floor. My back groaned at that decision and sent stiff pains into my shoulders as punishment while I sat up against the wall. The air in the room froze the sweat on my skin, but the heat from the sleeping bag pushed water out of me like a faucet.

I stood near the window to watch the stars. In the distance to the east I could see the sun hiding just below the horizon as it leaked a fine glow into the sky miles away. Thin cirrus clouds turned into capillaries of red and yellow against an otherwise dark, purple velvet sky littered with thousands of diamonds.

Beyond the window, small fenced yards from neighboring buildings connected like a quilt across the city with barbed wire and wooden posts acting as the stitching. Broken glass bottles, paper, and plastic bags littered the roofs and yards as if someone had dumped a huge trash can on everything. In silence I looked into the distance and imagined that I was the only survivor of some apocalypse.

The sound of crackling redirected my attention to the higher roof of the hotel beside us. A fire burned no more than a dozen yards away from the window and emitted a strong contrast against the blue and black that saturated the city before dawn. Flames licked the cold night air, and its glow engulfed a man tending it. A huge kettle sat on top of the blaze with pipes sticking out that ran into the building. Suddenly, I whispered to myself in the dark:

"Hot water."

I tiptoed past Luke like a cat burglar bypassing a high tech security system. After a few moments, the water turned brutally hot. I took a quick shower and dried off with my only clean towel. I feared it might be my last hot shower until I returned home, so I soaked up the warmth as much as possible.

I tried to go back to sleep but my mind raced. The same anticipation I got during early Christmas mornings rushed through me and made my veins tingle as stress coursed thick in my blood. Fear and excitement blended to form an intoxicating tonic. It felt as if the journey was quite a long way to come for her parents' blessing, but then again, who gets a chance to ask for it in such a unique circumstance?

I suddenly became aware of calling the disaster "unique." My trip so far had encompassed only hurried flights and a cramped room. I didn't yet appreciate the dire predicament that waited less than a day ahead. I only saw the perfect proposal to complement my already ideal life. Perhaps I'd ask at some campfire overlooking the city, or after the birth of a child from a pregnant woman we'd save. I wanted to make it as perfect as possible, amidst the most ideal of circumstances. I wanted to look good and to be seen by them as successful, charming, charitable, and strong.

I watched the sun rise from my window. Small veins of yellow and red turned to blankets of light as the rest of the world awoke from slumber. The rays covered me in a bath of heat that reminded me of the hot shower. I longed to get going and make the trip to Haiti.

A knock on our door followed shortly after sunrise. Jana wanted to take everyone to breakfast and plan our day. The daunting list convinced me we didn't have enough time. We needed medical supplies, water, food, and blankets. The agenda went on and on. We visited a small store across the street from the hotel that served egg sandwiches. All of us, it seemed, wanted different things from this trip. I obviously wanted to get Jana, Bob, and Marcus' blessing; Luke wanted to spend time helping the Haitians he grew attached to during his time at Crossroads; Megan came to prove her mettle to Jana.

At almost every opportunity Megan offered input for how to plan the day and the trip. With only four of us, we knew we'd need to split up to get all the supplies, so she found out where the right stores sat and broke up the list accordingly. I got the easy task of picking up food. The grocery store operated only a few blocks away so I got it done quickly. Afterward, Luke and I went to the hardware store to find batteries, flashlights, tools, and tape. Along the way Luke spoke incessantly about Faith. A week had passed since he'd seen her, and he knew he'd miss her terribly while spending the month or so at the orphanage. I knew he cared about the mission, but his words convinced me that if given the opportunity to return to Bonaire and see Faith, he'd accept. She'd moved to the tiny island off the Venezuelan coast to study medicine, and she planned to spend a few years there.

I decided to let Luke know about my plans with Amber's parents, half because I couldn't contain the secret anymore but also to get his mind off Faith. Even though I knew she could arrive any minute, it felt mean to let him torture his mind with longing. I only wanted him to squirm for a little, not drag it out continuously.

"So Luke, I'm going to ask Jana and Bob and Marcus for Amber's hand in marriage," I blurted out as he dredged midway through another story about him and Faith when they lived in California. He stopped speaking and turned, looking both excited and confused.

"What?" he replied, cocking his head back as he processed the sudden announcement. He thought for a moment then continued. "I guess this is the right place to do it. Does anyone know?"

"You do. And that's as far as I want it to go."

He nodded. "I get it, I get it. My lips are sealed." He put his bags down and gave me a handshake and a hug. He had to take me seriously now—I wanted to stick around the family for the long run.

We returned to the hotel mid-day. Jana and Megan sat outside at a table with a short Italian guy with a bulldog body and a big smile.

Jana introduced us to the new member of the team, Jared. She'd run into him at the gas station while picking up jugs of water. Once he found out our destination, he'd begged to be part of the group. Jana obliged, but warned him about the risks and that we didn't have a plan for return. He still wanted to come.

He held out his hand as we approached, greeting Luke and me. Jana brought us up to speed on the day. A few hours remained until Bob's convoy would pick us up and take us to Haiti. We'd acquired almost all the supplies, but Jared still needed to get ready.

"Luke," said Jana. "I need you to take Jared around so he has enough supplies for the trip. Can you get an empty gym bag? I left one up in your room."

He nodded and ascended the stairs.

"Who's Faith again?" Jared asked as Luke went just beyond earshot.

I looked back at Jana who smiled with Megan as they watched Luke go into the hotel.

From the ground we heard Faith scream as she surprised Luke from inside the room. I imagined what she must have done, waiting for him to open the door and then popping out of the dark in a sudden leap. I heard laughing, and then the two of them talking as they returned outside. He seemed stunned and completely surprised to see her.

"Who all knew about this?" Luke asked the group, giving me a smug stare.

We all replied that we did and he put his hand to his forehead and shook in disbelief. "I can't believe you kept this a secret." He turned back to Faith. "I didn't think I'd see you for a couple more months!"

"Of course I'm coming. This is my home." She replied, refusing at first to give him any affection over the surprise. Then she faltered, "But it didn't hurt that you are here too." She gave him a kiss on the cheek and he blushed in front of us. It felt nice to see someone else as vulnerable.

After a few exchanged laughs and a couple minutes of catching up, the group settled as Jana spoke. "Okay. We've got a lot to do in a little time. We are leaving in an hour, so get your bags down here and make any last minute stops."

Luke hugged Faith and left with Jared to fill the gym bag with supplies while Megan looked over plans and papers about the trip with Jana. For a brief moment Faith stood alone, and I walked up to her to talk. I pulled her aside and gave her a hug. A lot of time had passed since I'd first met her at Crossroads, but I'd heard her voice almost every night when she and Amber spoke on Skype. Often Amber left the room when they did, so I figured Faith knew everything about me. It took some guidance from Faith to convince Amber to date me seriously, and her inspiration to help Amber through our arguments. The few times I did speak with her on Skype or through Facebook we only discussed Amber. Her advice was like cheat codes in a video game—she knew her sister inside out and therefore always knew what to do.

In truth, though, Luke was only a small fraction of the reason she came to Haiti. She, like the remainder of her family, had spent her entire life living on the island and held a deep connection with the Haitian people. As a teenager she'd led groups of doctors and nurses through the ministries Crossroads conducted throughout Puerto Plata. It seemed like destiny that she eventually chose to go into medicine. She looked forward to working with her dad on patients, helping surgeons in the emergency room, planning logistics at hospitals, and feeding the thousands who needed the help of volunteers. I'd never witnessed anything but selflessness from her. She lived an incredibly simple life, and wanted to spend the rest of her days in developing countries as a doctor.

But when it came to Amber, she was just like any other big sister—older and protective.

"Good to see you, Faith," I said.

"You too, Sean. What's up?"

"Well, I want to get your take on something." Faith looked at me and smiled. I didn't feel as nervous around her as I did with Bob, Jana or Marcus. She possessed a gift for making people feel comfortable, almost as if she were already my sister too. "I want to ask your parents if I can marry Amber. What do you think?"

She didn't look surprised at all. She pulled me into a long, honest hug, and as she pulled away, she spoke. "Sean, this is amazing! What a perfect place to ask!"

"I take it you approve, then?"

"Of course! This is going to make them so happy. Who else knows?"

"Just you and Luke. I'd like to keep it quiet until I get to your mom. I need it to be perfect."

"Absolutely." She hugged me again. "I'm so happy, brother."

Brother. The term felt weird. I hadn't thought about all the brothers and sisters I stood to gain, too. It seemed she had already practiced using it though, or maybe she just dealt better with these things than I did.

The exchange lasted only for a moment but changed my mood completely. Talking to Faith helped calm my nerves about the issue, and getting her approval in person improved my confidence drastically. I really trusted her opinion when it came to Amber. I suddenly realized I was doing a terrible job keeping my plans a secret.

An hour later, the team regrouped at the hotel. Jana had called several taxis and they waited for us in the street. We packed the cars and drove off. We weaved through mid-day traffic, avoiding collisions with other cars by inches as we snaked in and out of lanes. Sometimes our drivers even used the shoulder when possible to push further ahead.

The drive felt like a thrill ride at an amusement park, and my stomach lurched as carsickness took over from the stale air and constant movement. We reached an expansive roundabout at the west end of town. As we approached I spotted a large Daihatsu parked on the side of the road with "Crossroads" painted across the bed. Outside the truck I could see Bob, Marcus, and several people I didn't know all standing under the shade of a nearby tree, patiently waiting for us. The taxi pulled to the side of the road behind the convoy. A massive statue sat in the middle of the roundabout. Cars zoomed past and blew wind that was hot, dry, and full of debris. The sky beamed blue and cloudless and let the sun beat down on the roadway while reflecting heat onto us.

Four people I'd never met before came with Bob and Marcus. Dean, a muscular guy in his late twenties, had come to Crossroads from Southern California. He worked as an EMT while finishing his pre-med work and used the money to pay for tuition. He wore a beanie over his straight black hair and always, I would come to learn, had a pack of gum handy. I'd also come to know that he joked a lot, mostly with Jared or Luke.

Justin always seemed serious. I sensed he possessed a much stricter and traditional background than Dean or Cameron. Highly intelligent and very personable, he wanted to be a doctor like his father. I didn't know if the goal started as his or his father's, but the pressure of applying for medical schools weighed heavily on him like a stack of books that kept him hunched. Every evening he wrote in his journal about what we did during the day as he watched the sun go down in the city or wherever we were ended up that night.

Cameron, another pre-med student from Berkeley, stood a bit taller than Justin and Dean and wore thinning black hair that sat in a small mop on his head. As the quietest of the group, he rarely sparked conversations but always sat and listened. I'd have a chance in the coming days to observe his gentle temperament, which complemented his judge-like confidence while treating victims. In the heat of the moment he'd often gave orders to Dean and Justin. He'd brought his mother Cindy along on the trip as well. As a registered nurse, she excelled at dealing with patients both physically and mentally. In the days that followed, I'd often see her playing with children and giving reassurance to parents. I would come to see that she often helped people feel good about tough situations, even if the circumstances felt dire.

Cameron had set up the Berkeley team's trip to Crossroads. He'd visited the mission several times but this was only the second one he'd planned himself. On previous endeavors, he'd built homes for the villages and did the regular mission work at the prison, hospital, and clinic. He'd organized this trip with others from his pre-med class to focus solely on medical work. He'd set the flights, the schedule, and recruited others to go. Coming to help the poor in Puerto Plata grew quickly into a passion of his, and he felt extremely connected to the people. He knew he wanted to be a doctor, but working with Crossroads had helped him realize that he wanted to dedicate his time to medical work in developing countries even more.

The detour to Haiti wasn't part of his group's original agenda. Cameron would enter his last semester the following week and couldn't graduate late. However, after calling his professors from Crossroads, he received not only a pass to miss the first few weeks, but also got the blessing of his advisor and professors to help as much as he could. Only Dean and Justin could stay with him; the rest of the volunteering team returned to California after finding out they couldn't miss classes, even for Haiti.

After a few minutes of introductions we boarded the vehicles. I got into the back of the Daihatsu with most of Jana's group. It was a clumsy vehicle, an older model Daihatsu flatbed truck that Amber's parents had repurposed into a personnel transport and painted blue and white with "Crossroads" written in big letters on the side. Two long, leatherette benches ran the length of the bed facing each other while a curved roof hung welded above it. Luggage, medical supplies, food, water, and fuel filled every inch of the bed and roof. There existed nowhere to sit on the ride so most of the group piled on top of gear during the trip. I sat next to Jared on the end of a bench. Supplies packed the back of the transport and left no room to stretch out our legs. Just as fast as we'd arrived we left again, finally on our way to Port-au-Prince.

Outside of Santo Domingo, the landscape surrounding the road stood lush and green. As we pushed west the terrain changed. At first we drove through countless miles of farm fields with sugar cane. Small groups of shacks dotted the edge of the road where impoverished Haitians lived, working fields owned by their Dominican employers. Most Haitians lived in the country illegally and did what they could do survive, working for a few dollars a day, if they got paid at all.

The landscape became dried and wilted as the terrain turned from plains to hills and then to craggy mountains. The truck worked hard as it pushed up the steep hills, while its brakes screamed when we flew down the bumpy, narrow descents. The trees completely disappeared, replaced by cacti and endless desert. The air tasted dry, like hot sand in my throat, and those of us sitting out in the open coughed from dust and dirt that the tires threw in the air.

The sun moved toward the western horizon, and the afternoon brought relief to us in the back as we hid in the shade. Ahead, the road cut sharply between two mountains as if a hatchet had breached them by force and left the slopes steep and jagged. Small bushes and cacti clung to the mountains at extreme angles, and loose rocks both big and small lay on the slopes, always threatening to topple onto the road. I hung my arms out the side of the truck to feel the rush of warm, dry air. The heat and wind dried sweat from my shirt. I'd sat in an awkward position among the supplies for several hours, and my body protested with aches and groans. I took solace in knowing that Haiti grew closer by the minute.

The monotonous tone of the desert was broken only by a few conversations. I learned more about Jared and why he chose to come. He'd felt empty in the past few years, and when the quake hit, something inside screamed to come. He couldn't quite explain it but he knew it was the right thing to do. Unlike me, he didn't care if his employer fired him or not for going. He'd find another job if they had a problem. He joked all the time, even in the dire circumstances. Even so, I never felt offended or out of line with him; in fact, most of the group often laughed fully at his acts. His personality let us know he was only kidding around. His ability to lighten the mood added a much-needed reprieve from the depressing backdrop of the trip. To me, everything he did seemed funny.

After the sun set, our conversations subsided, replaced with the quiet hum of vehicles. I strained to look for any sign of life. Only sand, rocks and desert vegetation populated the region. Though some of us managed to fall asleep, most of the group stared blankly at the landscape. Night overtook as darkness crept from the east and chased us perpetually west toward Haiti like cavalry forcing the enemy into the sea. The outside temperature sank with the sun, and I felt the cold night air lick my face.

I stuck my head out the side of the transport. In the distance I could see a dim set of lights partially hidden by a mountain range. We were still on the Dominican side of the border.

"Hey man, something's up ahead."

"Looks like a town."

We drove into a very small village overrun with military vehicles. Bob stopped at a guard station and spoke to the soldier on the road. He ran his flashlight over the vehicles and let us through. The convoy drove slowly into the center of town. Those of us in the back woke from the lights and popped our heads out the side to get a glimpse of the village.

A large military base sat in the center of town. Thick, red iron bars formed a gate connected to a wall that stood fifteen to twenty feet high and surrounded the facility. Armed guards stood along the top of the wall, and several men with guns walked along the side of the cars. I started to panic a little inside. Soldiers fell in line behind the transport. One walked directly behind us, just a few feet away from me. He looked up at the group in the back. We stared at him with concerned expressions.

Sensing our fear he smiled at us and said "Thank you for coming." As the convoy approached the main gate, the doors opened and we entered the base that sat just a few miles away from the border into Haiti.

Thursday, January 14th 2010
8:55pm
Port Au Prince, Haiti

Tasha let out a long groan as she slept. It woke Lucas from a shallow, almost lucid dream. Through the darkness of the tent he saw the orange glow of lanterns and small charcoal fires glimmer on thin plastic tarps that surrounded him. Shadows of people walking on the hospital grounds were reflected and danced on the walls of the shelter.

He'd spent the entire day building their new home in the small space they claimed along the road. He came without supplies, so he'd used the evening hours with Zac going back to their collapsed homes to collect blankets, tarps, clothing, and whatever food they found. Zac's brother Paul helped tie the tarp to trees against the fence and then to a light pole against the road. It would stop the rain but not much more. Ragged blankets and strips of plastic hung like meat from hooks in a butcher's freezer. Thicker blankets covered the grass and dirt inside to keep his mother off the bare earth. The rest of them had sat on the curb just outside during the day; now, at night, they huddled in fetal positions around Tasha while struggling to keep their feet and arms inside.

Lucas heard crying all around him. It formed an immersive cloud. Somewhere in the parking lot doctors and nurses rushed to as many people as possible. The first time he spotted one late the first night he'd tried to flag her down, but older and stronger men got in his way. Everyone thought his or her injuries were the most dire, and everyone wanted to be seen right away. Lucas pleaded with the man to come see his mother, but he wouldn't come.

Tasha coughed and gurgled when she slept. He crawled to her side and tilted her head so she could breathe. Blood trickled from her mouth but she couldn't spit it away. He gave her water every time she gained consciousness. An aid group came to the hospital with huge crates full of plastic bags filled with water. He grabbed as many as he could—everyone did. As it hit her lips, the blood diluted and flowed down her chin. He wiped her face and tried to keep her mouth clear. She got worse in the night; that much seemed obvious. Her chest had stopped bleeding but the flesh had begun to turn grey. Her leg looked purple and swollen, as if filled to the brink with rotten blood. Sweat and blood had destroyed any stickiness left in the tape that helped hold the brace to her leg, and it moved slightly whenever she did.

Tasha shifted to her side while trying to keep her leg still. She cried out softly in pain with every movement and constantly tried to get up. Lucas spent his energy to keep her steady.

"Be still mom; someone will come soon. Just rest."

She didn't look at him, but kept her eyes on the floor and slightly nodded as she tried to breathe slowly. "I know, Lucas."

He set her head on a bundle of sheets as she lay to ease each breath. She just couldn't get herself comfortable, and the waiting slowly chipped away at his sanity as each minute felt like one more step away from saving her. Even with so few doctors, how could it take this long just to be seen? Anger brewed in his chest. It slowly boiled as it rose to his head and blinded his vision. How could it take this long? Maybe they'd gone to sleep for the night. How could they sleep with so many out here in need of help?

Perhaps he couldn't make a doctor see her, but he wanted to know how long they'd have to wait. If he had a clue then maybe he could leave, get more supplies, or even move her to another hospital. Anything felt better than waiting. If he accepted waiting, then perhaps nothing would ever get done.

"Zac," he whispered as he poked his friend on the shoulder. "Zac."

Zac slept propped against the opening near the light pole. He rubbed his eyes and looked up slowly as he woke. "What? What? I was having a good dream."

"Forget that," he snapped back as he pushed his face closer. "Watch my mom for a while. I'm going to see what's going on out there."

Zac looked over at Tasha and his brother Paul, and then returned to Lucas. "Ok, sure man. I got it. Don't take too long."

Lucas stepped out of the tent and looked up and down the street. Hundreds of shelters filled the parking lot. From above, they looked like a patchwork quilt. No space remained save for the main roads, which made it hard to see far from his camp. He walked downhill toward the entrance of the hospital. Small fires glowed around him and kept the area lit. Even after walking a hundred feet or so, he never saw a single hospital employee. The expression he read on many of the faces in the glow of night fires told the same story as his: hopelessness, fatigue, pain, and frustration. Was anyone being helped at all, or were all the doctors just on the other side of the lot? The eerie quiet felt dangerous, like a ghost town filled with peering eyes that all stared through the shadows.

The main entrance looked dark but all of the windows on the second and third floors glowed with light. He saw people behind the frosted glass moving back and forth. Two armed guards stood at the door. They looked alert but tired. As he neared one held out his hand to stop him.

"Hold up. No one's allowed inside."

"I don't want to go inside. Where are the doctors?" He looked up at the windows again and pointed. "My mother's been wait-ing all day."

The one guard looked up at the window and then back at Lucas. "They're working. There's not many of them here. If she didn't get brought in then she wasn't serious enough."

"Wasn't serious enough? They didn't even look at her!" He got angrier with each second. "How can they know if they didn't see her?"

She hadn't even been given a chance. He started to believe that people had gotten in with broken toes and fractured wrists just because they'd pushed harder to the entrance. Suddenly he cursed himself—being polite didn't work. He'd let his mother down, and his decision to wait his turn soured in his mind. His fists quaked as he stared up at the windows.

The guard put down his hand and sighed. He suddenly looked less like a guard and more like a person as he wiped the sweat from his eyes. "I'm sorry boy. There's just too many people. We're being promised volunteers tomorrow. Be brave. Help her get through the night."

Lucas wanted to scream but knew it wouldn't do anything. He hated the guards too, even though he knew it wasn't their fault.

He thought for a moment about pushing them out of the way and running for the door. Maybe he could get past them, perhaps even take one of their guns. He'd make a doctor see his mother at gunpoint.

He felt a hand on his shoulder. He opened his eyes, stunned from the contact as he looked up. The guard stood over him with his dark eyes set deep in his strong, square face. "Go back, boy. You can't help her by standing here."

He nodded and left. It wasn't their fault, he repeated over and over again. They only wanted to keep order and probably had injured loved ones too. He wondered about that for a second and nodded slowly as he turned to leave.

He made his way back to camp feeling despair overtake him. His mother wouldn't last much longer and he knew she sat on the bottom of the list, if one even existed. He walked past a small tent with a few people inside. A small girl slept in her father's arms, both of her arms freshly amputated. Her father looked at him as he passed. Dried tears stained his tired face, but he stood straight and attempted to look strong for his girl. Behind him his wife slept with wounds on her legs and back that looked worse than his mother's. Red cloth filled the wounds to stop the bleeding. Each tent he passed held a similar horror story, and after a while he kept his eyes on the ground to avoid committing the scenes to memory.

At camp he sat down and hung his head between his knees. His mother and Paul slept and Zac drifted off while he left. The small coal fire burned out and he sat in the dark alone while listening again to the moans of the crowd around him. Zac rolled over to face Lucas.

"What'd they say?"

"They should be around any time now. We just have to wait a little longer."

"They've been saying that all day. Is that all they'd tell you?"

"No," he paused, not sure what to say. "It won't be until tomorrow. The guards said there are volunteers coming. We'll have a better shot with them."

Zac sighed deeply and cupped his face in his palms. He lay back on the ground and rolled next to his brother. Lucas sat next to his mother to keep her warm.

He awoke a few hours later as the sun gave hints of its ascent from behind the eastern horizon. Running engines idled in the background. From their tone he knew they belonged to something big. He looked outside. Just down the road near the main entrance sat two busses full of men and women dressed with scrubs. He felt his heartbeat as his eyes tried to spring from their sockets. Volunteers!

"Zac, wake up. The volunteers the guards told me about are here!"

He rubbed his eyes, "Huh? What are you talking about?"

Lucas didn't spend time to answer but instead leapt from the ground and ran down the hill to the growing crowd of Haitians. The volunteers wore large medical bags on their waists and shoulders. They carried boxes upon boxes of supplies. They brought water, food, and blankets. To Lucas the yellow buses looked like golden chariots sent from heaven, the well-rested and alert people in blue and white scrubs, angels. Their leader spoke in English. Lucas didn't speak it well, but enough that he understood the message.

"Okay everyone, you know what to do. Surgeons inside the hospital; doctors, physicians, and nurses outside. Let's get to work."

Like water on a rock the group split up and filtered into the eager crowd. At least fifty people came, and almost immediately dozens of Haitians surrounded each one. The one closest to him was white and at least fifty with thinning gray hair and thick round glasses. Men and women begged him to help.

He finally spoke up as he raised his hands in the air to get attention. "I'm starting at the top of the hill and going to every tent I can, one by one. That's the best I can do."

Lucas returned to his tent at the top of the hill where everyone else stood or sat just outside the shelter.

"Volunteers are here." Lucas shouted. His mother closed her eyes in a short, silent prayer as he spoke. "One of them will be here soon."

Tasha tried to sit up, and as she did Lucas went to her side and propped her against the light pole. Zac and Paul grabbed trash and shoved it just outside the tent walls to clean up the inside. Just as they finished, the white man stuck his head into the shelter.

"Hello, may I enter?" He spoke in basic French with an American accent.

Everyone looked at him, eager to be seen. Lucas spoke up. "Yes, please come in."

The man entered and got on one knee next to Lucas' mother. He looked at her leg first by scanning a flashlight over her flesh while gently adjusting the splint.

"This is a decent splint. Who set the leg?"

"I did sir."

"Did you set it properly?"

He fumbled with his English as he reached for the right words. "I'm not sure; I pulled the foot and tied the handlebar. Did I do it wrong?"

"Hard to tell. She'll need X-rays. I'll get her on the list for today. Now let's look at her chest."

He pulled a bottle of saline from his pack and soaked the blood stained cloth tucked into the openings. He pried them free carefully to reveal the deep tissue underneath and restart the flow of blood as the fabric peeled away dried flesh. He studied the wounds intently for a few minutes. He touched and probed with cotton swabs as Tasha struggled to keep still. After what felt like an eternity he spoke again.

"Well, you were smart for putting the cloth in; it kept them from getting infected. They're deep, but should heal with time and care. She's going to need quite a few stitches, though."

He pulled out bandages and antibiotic ointment from his pack. He wrapped her chest and wrote on his notepad before removing the bandages on Paul's face. His eye had swollen shut, and purple bruises covered his face. The man touched right below the eye. Paul pulled back in pain.

"I think you fractured the bone. Not much we can do for you here, but keep it clean and cared for. It will heal."

He stood and walked just outside the tent and Lucas followed him out the door. That seemed too quick and he didn't do anything. He wasn't getting away that fast.

"What about my mother? Will you take care of her?"

"I won't, but the hospital will. I'll have some people come up to get her later today. She'll need those X-rays to see if the leg is set and some stitching on her chest. You're doing a good job, just keep at it."

Lucas didn't believe him. After all this time waiting he couldn't trust that they would just "come back later." The man sensed the reservation. He put his hand on Lucas' shoulder.

"They'll come for her today, you have my word."

Lucas nodded. He desperately wanted to believe the man. "Thank you."

He smiled and nodded before walking into the next tent.

Thursday, January 14th, 2010
8:05 pm
Jimani, Dominican Republic

The road ended like the Nile delta as it fanned and faded into a grassy field. The Daihatsu stopped with the tires on rocky terrain hidden by tall grass. Several other vehicles were parked haphazardly in front and to either side of us. Behind and in the distance the lights from the military gate gleamed like a diamond and provided the only light in an otherwise black town. The stars bled light and covered everything with a milky radiance.

I'd felt tired, cranky, and bored with the long ride to Haiti's border, but the excitement of our entrance and subsequent parade quickly erased those feelings. I felt a second wind grow inside after I realized how close my goal of asking Amber's parents crept.

Jana and Faith went ahead of the group several minutes before we unloaded to scout for a suitable spot for tents. We planned to continue our journey across the border to an orphanage in Port-au-Prince when morning arrived. Before we finished unloading our gear, Jana returned and called the group to gather around her. She looked excited but exhausted as her eyes jumped back and forth from us to the hill behind.

"Everyone, this is Jimani," she announced, our small side conversations quelling as she spoke. "The road to Haiti is closed so we will camp here for the night. For those interested, there is a small relief camp over the hill that could use our help."

I groaned. I really felt like going to sleep, and doing some small relief work (or chores) didn't sound like a great idea. What did they need help with? Moving boxes? Sorting supplies? We needed our rest for the next day; the energy could be crucial once we reached the capital. Instead of walking with Jana I pulled out some tents and spoke with Jared and Dean, one of the new teammates I'd met with Bob and Marcus earlier in the day. No one expected much from the outpost other than to spend the night and move on the next day.

I sat quietly while Dean told us a story about his work as an EMT in Los Angeles. When he'd first started he believed the work mostly surrounded drug addicts, elderly people, and car crashes. He'd wanted to learn "on the fly" medicine—to handle extreme situations and save lives. He told us about his first emergency call. His team had arrived at a residential home in the middle of the night and found a four-year old boy bleeding to death on the concrete. An iron gate had fallen on him and a spike had impaled his skull. He died shortly after they arrived. Dean had never expected to deal with children as often as it occurred, and he lacked the preparation to see someone, especially a child, die under his care. After months of work he'd developed a strong stomach and a thick skin resistant to tragedy.

He'd decided to come to Crossroads to see how his experience and training applied to other people in need. Although he originally intended to take only a one-week trip to Crossroads, the quake quickly mutated the plan. He'd stuck with the dwindling medical team and came to Haiti to do what he could. He felt that everything he'd seen as an EMT would prepare him for anything in Haiti.

Faith broke up our conversation as she ran up to us from over the hill. Her eyes bulged, sweat streamed down her forehead and arms, her hair tossed in the wind, and her chest bulged in and out as she stopped to catch her breath.

"Everyone, come quick. This isn't some relief center. There's tons of injured people and no one is taking care of them." She paused and took in a breath. Whatever sat on the other side of the hill had rocked her. Her eyes fought back tears. Her voice cracked as she spoke again, "Just hurry up. We need everyone."

She turned and ran back toward the orphanage. Dean grabbed his medical bag and rushed after her along with the other three volunteers that had come with Bob: Cindy, Cameron, and Justin. Marcus shouted from the driver's seat of the truck.

"Guys, get the stretchers."

Jared and I pulled them from the truck and ran after the rest of the group toward the hill that stood between us and the lights on the other side. With each step the glow turned brighter and slowly the wail of cries grew from a whisper until the sound surrounded us. At the top of the small hill we stopped next to everyone else and stood frozen in our tracks. A scene reminiscent of a battlefield lay before us as far as the spotlights carried.

First I noticed the immense number of people on the ground. Two buildings sat in our view, the closest one at the end of a sixty-foot upward slope. People littered the ground under lights, on the sides of buildings, in the shadows, on the dirt, and across the lawn. They huddled in groups or lay in large piles so jumbled that I couldn't differentiate between the injured and their family members. Even more still sprawled out on the ground alone, thrashing or rocking as they writhed in pain, unaided. An older woman cried in the fetal position a few feet away while her blood-soaked arms covered a mangled chest wrapped in tattered clothes. Past her, several children slept together, all with severe lacerations to their faces and arms. The scene repeated over and over again, as if several grenades had just blown up, injuring hundreds of people and I'd just happened to walk in on the scene. Cries and pleas came from all directions, and wherever my eyes went they landed on someone who looked directly at me and begged for help. To my right I spotted an older man who sat against a post. The cloth wrapped around his head only partly restricted a stream of fluid as it oozed from his skull. I could almost see his brain. I wanted to puke and cry at the same time. At that moment time stood still as I tried to comprehend the scene that lay before me. Just seconds earlier I'd been thinking of nothing but how to ask for Amber's hand and to somehow convince her parents and Marcus that I fit their idea of a "perfect match." But suddenly, all of that evaporated as a rush of emotions boiled over in my stomach that coaxed me to cry. Something switched inside, and my only thought was how I could possibly help the screaming, crying people in front of me. I blanked out.

Dean, Cameron, Justin, and Cindy rushed down the hill and plunged deep into the crowd. They immediately began examining patients while furiously pulling supplies from their packs. Their small flashlights waved back and forth from person to person. The light let me see the gruesome wounds even from fifty feet away. They shouted while assisting each other and switching roles fluidly. I was still trying to catch up with what my eyes saw.

The rest of the group disappeared into the second dorm building, and I noticed Bob's white hair under the lights as people crowded around him for help. I stood dumb and quiet for a few more moments until Marcus hit me on the arm. Jared stood with him.

"Sean, Jared. Jana wants us to move everyone inside the buildings. Let's get to work."

For a moment I tried to count the number of people on the ground, but it seemed impossible. Jared paired up with a volunteer from another group while I worked with Marcus put people on the stretchers as gently as possible and move them inside.

I transported an elderly woman lying on the ground with wide punctures that covered her body and soaked her in red. Dirt masked her injuries, with small stones and sand clinging to the open flesh. Marcus searched for a spot on her legs to grab as I took hold of her shoulders. As we hoisted her onto the stretcher she lay back and closed her eyes while crying out. Marcus held a flashlight to her stomach. A large, jagged hole sat just above her bellybutton stuffed with cloth.

Jana stood at the main doorway of the dorm while Faith kept watch at the top of the second floor. Every time we brought someone in they pointed where to go. We gradually filled up rooms with people on thin mattresses in a tight grid. It felt like a morbid game of Tetris.

During the evening we recruited a man named Jacques to help us translate. He spoke English, Spanish, and Creole fluently. He'd brought his wife and son to the outpost on the back of a creaky pick-up truck. The surgeons had amputated his son's arm, but only because the ride to Jimani on the terrible roads had damaged it beyond recovery.

His wife had suffered a terrible blow to the chest. We couldn't tell how many ribs were broken or fractured, but with every breath she winced in pain as the swelling tightened around her lungs like a python gripping its prey. The injuries that didn't bleed proved the most dangerous because they didn't get immediate attention from volunteers. It became too easy to only notice the blood, bones, and burns while forgetting the internal damage. I lacked medical training and the ability to speak fluent

Creole, so my eyes did all the judging. If someone looked bad I took him or her first. Somehow those with the least amount of training ended up sorting the patients for the medical professionals. I knew later that I'd missed a few that had needed help right away, but I couldn't stop to think about it.

Jacques agreed to translate through the night only if we took his wife to surgery. The overwhelmed volunteers gladly accepted the deal. The surgery team kept him on board at the outpost to translate and in that capacity he excelled. He stayed up longer, moved faster, and pushed himself harder than anyone expected. "They're my people too," he'd say. Soon he was wearing scrubs while he accompanied the surgeons through rounds of examinations, patient questioning, and even surgery.

We didn't stop until every injured person lay inside. The last few I situated sideways, under canopies in walkways, in the showers, and even under the small shed roof near the back. My body ached from the work and my fingers popped and bled with blisters that formed on top of broken ones. I couldn't tell my blood from the rest after a while. Under the thick yellow glow from overhead lights my fingers appeared old, worn, and tattered. Dirt and blood outlined every parcel of skin and made it easy to see the gritty lines that covered my hands. I wondered how much filth had soaked through the thin protection, how much of the dirt and grime and sweat would float along in my body forever.

The night transitioned to stillness as the team dispersed. Some wanted to sleep while others chose to work all night. Faith worked in the surgery building. Cindy did rounds with Cameron until the morning. Megan and Marcus ventured to neighboring towns to find more mattresses for victims to use and bring injured Haitians to the compound. The team picked me, as the least experienced member of the group, to guard the cargo for the night.

The back of the truck faced the buildings and kept the sup-plies in the light to make them harder to steal. It also forced me out of the shadows where the cool night air and the deep black sky bursting with stars beckoned me to close my eyes. I sat on the lip of the bed and watched the evening glow of the spotlights fog with clouds of bugs that swarmed them. I listened to muttered chatter and singing coming from inside the dorms as parents did their best to help children sleep. It seemed unbelievable how they all knew the same songs and sang them in perfect harmony. The singing drowned out most of the crying and helped keep atten-tion away from the screams at the surgery building. They sang familiar songs like "What a friend we have in Jesus" and "Hark! The Herald Angels Sing," but in Creole. My limited French helped me pick up enough words to understand that much.

I thought about my house sitting on the hill, the feel of my dog's fur under my hand, and the smell of Amber's hair. One of my favorite things to do was rest with her on the cheap couch we found on Craigslist and watch movies while it rained or snowed outside. I, for the most part, hated to cuddle or spend any time whatsoever being unproductive, but with her I lose track of the day and my precious agenda.

I wanted desperately to be home. What was so wrong with presenting the big question to her parents over the phone again? I hadn't been at the compound more than a few hours and already I wanted out. The sheer amount of gore and blood I'd witnessed through carrying people already far outweighed any violence or brutality I'd seen in my entire life. I lost track of the million problems that seemed important just forty-eight hours ago. Thoughts about plant productivity, equipment failures, mortgage payments, interest rates, furnace filters—the little things that plagued my already stuffed head on a day-to-day basis—evapo-rated, replaced only by a general disdain for everything that had happened to the people in Haiti. I wanted to cuddle with Amber and forget the trip even happened. I didn't possess the mental strength to handle it.

A man walked toward me from the main building on the hill. From what little I overheard from others I knew surgeons had conducted amputations throughout the day before we arrived. His short, muscular stature seemed odd among the Haitians and his Crocodile Dundee hat and high socks reminded me of a safari guide. His weathered and tan face held a stern expression. He was American, the husband of a doctor that had worked on the site tirelessly since the quake. I straightened my posture as he approached and hoped until the last moment he didn't intend on speaking with me. He stopped in front of the truck and turned.

"Hey, you. What are you doing?"

I tried to answer quickly. "Watching the truck so nothing gets stolen."

He looked at me with a confused tilt of the head that immediately spawned embarrassment inside, as if I were an idiot for thinking people would steal medicine, food, and clothing. Well, I'd steal it all if I were in their shoes.

"No one's going to take anything. We need a few hands up at the other building. You in?" My slow response prompted him to prod again. "Just come up, we need the help in surgery." I didn't respond.

He picked up on my fear and uncertainty. "You'll be fine, I promise. You look like a tough guy." I didn't want to go, but his prodding of my manliness stirred a small flame of anger inside that proved just enough for me to follow. I nodded and secured the truck. I set up a sleeping bag to make it look like someone rested in the bed guarding supplies. I followed him up the hill and across an open field to the entrance of the main building. He pointed at a door guarded by two soldiers.

"Go in there, find the doctor, and say you're here to lend a hand."

"But I don't have any medical training."

"That doesn't matter. You'll be fine. Just remember why you're here, and you'll be okay. I've got to help upstairs with security, but I'll see you later."

With that he walked off. I stood confused for a moment, unsure as to why I agreed to leave the truck. Suddenly I started to panic about the supplies. Jana put me in charge of watching them, and now I'd left them unattended. The one time she'd put me in charge of something, I'd left it. I prayed silently that nothing happened to the truck. I didn't want to let Jana down. I'd just followed a total stranger and now stood in front of two guards that seemed to block the door to something I'd never planned to see. I knew nothing about surgery. I couldn't even stomach dissecting a frog in high school chemistry. Even so, something born inside me the moment I crested the hill shouted from within to go inside. I'm not sure why I listened.

"Fine." I muttered to myself at the arch of the main door. The man in the hat had convinced me to walk across the field; the least I could do was go inside and help clean the rooms or something. I prayed for the staff to ask me to watch the doors or take notes for the doctors. I hoped for something easy. The guards, like Cerberus at the gates of the underworld, let me pass.

Inside the smell of blood and the glare from bright fluorescent lights overwhelmed my senses. The transition from working in the dark to standing in a brightly lit hallway stung my pupils. My hat did little to shield me from the lights. Mint green walls and checkered floors made the hallway appear antiseptic. Along the sides countless severely injured people sat on the floor. Past the door to my right I heard someone scream and several others shout orders. I felt like I'd stepped into a horror movie. I looked at my hands and jumped at the sight of how dirty they appeared under the light. They quaked as my nerves wore thin. I walked up to a desk where a white woman sat writing in a notebook. I stood for a few moments until she noticed me.

"Yes?"

"Some guy told me to come up here to help. That's all I know."

She lifted her head at my comment after realizing I wasn't a Haitian asking for help. "Oh. Well—okay, do you have any medical training?"

"No. I told him I didn't but he said it doesn't matter."

"It doesn't, but having experience with trauma would be nice."

"What do you mean?"

"We need people to help in surgery. Clean up afterwards. Prep the tools. Hold down patients."

"Hold down patients?"

"Yeah." She didn't elaborate on it, but instructed me instead, "We'll start you off with clean up. The third room down on your right needs to be mopped. The supplies are in the room. Put on gloves, throw everything away on the floor, and don't touch anything with your hands if you can help it. Okay?"

"Okay."

Thursday, January 14th, 2010

11:50pm

Jimani, Dominican Republic

"Hold down patients."

I kept replaying the sentence in my head over and over again like a skipping record that etched a single message into my brain. She couldn't mean what I thought she meant. Maybe I needed to carry them, or help put them in beds, or pull them off tables. No. She'd said, "Hold down patients." Suddenly the cries and screams I heard earlier meant a lot more.

I pulled clean scrubs over my dirty clothes in a closet near the nurse's station. I pulled off my already filthy hat and inspected it as I replaced it with a plastic hairnet that stuck to my sweaty scalp. The brim had been soaked in sweat during the day, and now a thick white salt stain ran the length underneath. Dust covered all of it. I knocked it against my leg to release a small plume around my knee. It had aged quickly on the trip.

I entered the empty surgery room. A table sat in the center with bloodied sheets and towels draping off the sides. To its left a much smaller stainless steel pan balanced on a thin set of metal legs that resembled a TV dinner table. On it various tools lay on stained red rags and resembled saws, scissors, and hooks. Lights over the table hung from long arms that had been screwed into the base of the ceiling. It looked like a metal octopus installed to grope every inch of the person fastened to the altar.

I fought my nose as it reacted to the mess on the floor. The drains were clogged with wet bandages that covered the tiles in clumps around the table like hair at a barbershop. Everything appeared wet and red. I couldn't stomach thinking about it more than that, and I had to breathe through my mouth to avoid gagging. My knees felt weak, so I leaned against the door for a few moments to take in the scene.

I tried to imagine it as an apparition—or at least that I was watching it from somewhere else. I let my vision pan out until it seemed like I viewed the scene through a cloudy box inside my head. I tried to shut off my sense of smell and severely limit my vision to only what I had to. My legs wobbled and my head spun, but I managed to stand still until I believed the gore might be something less horrific.

I found the mop and bucket. Pushing the mess on the floor with the mop seemed useless. Oily streaks of red trailed everywhere. I moved as if making some grim abstract painting. Over and over I fought back vomit as the smell permeated my skin and surrounded me. Each time I gagged I tried to slow down, close my eyes, and breathe slowly through my mouth. I couldn't let myself puke. If I did that I'd have failed; I'd have to leave. My attempts at imagining myself outside the scene didn't work.

I kept mopping until only a slight pink haze covered the tiles. It took some water and time to get it clean to the point where the smell didn't gag me. I pulled off my gloves without my bare skin touching them. I finished the job and wanted to head back to the truck. One cleaning seemed like enough—I felt I'd done enough to call it quits for the night. I wanted to put on some new socks, get some water, and take a nap. I wanted to call Amber and play some games on my phone. More than anything I wanted to go home, but I'd be okay with the back of the truck for the rest of the night.

Just as I neared the door to the room I heard yelling down the hallway. A man in his late fifties spoke with the nurse, complaining about the conditions of the place. Her sunken eyes and deflated slouch gave away her exhaustion as she stared blankly at the furious man.

"This is crazy. We can't keep working like this. We're out of anesthetics and pins. We need those supplies tonight."

The Haitian woman responded, "I know, but the roads are closed. You just need to do what you can."

The man shook his head in disbelief and said something I couldn't hear before she nodded and walked away. Before I tried to slip out he turned and walked into the room and nearly ran into me. His eyes netted in bloodshot veins and his hair clumped into a messy pile that faded into erratic stubble across his face. He looked around at the floor and the table and then finally, at me.

"You clean the room?"

I'd hardly call it clean, but I didn't want to do any more. "I'm done, I think. I'm not sure I did it right." I started to motion toward the door but he spoke before I could leave.

"It looks fine." He looked me over and I felt him gauge me. "What are you here for?"

"Just to clean."

"Do you have any medical training?"

I paused. I knew what he really asked. I should have told the truth with a simple 'no.'

"I was a Boy Scout. Does that count?" I wasn't even sure why I said that. I wanted to get the hell out of there.

"That'll do—I need you in the next surgery to help hold a girl. The others are getting tired. We just need someone to help hold people. We don't have full anesthetics, so they are feeling most of the pain. You don't need to do anything special, nor would I want you to. Can you help us out?"

Time stopped right there. For a brief moment I saw the future, or at least the future as my mind saw it. I thought about Civil War hospital stories, blood, and screaming. I thought about home, making candy, and even taking a shower. He said they didn't have anesthetics. He said they didn't have pins. Could I handle it? I didn't think so, but I answered his question before I thought it through.

"Yes, I think I can."

He didn't waste a moment. "Good, let's get her in."

In a flash a tall, muscular man in his mid-thirties carried in the first girl. She looked six or seven years old and had passed out in his arms from the pain of her partially severed right leg. I saw some bone and muscle, but I turned away after a moment to try to block the image. My mind wouldn't let me accept that the leg belonged to another person. That running lie kept me from fainting.

A belt was bound the leg to stop the bleeding. I didn't let myself see below that point. I hovered closer to the girl while trying to remain in the background and out of sight. Perhaps I could just stand there and they'd go on without me. The doctor quickly dashed that dream when he turned and addressed me.

"Hold on to one of her arms."

With the others in place I approached the girl's arm. I shook terribly from the neck to my feet and my head heated up rapidly. They held her in place and numbed her locally but she still knew what the doctors planned. I put my weight on her shoulder and stood upright. With everyone in place a brief moment of silence blanketed the group until the doctor spoke.

"Okay everyone, just hold her still. This shouldn't take too long."

The doctor grabbed a long stainless steel saw with fine teeth and connected it to her wound. She tensed up and moaned while pushing against us.

"Just hold her still—a few more seconds."

The girl kept her eyes closed and continued to squirm as her jaw locked. Her hands balled into tight fists and small sections of white appeared on the tips of her fingers from squeezing.

Minutes passed. Eventually the doctor spoke. "Okay, we're done. Good job guys. The worst part is over."

I looked down at her leg. He completed what the quake had started by severing the rest of her tissue below the knee. He grabbed her lower leg and moved it off the table onto another tray. One of the men grabbed it and took it out of the room. I never did find out what they did with it. The doctor lifted her stump slightly and removed the bloodied cloth below it. He put new ones in its place and allowed the leg to return to rest. He resumed working, taking stitches to the inner parts. The girl struggled much less.

It took a while to close the leg. He folded the flesh over itself into a clean crease like a closed paper lunch bag. And then, just as quickly as she'd come in, one of the men carried her out. The doctor didn't seem fazed by the surgery, nor did anyone else. I stood in a state of shock, and felt my heavy feet stick to the ground as I stood motionless.

"You okay, son?" he asked me. I nodded blankly. "Good, cause I need you for the next one. But first I need a coffee." He stood and walked to the door. "Can you clean up this mess before the next surgery? Say ten minutes?"

"Sure."

"Good." He left the room, and once again I stood alone and surrounded by a mess of blood and bandages.

My hands shook as I stood next to the gore-soaked table. The rush of surgery came and went and I couldn't catch up. I held my hands to my chest and watched them shake rapidly in a subtle frequency. Pins and needles overtook my legs, and suddenly my head felt very hot. I felt blood rush through my veins, and my vision zoomed out to make the ground fall away.

Images of the severed leg and blood flooded my mind and turned my stomach sour. I took in a breath, and the smell of the room made its way to my gut to pull out anything I held inside. I vomited on the floor, bending over slightly as the muscles of my stomach contracted violently in protest of the surroundings.

I got to work and cleaned the room quicker and better than my first round. As I finished the doctor returned wearing a new set of scrubs. A Haitian man limped in the room with the help of a nurse. He removed a plastic bag that covered his right leg to reveal a crushed foot that had lost the flesh from his knee to the lower shin. Only the heel and part of the arch remained.

The doctor looked at me. "I don't need you for this one, but don't go anywhere." A weight lifted from my shoulder as I gratefully stood in the back of the room.

The man sat still as the doctor strapped his hands and left leg to the table while speaking in Creole for a few moments. The man nodded and closed his eyes. I watched, completely frozen and with the mop still in my hands as the doctor cleaned the foot. He clipped fragments of skin, muscle, and fat with surgical scissors. He worked fast, and continued to clean until the opening bled and all the ragged and dirty flesh sat on a rag on the surgeon's table.

During the process the Haitian kept very still as if in a state of meditation. I marveled at how he remained quiet while undergoing such an ordeal. The doctor stitched and bandaged the wound. The Haitian opened his eyes and smiled at the doctor while nodding and saying *"Merci"* again and again. They handed him a set of crutches and the nurse helped him walk out of the room.

I worked in the surgery room throughout the night assisting where I could and cleaning the room between each patient. My body ached from fatigue but adrenaline kept my muscles pumping and my mind alert. As the night closed I cleaned one last time. Afterward, the doctor walked in with a woman who carried a little girl with her arm wrapped in bandages. I saw her badly broken and partially severed elbow.

The doctor spoke to me and the others in the room. "We need to amputate her arm. The facility is out of pins, and I fear if we don't close her up she will get sepsis. I'm going to need everyone's help here. Most of the arm isn't severed, and I will need to work through a lot of tissue. We can give her a local to numb the pain, but it's going to be rough. If you're not comfortable with this I understand. I'm not asking anyone to stay."

Everyone, including me, agreed to help. They picked me to help hold her by the chest. They sat the girl on the bed and got her in position. She seemed so young, dressed in a sky blue outfit soaked in blood, dirt, and clay. Her beaded hair remained only in ragged and disjointed patches.

Friday, January 15th, 2010

6:20am

Jimani, Dominican Republic

The sun peeked over the eastern mountain range and fed its first rays into the shadowed valley. At first, lingering overwhelmed the light, consuming it like water on a drought-stricken plain. Rays pierced the morning mist on the ground and revealed the hidden fog that sat thick and heavy on the outpost. For a few minutes, the world sat in deadly silence as night transitioned into day to reveal the beauty of the Haitian countryside beyond the border.

The sun's crown rose above the ridge and painted the sky with shades of dark blue and purple followed by hues of magenta and red. Bursts of green and teal raced across the air like chariots as the sun claimed it for another day. I imagined the colors fought a great battle overhead. Blue and yellow overtook the purple and reds as they forced them to retreat west while sun reinforced from the east. The battle over, the sun claimed the spoils of war while evaporating the fog from the air and the dew from the grass.

The darkness of night had hidden carnage that the sun now put on display. I sat on a ledge of the larger building. Standing, I stretched my legs and looked around to survey the area. Two white buildings sat on the property, separated by five hundred feet of open field. A four foot stone wall ran the perimeter and worn dirt roads wove between the buildings and the entrance like snake trails, wavy but set on their destination.

Inside, the lower floor housed doctors' rooms, storage, and utilities. An enormous kitchen and seating area on the second floor with high ceilings and open windows let the weary rest on hot days. The other building acted as a dormitory for orphans. Its long, narrow wings connected with a large open common area. Painted completely white, the front faced northwest to watch the afternoon sun and keep it warmer when the night awoke again. Situated as it was, close to a large mountain range to the south and with a full view of the bay, I wondered what the compound felt like under normal circumstances.

I made out bodies in the grass and dirt directly to the side of the building. Many had died in the night, and the outpost lacked sufficient caskets. For both religious and hygienic reasons, the volunteers had wrapped them tightly in white sheets and laid them in rows. Only a dozen were visible from my perch, but I knew more lay just around the corner. The corpses seemed stark and hollow under the light of day.

The sun brought a chorus of fresh cries as those lucky enough to sleep through their pain woke to face another morning. Volunteers, including me, had worked through the night to move the injured into the dorms, and a rising wail of screams and moans pulsated across the field in waves that got closer and louder as minutes passed.

During the night, families of the injured had established camps in the grass field between the buildings. As the moans grew at the dorm I watched heads pierce the surface of the tall grass along with smoke from morning fires.

I focused on our truck parked in the distance. I needed a few hours' sleep before the day reached full swing. After twelve hours of nonstop work I'd reached my limit, exceeded it, hit another wall, broke it down, and fell forward a few more paces until I resembled a bloody and beaten sprinter on the ground dying for a drink.

I expected my legs to catch me as I jumped off the ledge. Drained of adrenaline and physically exhausted, I collapsed on the ground like a rag doll. I rolled my ankle and a sharp scream shot up my leg. "Damnit!" I spat out between my teeth as I grit them together to distract my brain from the ankle. I sat on the ground for a few moments with my forehead on my knee as I wondered why I'd done something so dumb. Slowly, I got to my feet and hobbled toward the truck while trying to keep the weight off my newly injured foot.

I yawned as I limped while the weight of my eyelids forced them closed. The sun grilled my body as I pulled my Ravens cap close to my eyes. The shadow it cast over my face created a sort of sanctuary. I felt like nothing could touch me if I remained under its brim. I ran my fingers across the crown to brush off dust and dirt and worked the fold of the arch to achieve the perfect curve. I constantly tinkered with it while feeling a sense of comfort from the ritual. It also kept me from biting my nails, which were too disgusting to think about, let alone pick at with my teeth. Perhaps I'd break the habit on the trip.

I walked with my eyes on the ground to avoid the throngs of people that begged for food or water. Even with my limited view I saw them lying on the ground on all sides. Children slept on the dirt while women made cooking fires and men built dwellings from whatever they scavenged. Some planned to stay at the outpost for a long time while their family members healed.

I closed in on the truck, anxious to fall asleep in the back under the shade of the metal roof. I noticed a pair of big feet hanging out of the cab. Intrigued, I crept up the side of the truck to see who owned them. Marcus slept soundly. Marcus had joined

Crossroads in the early Eighties after working with Jana and Bob on their jewelry business. His children often played with Amber and her siblings. When his children grew up and eventually moved away, he decided to move to Crossroads full time as the demands of the compound increased. His background in social work and his lifetime of experience working in the Caribbean made him an irreplaceable part of the managing faculty. He spent his time organizing groups and the work they completed when they visited as well as managing needs of the hundreds of volunteers that visited every year. Eventually, he'd taken over most of the logistics and planning for Crossroads.

I chuckled when I saw him in the cab. He crammed his six-foot-three-inch body between the driver and passenger doors like a jack-in-a-box ready to spring. His thick, wiry, fuzzy hair stood like an Afro as it traveled in all directions against the door. His thin frame glasses sat on his stomach and pulsated up and down as he breathed. Rainbows and flowers covered his scrub-style shirt and oversized cargo shorts hung off his thin legs. He snored loudly in the cramped bed and breathed in through his nose and out through his mouth in large, gasping breaths. I couldn't believe he hadn't woken himself up. I looked at my watch. 6:30 AM. I planned to grab two or three hours of sleep before someone inevitably woke me while rummaging through supplies in the back.

I grabbed the handrail and got in. The supplies had started in Santo Domingo as a neatly organized and efficient tower, but in one night of hurried emergency response the truck bed had been reduced to chaos. The tower had toppled, replaced by erratic piles of loose clothing, medical supplies, food packs, and water bottles. A propane tank lay on the floor, serving as a table for two cardboard boxes full of bandages and medication that teetered on the lip of the metal tank. Boxes of granola bars and crackers had exploded like grenades with empty wrappers blowing in the breeze. Crushed water bottles littered the floor and crunched under my feet as I crept inward. I looked around and noticed my propped sleeping bag still on the bench, but covered in more boxes. Nothing had been stolen, at least as far as I could tell.

At the front of the bed several bags of luggage created a messy pile in on the ground, I tiptoed around the boxes and fell into the soft bags of supplies. I pulled my hat down and pulled my arms over my face before falling asleep.

A dog barked nearby and woke me up. At first I thought that only a few minutes had passed. I checked my watch—several hours had slipped past in what felt like a moment. My stomach let out a long, deep groan. I hadn't eaten since early the day before, and the lack of nutrients caught up to me.

Hidden under the shade of the metal roof I peered outside. Less than a foot from my bed the merciless tropical sun beamed onto a black gym bag and caused it to glow with intensity. I reached out and touched it only to burn my fingers upon contact. It seemed like a taunt, as if the world outside wanted me to stay put. I sat still and tried to pretend I slept in my hotel in Virginia, still wrapped in thick covers to protect me from the frigid cold outside. I recalled what the winter air felt like on my skin, the bitter bite that dried my flesh and swelled my lips like bee stings. I wanted to feel cold again. I wanted to go home.

Marcus had left while I slept, and though the dorm sat far away the sound carried well in the open. Much of the crying had subsided, replaced by conversations, singing, and the sounds of children playing. I wondered for a moment if the night before existed in a dream and maybe I'd only slept while on a fun visit with Amber's parents. I loved to take naps at their pool or on the sand at the beach while Amber slept in a chair beside me with a cold *Presidente,* the national beer of choice in the D.R., in the cooler. When I sat up and saw the dorms, my heart dropped a little as I fell back to reality with a clumsy thud.

I walked toward the dorm to find my team. Thirty feet away a small group of children blocked my path. I looked each one over with intrigue as they did the same to me. The youngest boy had lost his left arm in the collapse and a clean set of bandages wrapped his shoulder. One of the girls wore gauze and tape over most of her skull and revealed only a mouth and an eye. The other girl's broken arm was slung in a cast along her chest. Regardless of their injuries they still seemed happy, and I smiled as they tried to take my hat. Bending on one knee, I took it off and put it on the girl with the full skull bandages. The rest of them looked at her and laughed as they chased her back into the dorms. I watched which room they entered; I couldn't go very long without my hat, especially with the sun rapidly cooking my pale skin.

Near the entrance of the common area, hundreds of new arrivals sat on the ground in small groups. Most of them had arrived during the night, and it appeared that quite a few had come while I'd slept. Many of the injuries, like the ones from the night before, looked severe and gruesome. Open wounds, infections, broken and exposed bones, burns, and missing limbs seemed ordinary in this surreal place. It seemed my stomach had hardened somewhat during the night, and I didn't feel as squeamish anymore.

"Where've you been, man?"

Jared stood behind me, carrying a large box of gauze and tape. I'd learned a little bit more about Jared since meeting him back in Santo Domingo. Originally from Arizona, he'd moved to St. Thomas to work in a hotel, then to bartend, and finally to work as a scuba diving instructor. I guess he'd felt some emptiness or something changed inside after the quake, because he left

St. Thomas and flew to Santo Domingo to try to find a way to Haiti. That seemed riskier than what I had done. At least a group waited for me when I arrived. Then he'd bumped into Jana by chance. He spoke Spanish but didn't possess any medical training. Jana had cared only that he wanted to help, though.

I told him I'd just woken up and pointed to the truck with an exaggerated, depressed look across my face.

"Oh," he paused, looking me over, "didn't you sleep last night either?"

"No." I looked at his arms. "Whatcha doing?"

"Helping Bob set up a clinic in the dorm." He looked closer at my face. "Where'd you disappear to last night anyway? I looked for you."

"Just around. Busy night I guess." I wasn't yet sure how to talk about the other building. My stomach rumbled. "Jared, is there any food?"

He laughed. "No man, we've been just grabbing what we can. I've got some extra crackers if you want them." He levered the box against his shoulder and left arm and pulled a handful of wrapped crackers out of his pocket.

"Thanks."

"You bet. I heard they're setting up something for lunch at the other building." He looked at the supplies as he shifted their weight in his arms. "I've got to get these to Bob." He walked past, juggling the box on his shoulder. He weaved between crowds of people in the confined area until he wandered out of view.

I walked to the building. Once inside, I stood in the middle of the common area surrounded by a sea of mattresses holding the injured. The sun flooded the room from the south and reflected off the white walls and white tile floors. The bright light burned my eyes even when I closed them. A boy stood at my side and peered with awe at the crackers in my hand. I sighed and handed over one of the two packets but ate the other myself. I pulled a half empty water bottle from my back pocket and finished it. My throat gasped for more, but I buried the feeling in hopes that the promise of lunch proved true.

The light of day revealed the severity of the injuries sustained by those in the common area. Everywhere I looked, it seemed lost limbs, third degree burns, and severe lacerations littered my view. In the daylight everything looked wet, sticky, and painful; some looked so mangled they prompted shivers to race down my spine. The fluorescent light of the surgery room dehumanized things a bit and provided a buffer for my stomach, but no such mercy lived under sunlight. Even with all the pain and suffering the majority seemed complacent, even happy just for the miracle of getting to the outpost at all.

A little girl with badly burned and bandaged hands sat on a cot on the far side of the room as her mother held her close. She smiled through dried tears as an older man applied a sticky ointment to her hands and gently patted her forehead. Tall, white and in his early sixties, Bob wore a flowered scrub that brushed against his fuzzy white beard. Amber's dad really did look just like Santa Claus. As he smiled, his rosy cheeks doubled over his eyes and lifted his thin frame glasses.

I thought back again to the first time I'd met him at the airport in Puerto Plata and the full, two-armed hug with which he'd welcomed me to his home. I'd only mustered the courage to get one arm around him while keeping the other back to maintain some manliness.

I didn't get the typical vibe from him that I expected after years of meeting the other girlfriends' dads. I expected him to be a bit cold and unwelcoming to let me know he only partially approved. I didn't get that at all from him; in fact, he revealed just how much he wanted to meet me. He took joy in revealing secrets Amber had shared regarding me and how she felt toward me. He told me he liked me, and that he liked me with Amber. By the time I reached their house, I felt at home. At the end of the trip I gave him a tight hug at the airport—using both arms.

Under the sun in the outpost he rubbed ointment on the girl's burns and, once completed, spoke to the mother and then moved to the next cot. I watched for a few moments more as he looked over a young man with gentle precision. He opened the man's shirt and cleaned several lacerations that ran up his chest. He worked quickly as he drained a bottle of saline. I knew he'd worked the entire first night, and I doubt he'd slept at all in the first forty-eight hours. Even so, he seemed completely alert and ready to go for another round.

He sat next to a man with a badly mangled foot. A few members of the team stood around him as he cried and shook his head. Bob pulled out a thick bottle filled with an elixir. Suddenly the man began to smile and nod and repeat, *"Merci, Merci."* Later in the trip I'd find out the man didn't want his foot amputated and had resolved to die rather than have the procedure done. He knew that without a foot a job would be impossible to find and he would end up broke and homeless. Even though the surgeons pushed him relentlessly to have the amputation he'd still refused. When Bob finally reached him he begged for another form of treatment. Bob created a mixture of honey and other ingredients that he used for infection and severe burns, so he promised to work on the man's foot and try to save it. Days later, the foot healed from the treatment. The man got to keep his foot and thus his livelihood.

I knew better than to interrupt him, so I walked toward the left wing to look for a way to help. Dozens of Haitians sat on the ground with untreated wounds. Everywhere I looked, people lay with signs and symptoms ranging from minor complaints of pain or headaches to broken bones and amputated limbs. An older woman with a head injury sat propped against the doorway to the left dorm. Her skull was split open with a crack that extended from her crown to left ear. Blood oozed slowly as she pressed a towel against her hair, the pressure only slightly slowing her bleeding.

I didn't speak Creole and I lacked medical training, so I tried to find Jana. I gave a woman my last full bottle of water before leaving to search the front of the building. I stood fifty feet away and scouted for her. Jana was easy to spot. Short and thin with wavy brown hair held in place with colorful bandanas, her figure stood out brightly in the crowd. She wore a light dress covered in a myriad of bright blues, greens, yellows, and reds.

I walked back in and traversed the crowded building. A breeze reached me on the balcony of the second floor as I entered, and I had to walk over people on the floor and around groups of Haitians that tended to their loved ones. I passed the group of children that took my hat and quickly reclaimed it from the girl's head to place it on my own. She jumped playfully to try and take it back, but I shook my head at her and said, "You can play with it later." The feel of it on my head steadied my nerves somewhat.

Jana knelt and gently cradled an elderly woman's head. Her experience with the sick, injured, and dying spanned a period of time far exceeding my years, and she seemed at ease and in her element amongst the chaos.

The Haitian woman had covered her right arm with a bloody sheet and appeared reluctant to let anyone help her. Jana spoke softly while creating privacy for the two of them as she explained our group and our intentions. We only wanted to help. The woman whimpered and nodded while glancing at the rest of the group and allowed Jana to remove the sheet. Her arm was cut off at the shoulder. Someone or something had sheared it without precision or care and left it as a heap of tattered flesh and muscle that hung in the wind. The bone was splintered. She or someone else had tried to close it, but now it festered. Later, we found out from some Haitians that she had slept against the wall the night before and refused to be treated by a white doctor out of fear. She'd preferred to sleep alone and endure a night of unthinkable pain.

I felt ill when looking at the wound. It appeared so mangled that I needed to step back for a moment to catch my breath. I put my weight against the wall and slowed my lungs as I tried to remain calm. Dean, Cameron, and Justin arrived moments after Jana removed the sheet.

Jana acted quickly. She ordered the three men to clean and dress the wound then take the woman to surgery across the property. They moved into action. The old woman sat still as they worked; I knew the wound would send me shrieking in pain. She tried to meditate as they worked, and I averted my eyes from the gore.

Jana turned to me. "Sean," she said, "I need your help."

Friday, January 15th 2010

11:30am

Jimani, Dominican Republic

Jana led me to a small room at the end of the hall. Dark, damp air filled the space. Dozens of people were crammed inside. They lay on dirty mattresses arranged in tight lines that filled the entire floor. Light crept in when we opened the door, waking people as it crawled across the living ground. Jana led me through a path that wound its way between sleeping and broken bodies. It reminded me of "Don't touch the ground," a game I played with my sister as a child. I wobbled with each step as I kept to my tiptoes. The breeze from outside didn't reach the rear of the room; instead, the air was choked with sweat and grime that floated like mist and stung my nostrils. I felt it soak my lungs and mouth with rot.

Along the farthest row against the rear wall, Jana knelt beside a man lying alone on a mattress. Though young, his face wore years of stress and labor like trophies in the forms of early wrinkles. His eyes sunk under their lids as if to bury themselves in his brain. A hard life had aged his body quickly, and left bones up against his thin black skin like poles stretching a nylon tent. Sparse, gray, flat hair was matted to his scalp. His clothes revealed minor cuts and bruises painted on his chest and arms. He had died in the night, but not even those sleeping right next to him had noticed.

"Sean, I need you to move him out back quickly and quietly, okay?" Jana looked around. "Try to find someone to help."

She looked at him again and placed her hand on his leg as she closed her eyes. She said a silent prayer and stood to leave. She kept a solemn expression around the Haitians, but I sometimes saw her alone at night sitting with her eyes closed in meditation. I imagined that she prayed or reflected to prepare for the next day. I never got too close, but could tell from her eyes she spent some of her alone time crying.

I had wanted to ask her about Amber as soon as we arrived, but the overwhelming need at the outpost ripped us apart and kept everyone busy at various duties. After everything I'd seen so far, I wasn't sure if I could even go through with it. It felt so selfish even to think about marriage here in this place of death and despair. During the first week I'd spent with Jana at Crossroads, I never met the rigid leader she'd become these past few days. I'd only seen a friendly but cautious mother. I'd met a woman who made meals and told us stories while we sat at a great mahogany dinner table. I only knew the woman who loved to talk to her daughter for hours every night on the phone. I didn't know this other Jana, and how could I ask someone I didn't really know such an important question?

I looked back at the man on the ground. I remembered bringing him in the room on a stretcher. He had complained about his stomach. We told him to rest, gave him some water, and let him go. We thought he came for a free medical exam and didn't pay attention. We focused instead on those with visually obvious wounds. I didn't know if his death had come by internal injuries or sickness, but either way, we didn't have the equipment to handle it. Even if we had, the shortage of doctors and nurses and the overwhelming number of women and children almost guaranteed his death. As a man with wounds we just couldn't see, he sat at the end of a very long line.

"Do you need help?" a man sitting close by asked. "I'll help… if I can have his mattress for my daughter."

I looked over at the man on the floor and nodded. He sat with two little girls, both crammed onto a single mattress. Nurses had treated the older daughter the night before and she now slept softly with her head and face covered with bandages. The younger daughter clung to the edge of the mat and attempted to sleep with smaller bandages on her arms and a splint on her left elbow.

I nodded and the father stood and took hold of the stretcher. I looked over the dead man and tried to formulate a plan to move him. He lay stiff, with his hands at his side, but his bowels had moved after he died and left a mess that covered his back, legs, and the mattress. There was really no clean way to move him. I took my hat off and wiped my face with it before placing it behind my waistband. Every day I spent here I got dirtier and dirtier. Would I ever shower again? I grabbed his shoulders and motioned to the father to grab his legs.

Moving the body stirred the smell and left an oily mess behind. I slipped my hands from behind his shoulders and stared in disbelief; feces covered them like greasy, brown glue. Nearly ready to break, I grabbed the wooden ends of the stretcher and lifted up the body. As the father and I moved, the little girl grabbed the mattress and pulled it close to her sister. She flipped it over and laid her blanket on it before closing her eyes to fall asleep.

Haitians avoided us as we walked. In the hall a breeze hit my nose and provided relief. Those standing outside moved as we pushed into the crowd. The back of the dorms sat out of view from the crowds on the compound. Long lines of bodies covered in white sheets soldiered the area and turned the clearing into a temporary grave. The beating sun worked hard to process the dead quicker than expected, and the stench of death flowed from the area. I stopped my lungs while near the bodies to keep from feeling sick. We laid the man on the ground and draped a sheet over him. The father turned and left as quickly as he could.

I looked at my hands. Under the sun the filth dried quickly and left a thick cake of smelly grit behind. The ground was charred and cracked, with sparse patches of thin dying grass dotting the area. I bent over and furiously rubbed my hands against the earth. After a few moments I stopped and inspected them. Most of the wet grime had rubbed off, but the thick, dry stuff remained and sucked the moisture from my skin.

I brushed my hands against my shorts and surveyed the area. The mountain range sat so close I noticed small stones and bushes clinging to the steep, rocky incline. It met with the ground a few hundred feet from the property and left red and brown rubble in heaps that clung to it like a child to its mother. Thin, wiry bushes jutted from the dry ground with tangled branches that provided little shade. To my right and down from the mountain, tall grasses grew in thick patches. The farther I looked from the mountain the more fertile the land turned, until nothing but thick grasses and trees filled the landscape to the edge of the lake below. It shimmered with a vibrant aqua that reflected the blue sky and the brown landscape against it like a mirror.

I felt the sun burn my forehead, so I reached for my hat. I had worked on the brim for several days, and admired the perfect arc. The purple was faded from sweat stains that crept up the hat and made it look as though it ate the color alive. The raven appeared clean, but blood and sweat covered the back. I put it on and hid from the sun under its brim. It fit perfectly, much better than new.

My khaki shorts were soaked from days of dirt, sweat, and blood. My shoes sopped in a soggy red mess. Bloodstained handprints and streaks of dirt from wiping my face covered my shirt. I thought about how dirty I felt at home when working at the candy plant. I'd get chocolate under my fingernails and peanut butter on my arms and clothes and hated the feeling of it on my skin. Now my fingernails were caked with human shit. Blood and bodily fluids had soaked into my skin. I'd happily jump into a pool of peanut butter just to get away from the outpost.

I stood over the man. It felt wrong leaving him to lie in the sun alone. I closed my eyes and muttered a short prayer.

Anxious to change, I jogged back to the truck. Luke, Faith's boyfriend, stood at the back handing out boxes of supplies to volunteers. Luke was kind and gentle, but often gave the vibe that his serious side beckoned to come out and overtake him. He seemed much older than his age. The first time I met Amber's family, he'd been midway through a several-months-long project where he lived in the Haitian village and taught the people how to make outdoor cookers in an effort to improve conditions caused by indoor charcoal fires. Many Haitian families traditionally cook using charcoal which, when burned indoors, can cause Tuberculosis, lung cancer, and even death due to carbon monoxide poisoning. It intimidated me to see how much he did for Crossroads when I did next to nothing. Now he planned to stay in Haiti for a month or so after we left. We weren't even in Haiti yet, and I already wanted to leave. It seemed crazy that someone planned to give so much under such risky circumstances.

Luke laughed as he carted the boxes from the back of the truck. He appeared full of energy even though his clothes looked filthy and his brow was soaked with sweat. Volunteers moved back and forth and took the boxes away as the truck was unloaded. I couldn't get to my bags without pushing through the crowd, so I walked up to the side of the bed and leaned into a small sliver of shade.

"Sean!" Luke yelled as I neared, bending over and handing out another box. "Help me unload this stuff."

I didn't want to help. "What's it for?"

"Dr. Bob's setting up a clinic in the dorm. Here, take this."

He placed a plastic tote on my shoulder, and I shrugged under the weight.

"Don't drop that, it's full of medicine." He turned before I could retort or complain, moving back into the bed and pulling another box from the pile I had used as a bed an hour ago.

I made my way up the small hill and into the common room. Bob stood at the doorway to direct traffic and inspect at each box as it came in. He smiled as I approached.

"Sean, put that in the back under the cabinet, okay?"

I nodded and moved into the small room. After unloading I went to leave, but he stopped me and placed his hand on my shoulder. I suddenly noticed that for a moment we stood alone.

"Are you doing okay with everything?"

The thought suddenly came over me to just ask him about Amber. I doubted the possibility of getting him and Jana together at the same time considering the chaos at the outpost. Things only seemed to get busier. I looked up and tried to build the courage. I rapidly practiced the lines in my head as I phrased the question a dozen different ways. "Can I marry your daughter?" or "I want to ask you for your permission to marry Amber," or maybe "I love Amber and I want to spend the rest of my life with her." I looked up to see him staring right through me. I suddenly didn't feel as comfortable around him as I did when we shared a few beers at his home last summer.

"You okay Sean? You look exhausted."

Suddenly, Cindy appeared in the doorway and interrupted. "Bob, we need you to come look at someone that just came in. They have pretty bad burns."

Bob pulled away, but momentarily stopped and turned his head. "Try to help Luke with the rest of the gear, okay?"

I nodded and shoved my nerves back to my stomach where they belonged. As the minutes passed I grew relieved by Cindy's abrupt entry. It didn't feel like it was time to ask yet. It would've felt cheap and forced. I did need to ask him soon. I shuffled back down the hill and grabbed another box.

After moving the gear I sat on a rear tire and opened a bottle of water. It felt hot in my hands but I emptied it in a few gulps. I hopped into the back of the Daihatsu to change. The place looked completely different. With most of it empty I moved freely throughout the bed. Luke had stacked the personal luggage into a pile toward the front. I rummaged through it until I found my bag lodged between the benches. I pulled on the handle, but it was stuck in place, wedged between the other bags. I reached and managed to grab the zipper. I pulled it open with an awkward jerk as I banged my elbow into the steel frame.

I jammed my hand into the bag and fumbled around until I found clean boxers. I pulled them out and held them up in the air like a prize as a wide grin extended across my face. The green checkered boxers smelled clean and looked soft. I pulled a tarp over my lap and peeled off my shorts. My boxers were soaked in sweat and grime, and a dark line had formed on my thighs. I wiggled out of them and sat for a moment while the breeze grazed my skin. The clean boxers felt amazing when I put them on. The fabric seemed softer than anything I'd ever worn before.

I held up my khaki shorts in the light. Dirt and blood soaked the fabric. Shades of brown, black, and red covered the front in the shape of handprints, and a dark brown stain had formed along the belt line. I pulled off my blood soaked shoes, and removed my socks like old Band-Aids. My fingers seemed permanently caked from wearing dozens of pairs of latex gloves during the previous twelve hours. I kept a large pile of them stuffed in my back pocket, and each time I took them off I could feel my skin celebrate as fresh air grazed over them. Any time I got close to blood I needed to put on a new pair. I lost count of how many I went through very early on.

From the bed I saw the entire compound. The day was in full swing. Trucks arrived hourly with new doctors and supplies, Haitians continued to file in the main entrance, and volunteers buzzed like bees throughout the property trying to fight the unending sea of need.

My stomach groaned. I looked at my watch. It was just after noon. I felt weak, tired, and slow, having gone almost a day without any real food. I noticed dozens of people on the kitchen balcony of the main building. I barely caught the smell of food. I hopped out of the truck to make my way toward it.

A dozen steps away from the dorms and into the field Jared caught up with me. Sweat soaked his scrubs around the armpits, back and upper chest, turning the light blue color of the fabric into a dark navy. He looked out of breath and in need of a smoke, his tired eyes sunk into his skull. Still, he wore a wide, sarcastic grin as he winked while pointing at the balcony.

"You hungry too?" he asked as he walked beside me in the field.

"Yeah, I guess the rumor is true."

"Good plan. Been busy today?"

I briefly told him about my morning but left out parts that threatened to ruin my appetite. Strangely enough I managed to keep thoughts of feces, blood, and gore out of my mind. I couldn't decide if my hunger or my fatigue did that, but either way I welcomed it as a break.

"Wonder if they got pizza?" I asked, prodding him on the side.

"Maybe some Coca-Cola and some cold-cuts too. Perhaps some strip steaks?"

"Yes, I'd love some lobster tail."

We laughed for a moment, probably a little too loud for where we stood. We caught glares from a few Haitians standing around a high-tech medical bus that had arrived in the night. The porch on the first floor of the main building sat packed with crates and boxes protected by security guards holding automatic weapons. Two large generators hummed with wires running to medical trailers. Buses idled in the field with lines of Haitians waiting to get inside.

On the second floor dozens of people stood eating. Our eyes lit up in unison.

We looked around until we found a small set of stairs clinging to the side of the building hidden by supplies and guarded by a soldier. He moved aside and nodded as we approached. Inside the building the kitchen buzzed with commotion. Jared and I weaved through the crowd unnoticed. Near the ovens, two Haitian women stirred giant pots of soup that smelled amazing as another two women made sandwiches. We got into line behind a few doctors and waited. At the front we each received a bowl of soup and a sandwich before the line pushed us aside.

We took our food and found a place to sit in the doctors' hall on the second floor. The area was reserved for doctors and nurses and so remained relatively quiet while everyone worked around the compound during the day. Upon closer inspection I realized the wonderful smell of the food had deceived me. Barely more than a few vegetables and chunks of bread bobbed on the surface of the hot chicken broth. A square of cheese and some bologna sat between two slices of white break to make a sandwich. Though the meal was meager, I felt extremely lucky to have any food at all. After a full day of seeing others deal with unthinkable pain and grief, the thought of any food at all dazzled me like a brand new car. I looked around the kitchen. Hardwood floors and painted ceilings didn't blend with the chaos outside. I felt stoned after eating, and I sank in the crack between two large cushions on the flimsy couch as Jared and I talked about home. I drifted off to sleep.

Friday, January 15th, 2010
1:30pm
Jimani, Dominican Republic

I sat up quickly and gauged the surroundings until my mind calmed and the sleepy fog lifted. I slouched on the leather couch in the common room. Lunch had put me to sleep. Even under the roof and the spinning rotors of a huge fan overhead, the heat from the midday sun outside had soaked my back in sweat while I slept and stuck me to the leather couch like a Band-Aid. I peeled myself forward to stand, but my muscles burned as if on fire and they groaned and cracked like a stone giant waking from a millennium long slumber. On either side of me and on the other couches small groups of people spoke in various languages as they ate. No one noticed, or cared, if I slept there.

I realized Jared had left. I couldn't help but feel bad for sleeping during the middle of the day—it seemed like a selfish thing to do. I could actually smell myself. I stunk badly and needed a shower. What time was it? It felt like I'd slept for days, and I didn't know how much time had passed.

Outside, under the sun, the compound ran at full speed. Huge semi-trucks held generators, trucks came in and out loaded with people, doctors scurried from bus to bus, and across the field hundreds of people worked at the dorms. I felt like I'd missed a lot, but after looking at my watch I realized only thirty minutes had passed since leaving for lunch.

After I took just a few steps into the field, the sun whipped its heated tentacles onto my neck as a loud buzzing noise came from overhead. I looked up and saw it: a blue helicopter paced toward us from the west. It stopped above me and hovered for a moment before slowly getting bigger as it descended while keeping completely stable. Tall grasses pushed out in all directions that rippled like waves on a stormy day. As soon as it touched down a small team came out of the main building and met several people carrying stretchers from the helicopter. Once they cleared the rotors it shot back into the sky and raced west as fast as it could, undoubtedly bound for Port-au-Prince.

What a transition in the last eighteen hours. When we'd first arrived, the ground was littered with people bleeding and dying from untreated wounds that the night hid and the dirt worsened. What had started as just a few doctors and a handful of nurses had transformed into teams with buses, generators, and medicine. The chaos of the night before seemed almost a distant dream as I heard the site organizers bark out orders to throngs of volunteers who'd arrived in the morning. The night before I'd helped in surgery; now I couldn't even get in that wing of the building. I'd like to admit that I felt relieved over the transition, but in truth the new compound brought on depression. I wanted to help with the patients, not be told to stand back as new volunteers shuffled in.

On the walk back to the dorms I decided to try asking Amber's parents for their blessing again. Bob liked to work on patients and Jana liked to organize and keep order, so they rarely ended up side by side. With all the new help at the compound it seemed plausible to finally get them together.

I found Bob sitting with Marcus near the truck. If I could just find Jana then I might get all three done at once. I knew how much it meant to Amber for me to ask Marcus, too. He saw Amber as a surrogate daughter; it only seemed right to include him in the moment.

Marcus and Bob were speaking about the tasks for the day so I decided to look for her myself. Marcus held his hands in the air as he spoke. Bob sat quietly with his leg crossed while sipping a bottle of water. Marcus is articulate and humorous and gets very excited about his topics, while Bob prefers to stay quiet and listen, choosing to speak only when he's crafted exactly the right words to say. I remembered the dinners at Crossroads the first time I visited; while most of the family spoke energetically about topics ranging from the mission to politics in America, Bob almost always stayed quiet, instead drinking a beer slowly from the head of the table as he watched his family interact, almost as if watching a TV show. When he did speak up most of the group tended to quiet, and when he and Jana carried a conversation it always lead to the rest of the family silently observing.

I started in the lower wings. I went from room to room as I scoured every inch. The daylight broke through the windows and made it easy to see inside, but I couldn't find Jana. I ran into Dean and Cameron. They hadn't seen her in a while, having themselves been stuck working with patients all morning. They hadn't gotten past the first few rooms over. Dean looked tired and dirty, with streaks of grime across his forehead and imprints of a hundred sweaty wipes on his shoulders. He excelled with children. Before starting on one he asked his name, held his hand and calmed him down. He laughed more than anyone else on the team, even during all the tragedy.

Cameron seemed so much quieter than Dean when they worked together, but I think that it looked that way because Dean grabbed the moment much more aggressively. In a lot of ways, Cameron reminded me of Bob. He took the time to look at an entire situation before acting, a trait I often lacked at work and at home. Often I saw Cameron stop, pausing next to people sitting on the ground or against the hallways to ask them questions, listen to their heartbeat, and inspect their bodies. He knew from his past visits that Haitians often didn't complain about pain or injuries and often neglected themselves to give the doctors time to work with those in the most danger. He discovered broken bones, fractured ribs, concussions, broken teeth, and other "easy to miss" injuries that often went unattended in Jimani. He knew how to appropriately spend his time and understood the need for prioritizing, but he made an effort to give everyone hope and care, even if they tried to deny his help.

On the first floor Cindy gave out toys to injured children. I found her sitting next to a little girl with a brace that went from her left hip to her foot. She held a new teddy bear close to her chest as Cindy checked her heartbeat. She let the girl play with the stethoscope while she listened to her pulse, all while smiling and giving reassuring hugs. She loved to work with children, and had chosen to skip sleep and a few meals since arriving in order to do as much as possible. I sat down next to the girl as she worked and played peek-a-boo with another girl until she finished. Every time I met a new child with life threatening wounds it caused my heart to ache. I'd thought about possibly having children with Amber in the future, and the thought of having them go through such pain pushed my emotions further.

"I haven't seen Jana since this morning." Cindy offered. "Have you checked up at the main building?"

I hadn't, but I couldn't get in there now anyway. The new organizers had tightened security and only let doctors and nurses into the surgery wing.

"I'll check up there." I wanted to find her before Bob got back to work. I thanked Cindy. As I was leaving, I noticed that the entire crowd was watching her closely as she worked. She grinned while sitting in the dank room right on the border of the Dominican Republic and Haiti.

I ran back to the main building. No Jana. I just couldn't find her anywhere. Finally I decided to ask Bob if he knew where she was. I failed miserably at keeping a secret and feared that he'd see right through me when I asked. When I got back to the Daihatsu he still sat on the rear steps with his eyes closed and his head tilted up, stretching, as if purging the stress of the last eighteen hours from his body. He looked a lot older when he was tired, but he didn't look frail. He reminded me of someone who had aged from a lifetime of seeing and doing extreme things. Walking up to him felt like climbing some great staircase in Nepal to confer with an ancient monk.

I stood in front of him for a moment to block the sun from beating down on the burnt scalp that shone through his white curly hair. For a moment I thought he was asleep until he spoke up.

"Sean. How are you doing?" he asked without opening his eyes. I wondered how long he'd felt my presence before speaking.

"Okay. I ate lunch up at the main building. There's a ton of food if you haven't been there yet."

He paused before opening his eyes to look at the dorms, "I'm afraid I won't have time. A burn victim just came in. I'm treating him every fifteen minutes." He crafted each sentence carefully, each word chosen as if he took everyone else's feelings into consideration. "I'm glad you got some food. I heard you were up all night."

"Yeah, I helped." He tried to make me feel better. It worked a bit, but it didn't completely shake my guilt for eating when he hadn't.

"Have you seen Jana?"

He looked up suddenly and seemed confused as he slightly tilted his head and readjusted his glasses. "She left for Port-au-Prince with Faith and Luke about an hour ago. You didn't know that?"

My heart sunk to my feet like a lead ball in the ocean.

"No. I didn't know they left. Are we going soon too?"

"You guys are leaving tomorrow, but I'm staying here. There's too much work to do, and they need my help. I need to get back to the vet clinic in a few days, and we aren't sure how long the team will stay in the capital."

I'd failed my primary mission. Jana and Bob had split paths and I'd missed my chance to ask them together. She'd left while I ate lunch and slept on that couch. I wanted to scream. I wanted to cry. I wanted to just go home and forget the entire trip. I lost myself for a few moments as I thought.

"Is everything okay?"

I looked at him again. For once it seemed at last I held his undivided attention. The rest of the group worked far away from us. Nothing about this trip had gone according to plan so far, so how could I expect this to be any different? Tomorrow the rest of the group left for Port-au-Prince, and I planned to go with them. I'd enter the belly of the beast as an unwilling participant, quietly wishing for my safe, sound home. I knew no chance existed of us speaking again alone.

As Bob sat on the step and looked at me my mind reverted to a time when I was a child at the mall with my mother. He did look exactly like Santa Claus, and the moment felt surreal as I remembered asking the king of Christmas for presents while I sat on his lap all those years ago. Now here I stood in front of him again as I decided how to ask for the biggest present of my entire life. Did he think I deserved his daughter? I quickly ran through the Rolodex of memories I shared with Amber, looking for something that would give him pause.

I asked him. I can't remember exactly what words I used, but I do know that they fumbled out like clothes bursting from overstuffed luggage. I didn't get the setup I planned, I didn't get time to prove myself to them in Haiti, and I couldn't quite tell him all my feelings in a way that accurately described them. I told him I loved his daughter, and that I wanted to spend the rest of my life with her. I told him the main reason I came to Haiti was to ask if I could marry her. I wanted to continue to explain myself to him, to further legitimize my request, but he stopped me before I rambled further.

All he replied at first was, "Yes, of course." Tears started to drip from his squinted eyes. Then he stood and wrapped his arms around me in a hug that felt surprisingly comfortable. My body didn't try to pull away from it either, and I stood there motionless while his answer set in. He stepped back from the hug to look at me. For the first time on the trip I saw him as Amber's dad and not one of the leaders of the mission group or the heroic doctor. His eyes puffed from crying and his cheeks balled into bright red lumps on his face as his smile reached from ear to ear. I felt that he knew all along I wanted to ask on the trip.

"I'm so happy you asked here. Jana and I both know that you are the one for Amber. We love you so much." He stepped back slightly but kept his hand on my shoulder.

"You wanted to ask us together, didn't you?"

"It was what I'd planned, but I guess I'll need to ask her in Port-au-Prince."

He let out a small chuckle as he wiped a few stranded tears from his face. I felt like a feather.

"I'll keep it secret until you ask her too. I'm sure she'll say yes." He gave me one more hug before grabbing his medical bag from the truck. "We can't wait to have you in the family." I smiled and nodded. I sat down as he went back into the dorms with a huge smile across his face.

Friday, January 15th, 2010
6:30pm
Jimani, Dominican Republic

The rest of the evening Bob smiled whenever he saw me, and I waved back with a sheepish grin. He promised not to tell anyone in fear of Jana and Marcus finding out before I'd had a chance to ask them myself. With the new rules in place I spent the rest of the day moving supplies and feeding the victims, no longer allowed to do any medical work because of my lack of training. I floated through my chores with my mind firmly planted on one subject: asking Jana and Marcus. I'd always felt more comfortable with Bob. He probably knew my intentions even before I'd approached him. Asking Jana presented something completely different. She moved so quickly during the trip that I feared the possibility of never getting her alone for even just a few minutes. Even if I did get a chance to talk to her I didn't have the slightest clue about how to ask. I still felt unworthy to request the blessing. Amber seemed fit to marry a doctor, or someone traveling the world and running a mission. Not a boring engineer from Pennsylvania. Asking for her hand seemed like getting permission to lock her in my mundane world.

I spent part of the evening talking to Justin and Jared about the whole proposal and my real reasons for coming down. They both decided to take a break around ten, and we just happened to converge at the truck at the same time. Justin had worked since the early morning and had stopped only to drink water and use the bathroom. Now overexertion hit him hard. Deep dark circles had formed around his eyes, and his neck was stiff from constant bending and twisting in the dark. An application to medical school consumed all his thoughts. Originally due home a few days earlier, he'd missed an interview with a prestigious school to stay and help. His entire family wanted him to get admitted, but now he didn't know if he even had an interview to attend when he returned. School had given him permission to come on the trip, but he still worried. "I just have to get in," he'd say to us when talking about it. During the few breaks he did take he either wrote in his journal or called home to check on the status of his application. He knew he couldn't stay in Haiti indefinitely, but he knew he'd made the right choice to come.

Jared had undergone a huge change in the first twenty-four hours. Whereas just the night before he'd joked around with me about anything we found, now a serious demeanor overtook him. The way he smoked seemed different, transitioning from shorter puffs to longer, drawn out, deeper breaths. Bob pushed him hard to set up the pharmacy, and I joked that he learned more in one day about medication than most students learned in several semesters.

As all three of us sat on the ground drinking water. When I told them that I missed the chance to ask Jana, Jared burst into laughter. "So I guess you're coming to Port-au-Prince?" he asked, obviously aware of the answer. He knew the truth—I didn't have a choice anymore. After speaking for a while, went to sleep to recharge for the excursion into Haiti.

The next morning the sun rose slowly above the mountaintops. Its morning glow breached the room to dance on the sleeping group as it fought back the shadows of the evening. Bob slept a few feet away, and I marveled as he slept on the bare floor with nothing but a bundled towel as a pillow. I stood slowly to keep from waking anyone and exited the room.

Outside I stood on the second story of the dorms at the end of the hall. The group had sectioned off a single room to store supplies and rest. Around us were fields filled with long grass that waved back and forth in praise of the sun. At the edge of the property sat a small stone wall with sections of barbed wire. A horse ate grass against it with his neck tied using a frayed rope. His ribs pressed against his sides as if to escape their prison of skin, and his mane appeared thin and wiry.

Past the horse a few miles of rolling hills and pastures continued until they met the lake, and boats dotted its surface like freckles to break the otherwise glass top sheen. In the west the stars shone weakly against a black and deep purple sky. In the east it transitioned to light blue with the halo of the sun pulsating light from just behind the mountain range.

To my right I watched the final transformation brought by the last few buses that had arrived in the night. Generators kept spot-lights lit over the entire property. Mountains of supplies sat around the main building like a protective wall. Armed guards patrolled the perimeter. I heard voices over loudspeakers, and everywhere I looked people moved back and forth wearing white coats. The established outpost didn't need a guerilla team anymore.

We said our final goodbyes to a few of the Haitian volunteers before we left. I gave Bob a hug before boarding the truck and settling in for the ride. At eight o'clock we left, ready to enter Haiti.

The truck crept as it made its way along the road that hugged Lake Azuei all the way to the border of Haiti and the Dominican Republic. Huge potholes and rocks made it impossible to drive straight for long distances; instead the vehicle snaked back and forth to avoid every big obstacle possible while hitting the small ones. Each turn, bump, and jerk heaved the supplies—and the people—in the back. It felt like a small ship being tossed about in the ocean.

The rest of the team struggled to stay awake or just stared into the distance. Marcus drove while Cindy and Cameron kept him company in the front seat. I watched Cameron rest his head on his mother's shoulder. Cindy looked out her window while holding his head.

Dean and Jared sat at the end of the truck bed and watched the road slip out from under us as we closed the gap between us and Haiti. Despite the heat, Dean managed to wear his knit beanie over his short, black hair as he sorted through his medical bag to update his checklist of what he'd used. Jared kept his legs up on the bench across from him as his head bobbled up and down while he fell in and out of sleep. He'd stayed up the entire night with Bob to set up the temporary pharmacy at the dorms. I heard him come in to sleep only an hour or so before I woke up to pack my things. The few days of adrenaline wore off somewhere during the drive.

Justin read a pamphlet he'd brought with him. I had an international cell phone so I let him call his school a couple times just to check in. Now he wrote in the journal he kept of the trip. He'd talked about Port-au-Prince over and over while we helped at the outpost, but he spent just as much time talking about getting home and applying for medical school.

Megan sat under the shade of the roof and stared at the countryside. She'd had only a few chances to lead the group so far and I knew from our talk at the airport that she wanted more. After the larger group of doctors arrived at Jimani they'd taken over her responsibilities and pushed her aside. I wondered how Crossroads would fare under her watchful eye. Her personality was split equally between compassion and no-nonsense, depending on the audience. When one moment she worked on the ground helping victims drink water or eat food the next she ordered volunteers and made firm decisions for the group. I, on the other hand, coped with the sheer immensity of the tragedy by telling jokes and trying to stay relaxed, a tactic she didn't understand or approve of. I wasn't sure if she didn't like me or if her desire to impress Jana just kept her on edge.

I tried to start a conversation about Crossroads. I asked her what she planned to do, when she would do it, and how. Would she keep it the same as Jana or would she change the way it worked? Would her husband come live with her in Puerto Plata or would she run it from Canada? I asked about hockey, and computers, and anything I could think of during the trip to try and spark some response, some conversation, but she didn't budge. I decided to try through actions once we got to Port-au-Prince. Maybe I could do something to get her to like me more. If she really planned to take over Crossroads, then our paths would intertwine indefinitely if I married Amber.

Heavy traffic and border control slowed the five-mile drive to the Haitian border. It took an hour to reach the guards that stood in the center of the road with rifles drawn. Finally, they let us pass into Haiti.

The road shadowed the coastline until the mountains veered away to leave a wide expanse of flat land between it and the ocean. Eventually the road deteriorated until it was nothing more than a series of large potholes connected by small patches of stone. All along it on either side sat one story homes and stores that displayed years of wear. As we passed, Haitians looked at us. I hoped the "Crossroads" sign on the truck signaled a white flag.

The surroundings transformed from sparsely populated towns to highly congested urban sprawl. Most traffic traveled against us; trucks, buses and cars pushed east toward the Dominican border. Luggage, furniture, lumber, and tools were lashed to every inch of the exteriors.

After driving for a few hours, we stopped in heavy traffic at the outskirts of Port-au-Prince. Immediately the bed heated up as the metal roof cooked us under the midday sun. Dust and dirt blanketed us within minutes. Vehicles sat on all sides and people moved between them like ants. I felt cornered amidst the massive crowd and chaos surrounding us. The flimsy walls of the truck suddenly felt like paper.

Here I first witnessed remnants of the earthquake's destructive force. Some of the buildings showed signs of cracking at the north end of the street. Long, jagged grooves traversed the walls, sometimes with sizable chunks missing. Several had collapsed completely, and as we inched forward on the road we approached the remains of a three-story office building.

The left, right, and rear walls stood solemnly in the daylight, and twisted rebar and concrete boulders filled up the space between them and spilled into the street. Large chunks of debris sat on two cars and had crushed them flat. People dug frantically at the chunks, and I couldn't tell if they were looking for survivors or possessions. Groups of men cut down metal and wire from the pile of concrete and took it way. Small fires burned beneath the rocks, and next to the building I noticed a row of bodies on the ground. Children lay next to women; men next to babies.

The destruction increased as we pushed toward the heart of the city. At one point virtually everything seemed partially or completely destroyed, and we needed to weave back and forth on the road to avoid piles of concrete and steel. Somehow Marcus navigated the narrow corridors and squeezed the large truck between wrecked cars and crowds of people.

A few miles in we approached a military base. The gate opened as we neared and closed immediately behind us. Haitians crowded the area and outstretched their hands into the courtyard through the bars. The soldiers looked disinterested and continued their patrol of the inner perimeter. The fence brimmed with Haitians begging for help and reminded me of a scene from a zombie movie.

Marcus came to the back. "Guys, we're stopping here for a few minutes. The truck that came with us is staying; they don't feel comfortable going all the way into the city. There's a small med station here; they want to stay and help. We'll leave in a few minutes."

Dean looked toward the street. "Guys, it's chaos out there."

I looked at the gate. People shook the fences, pushing up against them and trying to uproot the base. Although made of thick iron bars and at least twelve feet tall it swayed back and forth from the weight of the Haitian mob. Screams got louder and angrier, and with each passing minute my fear grew.

Six guards walked toward the gate with their weapons drawn and pointed at the crowd. The gate opened just enough to allow the wide vehicle to pass through. As soon as Marcus drove through, they closed and locked the perimeter. A mob of Haitians piled against it again like waves upon rocks. The crowds backed away from our truck and let us pass through the street unharmed. We continued west.

The truck drove through the northern edge of the city along the water. The smell of rotting food and human waste infiltrated my nose as we reached a huge market. On the street hundreds of small bazaars sold food and goods to shoppers. Pigs slept in trash covered in mud while vegetables and fruit sat on the ground. I'd known only the antibacterial grocery stores in America, and the sight made me sick.

Past the market the truck made a left on a road that went up a steep incline and acted as a main artery for the city. After a hundred yards we hit another roadblock. A white UN armored personnel vehicle sat with a soldier manning a gun mounted on roof. Past it the road stopped and a mountain of rubble filled the area from a hotel on the right.

Marcus turned sharply and drove down another hill. We passed a bulldozer pushing debris off an extremely narrow, broken road. We slowed to a crawl and navigated down as I stared at the steep drop off on either side of the path.

After countless turns, bumps, and hills the truck slowed in front of a long winding driveway that traversed a hill. Marcus got out of the truck and opened the gate to allow us inside. He floored the accelerator as the clumsy truck pushed to reach the top of a steep hill. At the crest we stopped in a quiet concrete courtyard in front of a single story building that overlooked the city. We'd arrived at the orphanage.

Saturday, January 16th, 2010
3:15pm
Port Au Prince, Haiti

The sun hung lazily in the sky above the western horizon and emitted a soft glow that wrapped the world in an orange hug. A warm, swirling breeze reached us in the back of the truck as it licked the hills and enveloped the courtyard in a slowing wake that chilled the sweat on my brow. I'd perspired from the moment I woke and my skin was stained with a salty chalk that dusted my flesh with a white hue. Even from atop the hill and far away from the city center a clamor sounded loudly in my ears. Vehicles, yelling, and music mixed together in a symphony half soothing and half chaotic. The orphanage existed past an imaginary barrier in my mind that cut us off from the danger. It was like an island amongst crashing waves as it sat atop a hill surrounded by cliffs and deep valleys within a residential part of the city.

A huge gate guarded the only entrance. A steep, narrow driveway flanked by sharp drop-offs provided the only pathway to the courtyard and enabled the owners to see people coming from far away.

The quake hadn't destroyed the stout, one-story structure that the orphans called home. Only webbed cracks that marred the gray walls in spots and a few missing red clay shingles gave hints as to what had occurred a few days before. A large swing set rocked in the quiet courtyard flanked with stone walls. My anxiety about sleeping in the disaster-struck city lifted as I took note of the security of our new home. This was the place Jana told us to meet her once we arrived; it would act as our base of operations for the rest of the trip.

After a few moments I heard giggles and laughs from inside the main entrance. Suddenly, a wave of children burst through the doors and ran at us with their arms outstretched, their guardians finally allowing them to come outside after giving us a minute to breathe. I stood still as a small throng of boys grabbed my arms, jumped up and down to get on my back, and danced around all the while screaming and laughing with wide smiles. Most of the boys wore faded t-shirts and shorts and ran barefoot while girls wore dresses made from light fabric dyed with bright garden colors, their hair braided with dozens of beads of all sizes that reminded me of the Haitian paintings sold in the Dominican Republic. Despite living in a poor city, they seemed well fed, clean, rested, and most of all, happy.

After the initial group more children ran out to meet us and further fill the courtyard with chatter and giggling. Little girls holding dolls or blankets made their way to us after the boys tested the water. They ranged from just old enough to walk to at least ten, with the ones older than that either working somewhere else or not in the mood to come see us.

I hadn't played for months, before Haiti and even before starting work in Virginia. The rowdy elementary school kid inside me suddenly came out and goofed around in the courtyard. Over the years all of my friends had transitioned into adulthood, but internally I never saw the change occur in me. Often at work I'd sit in meetings and answer questions or give advice to other adults and wonder why anyone took me seriously at all. I felt like a kid pretending to be an adult while putting on a show for the world. I felt comfortable letting my guard down with the children.

Three boys pulled my arm as they led me to a short wall under an ancient tree over the courtyard. They climbed atop the ledge to jump on my shoulders and back, all the while screaming wildly. One of them grabbed my hat and ran off with it. He disappeared around a corner before I got the rest of the kids off me so I yelled at Dean to stop him as he ran. He looked back and shrugged his shoulders—children swamped him, too.

The group split up and each took on a group of kids. We got tired just from watching them play. Megan sat on the main steps with a few girls and tried to teach them English words. Several of them repeated after her as she pointed to things. She sat one girl on her lap that held a blanket tightly as she nuzzled into Megan's shoulder and chest and almost fell asleep. Megan rocked her back and forth gently while playing with the others. Dean played tag with a small group around the truck that chased him wildly. Each time they got close he jumped and kept them just a few inches apart.

Cameron and Cindy rested in the back of the truck after spending some time giving out coloring books, crayons, small toys, and a soccer ball. Dozens of children sat on the ground coloring with whatever crayons they grabbed from the pile. Everyone wanted red and green, but the orphanage's guardians that stood by settled any quarrels as they watched.

I noticed Justin sitting near the swings on a bench that faced the city. His attention constantly transitioned from writing in his journal to the view of the city and the setting sun.

The lighting of hundreds of small fires in the valley below and in the city beyond tricked my eyes into believing that the starry night extended onto the ground. As goose bumps formed on my legs and arms from the suddenly cool breeze, I wondered if Amber looked at the same night sky. The sunset looked much different at home. At home the ground sat frozen and covered with snow and naked trees swayed in the bitter breeze. I missed her terribly. I wanted to call her and tell her about talking to Bob.

Jared approached carrying his pack and wearing a headlamp.

"Sean, let's get our tent up."

I nodded and followed him to the edge of the swing set where a single tent sat against a wall.

"That's Jana's." I said, pointing to it. "Let's set up near that one."

We worked despite increasing winds and fleeting sunlight, and managed to get stones on the corners before darkness made it impossible to see. Back in the courtyard, the guardians set up large white sheets that hung from the building to the wall to create a roof for the orphans to sleep under. No one slept inside anymore—fear of a collapse with the multiple aftershocks overwhelmed everyone. Even a small tremor could turn a crack into a falling building.

A few of us sat and chatted near the truck as night settled in. Jared told a story about a time he taught a completely overweight man to scuba dive. He did an impression of the man's breathing and showed the air tank emptying with each breath. Then he pretended to swim as he flailed his arms and legs around as if drowning. We laughed at the story and the impression. As I looked around I saw everyone smiling at once for the first time on the trip. I almost forgot we were in Haiti.

The sound of a pickup truck groaning up the driveway cut his story short. As it pulled into the courtyard I noticed the familiar green paint as younger children fled the outdoor beds and surrounded it. Luke, Faith, and Jana got out. They looked dirty, sweaty, and tired, but happy to see the group.

Jana and Marcus spoke about the trip, our journey here, and the afternoon at the orphanage. Luke left Faith standing alone when he went to unload their gear. I approached her after Cindy and Cameron finished asking about her day in Port-au-Prince.

"Hey, Sean," she said as I approached. She put her arms around me and gave me a quick hug before I stood at her side, both of us looking ahead at the orphanage. "I guess you didn't get it done the way you thought?"

"No," I slumped my head, "I guess not." I paused for a moment. I figured she knew already, but I wanted to tell her anyway. "I asked your dad before I left."

"Yeah?"

"Yeah." I smiled, and she returned a knowing grin.

"Just Jana and Marcus left then?"

"Yep. We'll see how that goes."

She put her hand on my shoulder and playfully shoved me, "You'll be fine." We stood and talked about the day. Jana spoke with the rest of the group and caught up with Megan, who seemed eager to start leading the team. Faith had spent the entire day in a hospital working with patients and helping doctors. Although she had already learned a great deal at school, she couldn't compare it to what she picked up working in the field. To her Port-au-Prince represented everything she wanted to do with her life and being here provided a chance, despite the horrific tragedy that made it possible, to experience her dream first-hand.

Months before and at home, I had asked Amber why Faith didn't choose an American medical school and why she didn't want to work in the States. She told me that her sister had always believed that working in developing countries had called to her throughout her teenage years. Growing up around Haitians and coming of age in a world full of joy and laughter mixed with poverty and sickness gave her a deep and profound devotion to helping the world. She wanted to emulate her parents and wanted to live in places like Port-au-Prince for the rest of her life. Standing next to her I sensed her inner joy with being in Haiti again. Her confidence in this place overshadowed any sense of comfort I believed I'd accrued over the first days in country. She looked as if she bundled more energy than her body could fit just under the skin, and she couldn't wait to do it all over again the next day.

Jana stood outside her tent alone when I passed it. She paced back and forth while fumbling with a cell phone and putting it to her ear over and over. I slunk in the shadows to wait until she put it away and watched the city glow instead. I thought about asking her right there. The fear of waiting too long slowly grew inside me, and I worried that somehow she'd find out before I could talk to her. She hung up the phone and rubbed her eyes. She looked exhausted, and frankly, I too could barely keep my eyes open. For the first time during the entire trip I found her by herself but I felt too tired to ask. I walked past her toward the truck when she spotted me and called me over.

She gave me a hug when I approached and spoke softly. "I'm glad you made the trip, Sean. How are you doing? Have you called Amber?" I wondered if she felt just as awkward around me as I did with her.

"I'm doing fine. Just a little tired." I wimped out again. She'd given me a genuine chance to bring up Amber, but I held back. I brimmed with fear at the thought of her rejecting me. What if I asked too soon, she said no, and I had to spend the rest of the trip working next to her?

"Well, get some rest tonight. We're going to a hospital bright and early. Maybe you'll get to help a little more tomorrow?" She phrased it innocently enough but I understood her meaning. Up until now, the things I'd done in the operating room the first night had gone completely unnoticed. While I initially thought the experience might have helped me look good in front of the team, since then I'd failed even at processing it myself. I'd barely dealt with the images that dwelled in my head. As far as Jana knew, all I'd done so far was move people and supplies from point to point and sleep. I knew how useless I appeared. It was the main reason I wasn't ready to ask her about Amber.

I said goodnight and went on my way as she crawled into the tent to sleep. I walked alone to the truck to find my belongings. I hadn't made a complete clothing change since I'd arrived in Santo Domingo. Bags, totes, and crates were stacked high, and the bumpy ride had knocked several of them over. I found my bag lodged under a bench and pulled it from its crevice. The smell of clean clothes teased my nose, and the sensation transported me home. I could see Amber, my house, and my dogs. I wanted desperately at that moment to be back in Pennsylvania and in her arms. I missed her terribly.

I pulled my cell phone out of my bag and turned it on, having kept it off for most of the trip to conserve the battery. After connecting to a local network it flashed an update across my screen "27 missed calls, 18 voicemails, and 42 missed texts." The updates repeated one after another as the phone tried to catch up to the backlog. I didn't want to waste any battery life checking messages so I just looked at the missed calls and texts. All of my friends, parents, sisters, and even several people from work called and left messages for me. No one could believe I was here.

Everyone was watching the news. "Be careful" and "Come home soon" seemed to repeat the most. It felt reassuring to see so many messages, and it brought a full smile to my face.

I dialed Amber, and after a few rings she answered.

"Hello?"

"Hey, it's Sean."

She erupted with words like a volcano after a dormant spell. She asked how I was doing, what Haiti was like, and what work we'd completed so far. She asked about her family and the group, but most of all about me.

"Things are going fine." I kept telling her over and over again. It seemed too hard to try and describe the events of the day, and my brain still was trying to process the events from our first night in Jimani. "I love you, and I miss you," I repeated a few times.

We spent a short time talking about our home and dogs, the weather, and people's reaction to my decision to come on the trip. No one believed that I'd gone through with it—it was completely out of my normal character. I felt some sense of victory when I heard that.

After a few minutes I pried myself from the phone. "I have to go. I need the battery for the whole week."

She didn't want to let me go. "Sean, just a few more minutes," she repeated over and over again. Eventually I needed to hang up. I didn't expect to be able to charge my phone, and every second of battery life mattered.

"I love you," I said softly to her before going to hang up the phone. "You are my sunshine, and I love you very much."

"I love you too. Goodnight." I heard the phone click after a few moments where neither of us wanted to hang up. A small knot welled in my throat; speaking to her only made me miss her more. I turned off my phone and put it in my pocket before digging through my pack for clothes.

Suddenly, I spotted Cindy drying her hair and wearing a clean set of clothing. I stood convinced that my eyes tried to trick me. She looked clean. My skin crawled at the thought of washing away the dirt and grime from the last few days. Instantly my clothes itched to fly off, if indeed my far-flung hopes came true.

"Hey Cindy, why is your hair wet?"

"They have some water here. I just took a shower," She replied with a wide grin across her face.

"Wow! Where? I haven't showered in days!"

"Inside, but the water's almost gone. Good luck!"

I grabbed my soap and a towel and walked toward the orphanage to find it. Near the entrance I ran into Dean sitting on the steps. Next to him sat one of the young boys, wearing my Raven's cap. It looked funny with him sitting next to a kid while the boy looked up at him in wonder. They sat like old friends, the boy leaning back with his hands behind his head and his feet crossed, Dean sitting Indian style with his beanie on his knee, looking back at the kid and nodding as they spoke without words.

"There's my hat." I grabbed it off his head and put it on my own. He looked up and frowned while folding his arms in a pouty display.

"Careful Sean," Dean replied, "He wore that hat all day."

I looked at it lovingly, happy to have it again. "I'll take my chances."

The part of the city we camped in had lost power with the quake, so only the moon lit the hall inside. I found the large, white tiled bathroom. A rusty sprinkler jutted from the wall in a corner flanked with a small tile ledge that kept the water collected.

I disrobed and got in while still wearing the flashlight affixed to my head. I slowly turned on the water, but nothing came out. Confused, I tried to turn the valve the other way, thinking that someone had installed the plumbing backwards. Still no water. I shook the faucet—maybe a clog or air bubble held up the flow. Nothing worked. I stood for a moment stunned and fuming mad. I looked at my disgusting clothes on the floor. I couldn't imagine putting them back on and crawling into bed with the skin I wore. I thought about the water pressure at the hotel in Virginia and how strong and hot the water felt on my back. I'd stand in it forever and let it turn my skin red and sensitive.

Deflated, I looked down to step out of the shower when I noticed several buckets on the floor that glimmered when my flashlight ran across them. I dipped my hand into one and felt the ice-cold water. I brought a small pool to my nose—it smelled clean.

I hopped back into the shower and placed one of the buckets in front of me. I took a few short breaths for fear of the shock of cold water on my skin. I clenched my teeth and poured half a bucket over my head as I screamed in shock. Goosebumps shot out from my shivering flesh as I stood naked in the dark. I lathered up in a hurry as dark brown suds formed on my skin and dropped to the floor until I stood in a puddle of bubbles. I looked at my hands. For the first time in days, entire patches of skin returned to their normal hue. The arid breeze quickly dried the soap so I scrubbed harder in a race against the clock to avoid using more of the frigid water. Once I finished with the majority of my body I dumped the rest of the bucket over my head and rinsed off.

Out of the shower, I trembled as my teeth chattered. I dried off and left the room wearing only a towel around my waist. I now understood how Cindy had felt. My skin had never felt cleaner and my hair had never felt lighter. As I walked across the courtyard dozens of children watched me and giggled as I tiptoed barefoot in the night. Jared slept in the tent. I grabbed a pair of boxers and got in my sleeping bag before falling asleep.

A few hours later I awoke to a tremor. It felt as if someone pulled our tent across the ground.

"Jared, wake up." He looked over at me, his eyes puffy from sleeping. "What is that?"

He looked around the tent for another moment, still in a sleepy stupor. "I think it's another earthquake."

The ground shook for a few more moments. It felt like riding a sled pulled in the snow. Just as suddenly it stopped. A few moments of eerie silence were followed by sounds of screams, car alarms, and police sirens that grew louder until they surrounded us.

Dean turned in his sleeping bag to face Jared and me. "Good thing we're getting some sleep. Tomorrow's going to be crazy."

Sunday, January 17th, 2010
6:35am
Port Au Prince, Haiti

"Wake up, everyone! Time to get going!" Megan shouted near the tents. She led the charge for the team, and I knew she planned to keep order all day.

I groaned in protest at waking up before the sun rose. I'd slept a full eight hours—the longest since leaving the United States, but it felt like just a few minutes to my body.

"Breakfast in five minutes. We leave in ten. Coffee is hot, guys. Let's go!"

"Coffee?" Jared jumped out of his sleeping bag faster than I'd seen him move the entire trip. "I haven't had coffee in days."

He leapt outside while pulling up his pants. Dean's sleeping bag looked long vacated. The smell of coffee didn't stir me, but the threat of a disappearing breakfast did. My stomach grumbled and rumbled at me to get up and feed it.

I didn't need to try to find the rest of the group—the smell of coffee drew me to them like an imaginary magnet. Jared and Dean stood at the arch of a small room at the end of the building that Jana had designated for storage and cooking. Everyone stood dressed and ready to go—everyone except for me.

Megan sat on the floor stirring a large bowl of oatmeal as Cameron dumped piles of raisins and brown sugar into the mix.

Brown sugar? My tongue didn't believe my eyes, and I felt my mouth salivate like a dog. Cindy, Faith, and Jana all sat on a small bed with their cups of coffee held to their mouths in protective grips. Luke stood against the wall looking outside with an empty cup in his hand while the kettle prepared another batch of the strong brew. I shuffled in line behind Jared and Dean for a chance to get inside and grab some breakfast. Each time Megan stirred the wooden spoon I felt my stomach lurch with it. I wanted to jump past everyone and inhale the entire bowl myself.

After a few minutes of waiting and clumsy shuffling in the small room, I received a big bowl of oatmeal and a glass of water. I went to retreat outside when suddenly Jana stopped me. "Sean, hold on a minute—we're going to pray before we eat." I winched. I'm sure it looked terrible trying to leave the room so quickly. "Sorry, Jana," was all I replied. I took a spot on the far wall near Dean and leaned against it as the group settled for prayers. Luke looked at me and shook his head while quietly giggling at my misstep. "Nice one," he mouthed. I rolled my eyes back and bared my bottom teeth, gesturing embarrassment and absent-mindedness. Jana turned her attention from me but still I felt red in the face. I was making no progress with her, and I needed to get my act together.

Jana nodded to Megan to lead the group. Megan put her hands out and grabbed Cindy and Jana's to form a circle. I joined in next to Dean and Luke while holding my oatmeal between my elbow and my waist. The group bowed their heads and prayed. Megan led the effort and asked for blessings on us, our work ahead, and the lives of all the Haitians affected by the quake. I actually said a little prayer silently while we held hands, and found myself asking God to help the people in the country and our group. I didn't quite believe it, but a part of me actually felt someone listened.

I gobbled the food faster than I'd put it in my bowl and jogged back to the tent to get ready for the day. I put on some fresh clothes and even applied deodorant for the first time. I didn't think I smelled but I wanted to be cautious. Even if I didn't stink, it made me feel cleaner to apply it. A terrible rash had started to form on my inner thighs from sweating all day and night while walking back and forth and rubbing the dirt from the day deeper into my skin. It didn't itch yet, but it looked like it could start at any time.

The truck left the orphanage and barreled down the streets into the city before the sun rose. In the early hours it felt quiet, and getting to the hospital now meant fighting less traffic than Marcus had upon our arrival. A morning fog blanketed many of the low-lying streets while dew covered the higher parts. The effect was to create a thick, heavy weight that sat on our clothes and soaked us with humidity. People slept on both sides of the street, sidewalks, and in makeshift camps. The small tremors the night before had caused additional damage. Fresh fires burned on side streets and engulfed trash and rubble in black smoke. It felt like driving through a battlefield just after a great clash.

On the way to the hospital I asked Dean some questions about treating patients. Up until now I'd only worked in the surgery room the first night, and my experience was limited to holding down people or mopping up gore. He pulled out a bag of saline and some bandages and showed me how to apply them to a wound. He did a test on his arm and let me try. I wanted to bring more value to the group and to the injured. Standing by and helping half-heartedly no longer felt sufficient.

Thirty minutes into the trip we drove down a narrow side street until we hit a fork in the road. One side continued down to the bay and the other disappeared into a steep incline covered in trees that hid the hospital at the top of the hill.

Jana got out of the cab and came to the back. "Ok everyone, listen up!" She yelled over the rumble of cars zooming past on the main street. "This is one of the main hospitals for Port-au-Prince. It's really crowded and needs our help. Our job today is to treat, disinfect and re-bandage as many as we can. Stick in groups of two and we will regroup at the truck at noon. Sound good?" Most of the team nodded quietly.

"How you feeling?" I asked Jared.

He wore a clean set of scrubs given to him in Jimani. "I'm good, a little nervous."

Most of the team felt the same way. We'd seen a lot in a short period of time. Between the gore in Jimani and the chaos on the drive in I figured the hospital would look like a horror show. Several days had now passed since the quake, so injuries had gained time to fester in the heat. I shuddered at the thought of living with an untreated and possibly necrotic wound in the sun for days on end. The strength of Haitians dwarfed any toughness I believed I held personally. I thought about a few moments from the first night in surgery to prep my mind for the day. I needed to pull it together to help as many as possible. The Haitians made it easier to find strength. They showed us how to deal with great pain and grief by using songs and each other to make it through. I wished for a moment that I also belonged to such a loving community.

As we reached the parking lot, tents dotted the grass on either side of the hill. We passed one with Haitians packed into it like sardines. Two lay on tables surrounded by the others. One victim wore nothing save for thick bandages wrapping her thighs and ribs. The second was an amputee with his left leg severed slightly below the knee. Thick, bloodied bandages wrapped the stub, and as we walked by he lifted his head to watch. I turned away from the scene, not wanting to offend them by staring, and not ready to commit another gruesome picture to memory.

At the perimeter of the hospital the tents were grouped closer and closer until they appeared as one continual canopy. Hundreds of ropes and tarps were tied to every possible point and resembled a gigantic spider web. Haitian men stood guard while women cooked rice in small black pots over charcoal burning in holes dug in the ground. The morning buzz of activity filled the air with loud and chaotic noises. Smells permeated from all directions and mixed into a sweet odor that I couldn't quite conclude was good or bad.

We pulled in front of the main entrance and shuffled through as two armed guards stepped aside and let us pass. Sunlight and a few lamps connected to generators tried to brighten the dark hallways for the patients and doctors who scurried back and forth. Haitians sat all along the walls. Some looked ready to camp for a long time with blankets rolled out and supplies organized between them. Any spot clear of squatters was filled with boxes of supplies. Near the center a large outdoor courtyard was filled with more people waiting for family. It felt like a village had popped up overnight. Some fought over spots or supplies, but guards quickly settled quarrels before they grew.

At the far end of the hospital we reached the supply room and fanned out to fill our bags with antibiotics, bandages, tape, pain relievers, and other medical equipment for the day's work. With my pack full I went outside to start my rounds. Jana and Faith stayed inside working with doctors on surgeries. They spent the entire day sorting tools, comforting patients, and taking orders. By the evening they'd participated in everything ranging from amputations to infections, each success a miracle in its execution and result given the short supply of tools and medication. Necrosis, sepsis, blood clots, gangrene, and filth compounded each surgery with additional hurdles to surmount. Jana held the hands of patients, found new victims hidden in the hallways to move to surgery, and helped translate Creole for doctors. Faith ran into a wealth of opportunity for a first year medical student. Doctors allowed her to work in surgery, administration leaned on her to coordinate schedules and prioritize patients, and she constantly translated for visiting doctors and nurses. Later that night she spoke about working on a woman with a broken hip. Though in brutal pain, the hospital just didn't have the right medication to ease it. As they put her in a cast she continually screamed and cried, and all Faith could do to help was talk to the woman and try to keep her focus off of what they tried to do for her. The doctors asked Faith to stay and take on a hospital coordinator role, but she turned it down to stay with the group as we trekked across the city day after day.

The rest of the group split into pairs and dispersed into the huge throng of people anxiously awaiting care in the parking lot and beyond. Megan specifically went alone as the odd one out, but didn't falter in working on over thirty people by the time we left. She, like me, lacked the experience to deal with so much gore and pain. Like me she was just another normal person that came down to help, unaware of how badly the situation had escalated. She needed to lead our group and put on a good example. When the rest of us goofed off during rides back and forth she usually remained stoic or reserved and chose not to tell jokes or make small talk. Later she admitted to loving those rides, those small chances to forget about where we were, even if only for a second.

I paired with Marcus and we made our way to the closest tent. We hadn't spent any time together on the trip, and to be honest, I didn't know much about him other than what Amber had told me. She loved him like a second father and often reminisced about the cross-country trips that he, Jana, and Bob had taken all the children on. He'd taught her how to surf, showed the perfect way to tell a joke, and always made time to sit and listen to any problem she dealt with.

"You having a good time?" I asked, trying to spur some dialogue. "I mean, how are you doing?"

"I'm fine. As good as I can be."

"What do you think about the orphanage?" I asked, trying to keep our minds off the current location until we got to the first tent. He liked it, a fact made evident by his relaxed disposition during our evening there. I tried to talk further, partly to learn more about him and partly to look for an opening to ask about marrying Amber, but we reached the tent before I fit it in.

It wasn't even a tent, but really just a few blue and black tarps strung together and held down with rocks. Under them a small group of women sat on a blanket. As I approached, they turned their eyes as one of them rose to greet us.

"Morning sir. Can you help?" the woman asked as I approached. It surprised and relieved me that she spoke such fluent English.

"Absolutely. What do you need? Who's hurt?"

"My daughters and my mother. Doctors saw them two days ago but haven't seen them since."

I looked at her family. The older of the two daughters seemed to be in her early teens, but the younger one appeared three or less. Thick bandages stained red and yellow wrapped the older girl's left shin. Gauze covered the toddler's left arm from shoulder to wrist. Both of the girls needed the bandages to be changed to reduce the chance of infection.

Behind the girls I spotted their grandmother. Doctors had amputated both arms at the shoulders. She stared blankly to her right and avoided eye contact with me as I inspected her for any other wounds that needed to be dressed.

"Okay," I addressed the lead woman. "I'll start with your older daughter."

"I'll work on your mother," Marcus said to the woman.

I got on the ground and kneeled over her leg. Skin clung to the edges of the bandage as if glued on. I tried to follow Dean's short lesson as I pulled out a bottle of saline and soaked the bandages. I picked at it as I sprayed and peeled it off inch by inch as fresh blood poured out of her leg. I let the saline soak into the flesh until the rest of the bandages fell to the ground.

With the covering gone I inspected the wound. A large, clean incision ran from just below her knee to her foot to create an oval opening as big as a shoeprint. Two days ago, doctors had removed a large section of infected skin and fat tissue. It prevented an amputation. I saw deep muscle and bone through fresh blood that wept continually. I cringed and tried to keep it together. I steadied my breathing and concentrated on slowing down my heart. I needed to disinfect and bandage it quickly.

Her mother held the leg still as I applied antibiotic ointment with a gloved finger. As I cleaned, blood mixed with the ointment and created a red emulsion that dripped off her leg and onto the ground. I broke open the bottle of ointment and covered the wound with a thick layer in an effort to stop the flow of blood. Afterwards I bandaged her shin.

I sat back and removed my gloves. The girl straightened her leg flat against the ground and rolled to her side while sobbing quietly in pain. I felt awful, but she'd needed the new bandages.

My work on the first girl left the toddler terrified. She cried when her mother brought her to me. Marcus finished working on the grandmother and came to my side.

The woman spoke while holding the little girl close as she rocked back and forth. I sat next to them and took the toddler's hand in mine. She tolerated my touch, but once I poured cold saline on her bandages she cried.

"Make it fast, Sean," said Marcus.

I took my scissors and cut the soaked bandage away from the arm. Deep slices that splayed her flesh ran from wrist to shoulder. Stitches dotted the wounds and kept the larger ones barely shut. I cleaned with saline and applied ointment before wrapping fresh bandages around her arm. Once I finished the mother let her go and she ran to the back of the tent and out of sight.

"Thank you sir," the mother replied.

We nodded and stood. Walking back to the road we surveyed the area. The parking lot was jammed with traffic.

"We're outnumbered here," Marcus said. "I think we should split up and try to handle more people at once. You okay by yourself?"

"Sure, no problem."

He left and walked down the hill to the next set of tents. I stood alone under the sun as the heat of the day seared the pale flesh on my back and neck. I removed my hat and wiped my forehead. The sweat felt cool to the touch against my arms, and I grimaced as grime rolled against my forehead when I wiped. Up the hill I saw Dean working with a boy on a stretcher. Cameron and Cindy spoke with a surgeon at an aid station, and I spotted Jared with two kids near the main entrance of the hospital, each with fresh bandages on their arms. Everyone worked hard to help, but the need still overwhelmed the capacity of the hospital.

Tents sprawled endlessly over the parking lot and even spilled into gutters and sidewalks. Families huddled in hallways, under overhangs, and next to parked vehicles. A woman with a broken femur lay in the backseat of a nearby car. A large rock was attached to her foot with rope, and hung out the window to provide traction for the break. Crates of bagged water sat empty a few feet away as men and women ripped the wood from them to use for shelters. Police stood guard with automatic weapons and body armor near the hospital doors, and most men carried machetes at their waists.

I took a deep breath and put my hat back on. I walked to the next tent, averting my eyes from the endless rows that sat beyond.

Sunday, January 17th, 2010
2:50pm
Port Au Prince, Haiti

Zac and Paul left the hospital after getting the final diagnosis. Paul had fractured his eye socket and the doctors told him to rest and keep it protected. After receiving the news they stayed at the tent to stop looters while Lucas took Tasha with the guidance of a doctor for an examination in the hospital. When they finally returned in the evening, Zac and Paul took the truck home. They returned to the neighborhood to help their family gather belongings before moving to a relief shelter set up just outside of town. Lucas knew he and Tasha would likely be spending a much longer time at the hospital.

The ordeal over the last few days had forced Lucas to abandon sleep, most meals, and any time at all to relax. Instead he'd spent every waking moment caring for his mother's wounds, feeding her whenever they got rations, and carting her back and forth to the hospital whenever her bandages needed to be changed.

Often he sat alone and watched people walk past his tent while his mother slept. Just a week ago his motorbike had held the most important spot in his thoughts. He'd wanted it for so long and worked hard for it. In the end it probably saved his mother's life, first by digging her from their home and last by keeping her leg set correctly. Even though he'd adored it from the first moment he bought it, of course he loved his mother much more.

When the doctor revealed that he'd set his mother's leg properly he'd almost cried. She broke her shin in only one place, so pulling on her foot barely worked. They called it a miracle. Doing it wrong would have guaranteed death through infection. They gave her a set of crutches at the hospital to use when she tried to walk.

Her chest didn't fare as well. She received over a hundred stitches across her breast and side. She lost muscle in her shoulder and chest, resulting in limited mobility. Time and rest remained the only prescriptions left to give.

She sat on a blanket when he returned from getting the daily food and water handouts from the Red Cross. The long line was always filled with people cutting. Except for him, it seemed that everyone always knew someone in line. He swore that twice the number of people received aid each day before him due to the practice. Anger swelled inside as it happened but he didn't dare speak up and risk starting a fight. Guards quickly kicked troublesome people off the property, and he needed to stay for his mother.

She cooked some rice over a coal fire. She grew more active every day and the change helped brighten his mood. The color had returned to her skin and her eyes looked alert. She noticed him returning from halfway across the yard.

"Hey, just making some dinner," she said as he sat down next to her. He knew she didn't want to dwell on her being up and about, so he tried to focus on the food instead.

"Yeah, smells good. I'm hungry."

Two days had passed since she'd changed the bandages around her chest. Yellow and red leaked through and created faint polka dots that covered the surface.

One of his new neighbors had brought a deck of cards to the hospital. They played almost every afternoon and always at night under the light poles powered by nearby generators. Lucas joined in whenever he had a chance—they sat close enough that he could hear his mother if she needed anything.

She noticed him staring at the other teenagers. "Why don't you go for a while?" she asked. He shrugged, unsure if he should. He didn't want to leave her alone. "Go ahead, I'll be fine. I'll call you when the rice is ready."

He looked over at them and then back at her to smile before getting up. Just as he stood, a short white man in his mid-twenties with short blond hair approached their tent from down the hill. He wore a brown shirt, khaki shorts, and a purple hat.

Lucas stood and waved. "Over here." The card game needed to wait—he jumped on any chance to get bandages changed.

They met at the entrance of the tent. Lucas' neighbor knew better English than he did and stood up to help him with the man. For a few minutes they spoke while the neighbor pointed at Lucas or Tasha. The man nodded and held out his hand to shake Lucas'. He then pointed to his own chest and said "Sean."

"He isn't a doctor, but is cleaning and redressing wounds," the neighbor added.

Lucas welcomed them both inside his tent and Sean sat next to Tasha and inspected her chest and leg. He spoke some more to the neighbor, who gave more information about the history of the wounds.

Sean laid a towel on the floor and pulled out bottles of saline, rolls of new bandages, gauze pads, and bottles of ointment. He spoke again, pointing to the woman's chest and then at Lucas. After a minute the neighbor spoke to the mother.

"You need to raise your mother's arms; he is going to change the bandages."

Lucas went to the man's side and helped him situate her. He raised her arms and the man unrolled the bandages slowly, stopping to soak them in saline whenever they stuck. He worked quickly to pull away the gauze under the bandage and reveal her stitched openings. The swelling in the skin had subsided and the flesh had worked hard to scab in and around the stitches. Sean put on a set of latex gloves and wiped dried blood from the skin with a saline soaked rag. The cold solution made Tasha shudder, but she tried to hold still as he worked. She turned her head, ashamed with her bare breasts in the daylight in front of the young man. He spoke to the neighbor who translated for the mother.

"He says your wounds look good. It's all old blood he is wiping. The stitches are holding well. He says you're going to be fine."

She looked back to him and smiled as she nodded with small streams of tears running down her face.

He squirted saline directly on the incisions and allowed the rest of the blood and grime to wash away. He used a clean cloth from his bag to dry the skin and applied several tubes of antibiotic ointment to the openings. Lucas helped hold clean gauze pads in place while the man wrapped her chest with new bandages. After a few minutes he finished and repacked his bag. Lucas helped his mother put on her shirt and laid her down. The man spoke to the neighbor again.

"He says that he can't do anything for the leg, but that the bandages on her chest will need changed again in two days."

Lucas and the neighbor walked Sean to the entrance of the tent and thanked him. Lucas worked through his limited English. "Thank you," was all he could muster. The young blonde man spoke with the neighbor for a few minutes, who then asked Lucas where they planned to go next. "To the outpost shelters, I think," he told the neighbor. The neighbor continued to speak with the American for a while longer. Later he told Lucas that the man had wanted to know where they lived and how they got to the hospital. After a moment, Sean shook Lucas' hand and said "*Merci*" before pointing to the long row of shelters up the street. A few feet from the tent, another group pulled him into their makeshift home.

Lucas sat down with his mother, happy to have the bandages changed and her leg in a strong cast. He pulled a sheet over her to rest. He closed the entrance of the tent and stood to leave.

The bowl of rice she made sat cold and partially cooked on the ground. The painful process of redressing the wounds had put her to sleep. He picked up the bowl and ate everything before placing the empty cookware inside.

Sunday, January 17th 2010
9:00am
Port Au Prince, Haiti

When not in the parking lot reapplying bandages I ran to the hospital supply room to restock my bag. I used an entire pack of supplies on a woman with a deep shear that traversed her thigh. It took three bottles of saline to peel off the old gauze that firmly stuck to her tissue as if glued on, and I used every roll of gauze and every tube of antibiotic ointment in my pack to dress the opening. I even gave her my reserve painkillers just to help her through the day, even though it felt cruel knowing that receiving a steady supply of medication looked impossible. I had sweat so badly that eventually it stopped altogether, and left me dangerously dry while the sun crested over me.

I'd never felt so important and so woefully unprepared before. The injuries surpassed anything I'd ever seen, and the pain endured by the people was inhumane. Pins and frames dug into shattered bones through patchy flesh, fat tissue dried and cracked from the heat, and the blood and skin attracted legions of flies to add insult to injury. Families grew tired of waiting for help and often pushed the frustration onto us when we did less than they expected.

The compound brimmed on the edge of revolt and I teetered along with it.

Each time I started a new round, the crowd that gathered around the main doors grew bigger and louder. I only made it a few steps before someone pulled me by the arm into a blazing hot tent stuffed with people begging for help. Fathers and mothers, husbands and wives, children and grandchildren stood at my back and emitted pressure that kept me moving forward. I didn't dare walk out on anyone without doing what I could. The part of me that wanted to go home screamed to be heard, but I bottled it deep inside. I worked amongst people with no place to go, no one to help them, and no future relief in sight. I believed that if I let my thoughts of home and quitting overtake me, the Haitians would sense it and lose hope, too. I believed they only saw me as a tourist; that this wasn't my reality. I wanted them to see me as more than that.

Halfway up a hill leading to the hospital entrance I met with two men standing outside their tent, beckoning me to enter. One of them, Patrice, spoke some English and introduced himself and his new neighbor at the hospital, Lucas. I shook both of their hands as Patrice spoke for the group. Lucas had brought his mother from a few miles away in a wheelbarrow to get help and they'd spent every day since the quake keeping her wounds clean and fighting in lines for food and water. After a few minutes I entered the tent to work on his mother. They had already set her badly broken leg, but the wounds on her chest and stomach needed to be cleaned and the bandage changed. She seemed exhausted and in constant pain, so I attempted to work quickly so that she could lie back down. I felt Lucas standing behind me the whole time, anxiously awaiting me to finish.

After cleaning the wounds and giving them some fresh bottles of water I stood to leave. Outside the tent I stopped to drink some water and eat a few crackers. Lucas and Patrice both came out to speak with me. Patrice came to the hospital with his wife, who was pregnant at the time of the quake. They found out she'd lost the baby shortly afterwards due to internal bleeding and trauma. Lucas' mother, on the other hand, had a much longer road to recovery. The doctors told them her leg would take weeks to heal, and until then she needed to stay still. The hospitals in Haiti didn't possess the in depth care and proper materials that facilities at home did, especially during a crisis. We spoke for a while longer and they told me about their journey to the hospital, the treatment they'd received, and where they planned to go once they left the hospital. I showed Lucas where I planned to go if he needed anything else. I doubt he understood what I said. When his mother started to moan again he shook my hand and returned to the tent. I said goodbye to Patrice and continued my walk up the hill.

I lost my weak stomach for blood and gore in one day. I looked at broken bones, smelled infection, and touched ruined flesh without feeling the churn in my gut. My inability to speak Creole and the short time available to work pushed me into a mode where I worked like a machine. Somewhere during the day I gained the ability to narrow my vision only to the body parts that needed attention. I imagined them as simple machines made of meat and not much different from the equipment I fixed at home. A broken bone needed to be held in place and bleeding flesh required clotting and wraps. Do doctors do the same thing in their minds? I'd found the weird tunnel vision through necessity. I knew the others that spoke Creole formed emotional connections with their patients as they worked in order to build trust, but my inability to speak their language cheated me out of making those connections. But maybe, in a way, this was precisely what helped me press on so efficiently.

I cleaned an older man's broken leg. Surgeons had worked on it a few days earlier. They'd implanted several iron rods into the shin and screwed them into a steel housing that wrapped around the knee. His family stood over me as I worked, and I felt his wife right behind me as she breathed down my neck.

"Can you give me some room?" I asked forcefully as I turned my head. She didn't let me concentrate while standing so close, and after a moment of staring she took a few steps back. The urge to stand up and leave came suddenly to mind, but I dismissed it just as quickly. After cleaning and dressing the wound I stood to leave. No one said thank you; in fact, I felt they detested my presence.

Cameron approached me from down the hill. His eyes appeared sunken into his head and he walked with a drained posture hidden by his filthy scrubs. He worked much faster than I did and completed better work. Where I fumbled over gauze or bandage he glided through as if he'd done it a thousand times.

He stopped next to me. "Ready to go? Jana's rounding up the troops."

I looked down the row of tents beyond. At the next one a man stood frantically waving both hands as he gestured for us to come. I turned back to Cameron. "Got supplies for one more before we go?"

He looked over at the man and nodded slowly. "Yeah, let's do it quick."

"One person." Cameron said to the man as we entered, "That's all we have time for today."

He nodded and pointed to a boy lying on a blanket on the ground, his left leg covered with towels. The boy cried out as Cameron moved them and air struck the wound. I gasped at the sight.

Four iron rods extended from his thigh to heel connected by circular pieces of steel that wrapped around the leg. Over twenty metal pins jutted from the flesh and screwed into the housing to keep everything still. He wasn't bandaged, and sticky scabs stuck to the pins and stretched with the metal. Muscle tissue and bone sat exposed everywhere.

"Shit." Cameron muttered as he looked over the boy's leg. "We'll need some help with this."

I stepped back and looked out the entrance. To our luck I saw Dean just a few steps away on a path headed toward the truck. Blood and dirt covered his scrubs and his medical bag looked empty as it swung around his waist. I called out to him and he waved and jogged up to me. He smiled despite the surroundings and appeared full of energy.

"Hey. We're heading out," he said. "What's going on?"

I stepped to the side and let him look inside. "We need your help, got time for one more before we go?"

"Let me see." He cocked his neck to see past Cameron. "Oh, shit. Yeah, I'll help."

He entered the tent and got down on the ground next to Cameron before opening his bag and shuffling through the remaining supplies. He let out an annoyed moan as he shook the pack.

"Sean, you got any saline left?"

I opened my nearly empty pack hoping for some luck. A bottle sat at the bottom. Cameron helped hold the leg still as Dean doused the solution from one end to the other. The dirt and grime gently washed away with ease and reminded me just how much better they worked with patients. Cameron handed me his bottle.

"Here, help keep it wet."

I got on my knees to the right of Cameron so that all three of us sat in a row in front of the boy. Dean used a scrubber to gently rub away the infected flesh starting with rods near the thigh. Fresh blood poured out around them as he cleaned and I followed with saline as he moved down the leg. Cameron inspected and applied antibiotic ointment to each opening after I cleaned it and then carefully wrapped with new bandage. He worked meticulously to create an organized web that surrounded each rod. The boy managed to hold his leg still but grabbed at my hat and put it on his head to play. He kept distracted during the procedure by manipulating the brim and wearing it in different ways.

Cameron completed a masterpiece of triage that left every pin clean and every inch of flesh tightly covered with fresh bandage over a solid coating of ointment. He took a picture of it for his records. As we stood the boy gave me back my hat and I shook his hand. He smiled and rolled onto his side before falling asleep.

We walked toward the convoy. The setting sun cast long shadows over the gradually darkening tent city. Red coals burned in small pots in front of shelters, and the smell of meager meals saturated the area. The hospital parking lot provided a vast view of the city. Glow from the fires and lights scattered throughout appeared like veins on craggy flesh that pulsated with flickering energy. Smoke rose to the evening sky, and the ocean in the distance reflected the sunset, broken only by the large cargo and military ships clogging the port.

As we walked Cameron suddenly spoke. "What happens after everyone leaves?"

Dean looked toward the tents and took a deep breath while pulling out his pack of gum. "Don't want to think about it."

I looked around as we neared the truck. Luke and Marcus packed a few totes in the rear, and Jared sat on the roof of the cab as he lashed gear to the frame. I climbed into the truck and slumped on the bench. My legs throbbed and my eyes begged to close. I drifted off as exhaustion overtook me and my vision reduced to blurred slivers of light.

I woke and recognized the narrow street lined with burned cars followed by the steep decline that our truck barely passed each time. Rushing through a small market square and into a neighborhood, we reached the iron gates that led to our new home. The truck drove up to a much quieter setting than the day before. Outside the children slept in their beds under the evening stars. A few lights cast a glow over them, and several women sat in chairs creating a protective ring like caravans in the Old West. We unloaded our gear and congregated near the courtyard. I wanted to eat. I expected granola bars and freeze-dried fish when Jana made the announcement.

"There's food inside."

My eyes perked up before she continued.

"The women at the orphanage left us some food from the children's dinner. It's in the kitchen."

I shuffled into the kitchen at the end of the building. I took a bowl and filled it with the steamy stuff, eager to fill my belly. No one made it out of the galley area with food; it disappeared before we even gained a chance to enjoy it. I wanted to eat more but my stomach pressed tightly against my skin. The warm feeling in my gut and the lingering taste of spices on my tongue surprised my senses. My stomach had definitely shrunk. I thought about the huge dinners I ate at the Outback in Virginia supplemented with full beers and finished off with ice cream or apple pie. How did I have the room for so much food? I licked my lips thinking about ice cream and its cold, wet texture melting on my tongue.

I headed back to the tent to change before playing cards with some of the guys. I chuckled at myself for getting so excited for such a simple thing, but I wanted to keep myself busy to prevent dealing with memories of the day. I generally go stone cold when faced with emotional stress; I feared that reflecting on the events might break my spirit and plunge me into depression. I needed to stay strong for a while longer. Jana went to bed right away and so did my chances of asking her my question. I'd only seen her a few times during the day, but she was always in the middle of something and always in a rush.

I ran into Marcus standing alone by the crest of the driveway. He watched the sunset while a chilly, quiet aura surrounded him. He didn't speak, and he kept his left hand on the wall and his head tilted toward the sky. I tried to imagine what he thought about. We'd missed a few chances to talk—most of the time either he'd been driving or I'd been working. When he left the driver's seat he watched over the group, planned our route to the next destination, and spoke to locals to help plan our next objective. I wanted to talk to him, even if just for a few minutes. He turned as I stopped at his side and nodded with a smile.

"Hey Marcus. Not hungry?"

"I ate."

We stood silently for a few moments as the awkward air covered us with a blanket from which I struggled to wriggle free. I needed to ask him about Amber, but I fruitlessly tried to think of the right words to say. I wanted him to know how much his permission meant to both Amber and me.

"So, I got something I want to talk about."

He looked over, worried. He truly had no idea what was on my mind. How could he, though, after the day at the hospital. I preferred it this way—the question being a surprise and the person unable to guess at my words as I formed them. I lacked a decent poker face and my words left shakily as I spoke.

"Well, I wanted to ask you something. I've been thinking about it for a while actually, but...uhh...I've just been looking for the right time to...to ask." I fell over my words and it felt like a train wreck about to happen. I tried to get a grip. I kept telling myself how important this moment was for Amber.

"What's that? Is everything okay?" He asked, oblivious to my impeding question.

"Well," I needed to spit it out. "Would you give me your blessing to marry Amber?"

All at once he turned, grinned, and teared as he faced me. He stuttered over his words, and it took a few seconds between nervous coughs and clearing his throat to form a sentence.

"Sean, you don't have to ask my permission, I ..."

"I want to." I felt more confident with him shaken. "It means a lot to Amber, and it means a lot to me."

He started to cry, but he didn't sob, instead letting only a few stray tears escape down his cheek. He tried to fight it back. I put my hand on his back and stood closer to him as he took off his glasses and wiped them clean. Then, after a few precious seconds of gathering strength, he gave me his reply.

"Sean, of course you have my permission. You're already family in my eyes." He pulled me in for a hug and I let him hold me for a few long seconds. I was getting better with Crossroads hugs and with being around Amber's family. They were slowly starting to feel like my family, too. In that moment I forgot that we stood in Port-au-Prince just after a massive earthquake had rocked the country. It seemed that I no longer stood next to a stranger, but instead a friend, and maybe even an Uncle.

Monday, January 18th 2010

2:30am

Port Au Prince, Haiti

I heard the rustling again. I had sweat profusely from the sleeping bag and soaked the inner lining until the night air had chilled it. I scooted out of my cocoon and peeked out the front flap of the tent as voices mumbled a few feet away.

A woman stood with Marcus outside Cindy and Cameron's tent entrance. Cindy's flashlight moved frantically inside as the beam created an erratic show through the mesh roof. They spoke in a hurried but hushed tone.

"What's going on?" I asked in a strained whisper.

The woman outside looked at me. I didn't recognize her specifically, but I knew she belonged to the other group of doctors that stayed at the orphanage. "We need Cindy for a procedure at the bottom of the hill."

She turned her head back to the tent and I sat at the entrance of mine until Cindy and Cameron got out and followed the woman and Marcus. After they disappeared I got back in my sleeping bag and tried to close my eyes. I wished they'd asked me to go too, but I knew that I'd only get in the way. At some point I drifted off to sleep, but it wasn't long before the sun rose.

The morning filled the tent with light as I sat up and looked around. Jared and Dean had left before I woke. I got up and stood outside under warm rays of heat. The hours had passed too quickly, but I thanked God for a second night of restful sleep.

I turned on my phone. It was early, but I called my dad anyway. Running a construction company meant you woke up early and went to bed late. I knew he would be awake, but hoped he had time to answer my call, if he was near the phone at all.

It rang once or twice before he picked up.

"Hello? Sean, are you there?" he shouted into the phone as if being in another country meant that he had to speak louder.

"Dad, I'm here. Good morning." The reply seemed overly normal given my current circumstance.

"How is everything going? What is it like there? Are you safe?" He shot off questions rapidly and they hit me too fast to answer them all, so I tried to answer his questions with my own.

"Everything is great. How are you and mom? What's it like back at home?" I was interested for egotistical reasons to find out what others at home thought of my trip.

"Well, your friends and almost everyone in the family has called us. The phone just keeps ringing. Amber made an update on Facebook about you going, and no one really believes it. I still don't believe it."

I thought about the comment for a moment. I'd only really started to believe it myself a few days after arriving. My memories of the first night in Jimani still felt like a dream; my mind hadn't yet caught up with the completely new and unique situation.

"Yeah, it's crazy that I'm here." I couldn't think of anything else to say, but I didn't want to hang up the phone either. I couldn't quite articulate my experience, and all he wanted was to hear about it. I was just happy to hear his voice. It allowed me momentarily to pretend I was home, even if only in my thoughts.

"So, did you ask them yet?"

I put my hand over the phone as if someone could possibly hear the conversation from far away. "I asked Bob and Marcus— they both said yes. I still need to talk to Jana."

I could almost see him smiling as he stood in the company shop, perhaps some of his employees standing around. He probably held a large cup of coffee in his left hand as he silently directed his people to get to work at different projects around town, all while maintaining focus on our conversation. "That's good, Sean. I'm glad to hear that. Just one more to go then."

I smirked, knowing the one I was most scared of asking was left. The job seemed very far from over. "Yeah I know."

We spoke for a few more minutes before I said goodbye and hung up the phone. Then I made my way to the truck to leave for the day with the group.

Cindy and Cameron sat along the bench in the Daihatsu and spoke with others in the group as I jumped into the back. Their eyes were sunken. Cindy rested her head on Cameron's shoulder and told Faith and Jana about their night.

It turned out that a woman had gone into labor nearby. The villagers knew about the doctors at the orphanage and sent for help. They woke Cindy and Cameron and they jumped at the chance to help. Cindy had always wanted to deliver a baby in a remote part of the world, disconnected from the tools and guide-lines in traditional American hospitals. She wanted to experience true medicine without safety and back up plans—to understand what it felt like to depend on her skills and experience in bring-ing a new life into the world.

At four o'clock they had reached the woman and her sister a few miles from the orphanage. The sister informed Cindy that the woman had given birth before through a cesarean. The risk of complications with a traditional birth outweighed those asso-ciated with performing another cesarean. They needed to act quickly; she was already fully dilated and no longer could walk.

Cindy made a translator flag down a vehicle and rush them to the nearest hospital. When they arrived an hour later, they found the place empty and the doctors gone for the night. With the rescue efforts already a few days in, the doctors usu-ally went home to sleep at night. With no power, Cindy and Cameron brought the woman into the closest empty room and set her up for surgery. The translator ran for ten minutes to find the medical staff.

While waiting for help, Cindy built an IV using German flu-ids, Canadian tubing, and a catheter from the United States. It took several minutes to get all the parts to fit and in the end she needed tape and clips to hold all the incompatible pieces together. Using a rubber glove as a tourniquet, she inserted it into the pant-ing woman—all while trying to keep her calm.

Cameron looked around the room with his flashlight. The floors sat buried under dirty gauze, bandages, and papers. Piles of surgery tools sat in filthy heaps that soaked in murky bowls of water on countertops around the perimeter. Rust dotted outdated equipment. He scanned frantically for clean supplies until he found a few sealed packets of bandage and a handful of tools in a cabinet. He brought everything to Cindy and she rummaged through them until she found the instruments she knew they needed to save the woman's life and the life of her baby.

Finally the doctors, two Koreans and three Germans, arrived with the translator from their camp. As soon as they saw the woman they jumped to action.

After some translation and hand signals Cindy realized that no one in the room had ever led a cesarean before. One of them finally volunteered to lead, but each doctor and Cindy played a big part. Cindy kept the tools clean and comforted the patient while Cameron held the woman down. She underwent the procedure feeling every sensation. No epidural or spinal injection. They only gave conscious sedation, which did little to dull the extreme pain from each cut and dig.

When they sliced her belly she tensed up and gritted her teeth. Several men kept her still. If she jerked too quickly the staff feared that the knife could sever one of her vital arteries or even kill the baby. After a few moments she adjusted to the pain and started to sing. Blood soaked everything, but she kept her eyes on the ceiling and her hands clenched tightly around the bars of the bed.

At seven twenty-eight, the lead doctor pulled a baby girl from her mother. She screamed immediately and after a short inspection they deemed her completely healthy. Cameron cut the cord as the doctors congratulated and hugged each other in an overwhelming euphoria of joy and excitement. The birth brought a much-needed lift in morale after endless days of amputations, infection, and death.

Cindy put the baby in the woman's arms. She rocked her back and forth as she quietly sang and closed her eyes.

Cindy's mouth formed a big smile as she told the story to the group. Cameron pulled his camera out and flipped through pictures of the ordeal with the team as we crowded around them in the cramped space in the back of the truck.

Marcus took us back into the heart of city. We stopped at another facility run by the orphanage a few miles from our camp. The injured spilled out of the doors and into the courtyard where temporary beds and shelters crammed against each other and fought for space. We stopped to gather supplies and provide transportation for several doctors to a different hospital deeper in the city.

Walking down the driveway I noticed a crib nestled under a tarp. In it a baby slept against one of the walls with her legs hoisted in place and secured to the rails. Thick ropes tied both of her ankles to heavy rocks that dangled over the edge. Falling debris had broken both of her femurs during the quake and the rocks created traction to keep the bones in place. Her mother slept on the ground on a thin mattress next to her, and x-rays clipped to the bed frame showed the breaks.

Haitian women moved in all directions to bring water and food from inside the building. Electrical cords ran endlessly throughout the courtyard in chaos after starting either at one of the few generators set up outside or from inside the building. Expensive monitoring equipment sat under several of the tarps with the more severe patients. A large crate half full of square plastic bags of drinkable water sat near palettes of food. Volunteers had built an entire hospital out of borrowed equipment and spare parts.

I walked inside the entrance to the main building and into an open room. Red paint and Haitian art covered the walls, and the few dim lights cast a yellow glow over everyone inside. Men, women, and children sat either on plastic chairs or on the floor in a long line. At the other end of the room a few doctors looked at injuries under a bright lamp. A small boy sat on the table with his mother close by as one of the doctors inspected his badly injured knee.

"Sean, help us out over here," Justin said from across the room.

I followed him through a doorway and down a flight of steps to a storage room. Wheelchairs, crutches, boxes of triage equipment, and splints sat in piles near a garage door. Justin opened it and allowed the sun to flood the dark space. I followed his lead and brought a wheelchair to the truck. After several trips I packed a box with water bottles and hopped into the truck as we pulled out of the driveway. To my surprise, ten new volunteers sat with our group, all of them either doctors or nurses. I sat down next to one of them and listened to their conversations as they recounted the morning and their trip.

They all belonged to the same church in Arkansas. One of the nurses coordinated the effort to Haiti, and they'd arrived two days after we had. They spent most of their time in Port-au-Prince's hospitals while using the orphanage as a base camp. They performed surgeries, led hospital administration, and provided as much post-surgery care as possible.

We dropped off the doctors at a nearby hospital before continuing deeper into the city. Marcus maneuvered around wreckage and debris that littered every street. The truck stopped in traffic near a collapsed apartment building. Dozens of people climbed over the rubble and shouted as they pulled twisted steel and chunks of concrete from the heap. The city's inhabitants continued to look for survivors, even though several days had passed and reports of live survivors dwindled.

We broke free of traffic and reached our destination, a hospital on the northwest side of town. Unlike the first one perched on a cliff, this hospital huddled on the city streets amidst the crumbled remains of its neighbors. A new blue and gray paint job covered the curved walls and framed in massive glass windows. The contemporary architecture made it look like several huge cubes that sat on each other offset by slight distances and held up with thick round beams.

As we unloaded a group of men approached us on the sidewalk.

"Welcome, thanks for coming," one of them spoke in perfect English. The other two introduced themselves as well. All three wore clean clothes and appeared refreshed and well fed.

"Are you doctors?" Jana asked.

"No, we are translators from the University. We speak English, Spanish, and Creole. We've been here for days helping foreign doctors and nurses."

Cindy introduced herself as a nurse and one of the men immediately escorted her and Cameron inside the hospital. "We need your help," one of the translators told her as he cleared the way. The second translator pulled in Faith, Dean, and Justin after they revealed their pre-med background. Megan rounded up the rest of us to help outside with redressing wounds and bringing food and water to patients.

The third translator walked us inside the perimeter of the hospital wall through a narrow door guarded by a soldier. As we turned the corner, the side of the building sat in plain view and free from the trees that lined the main street. I noticed the huge cracks that ran both vertically and horizontally across the major support beams. I gasped. The third translator overheard me talking about the stress fractures to Marcus.

"Do you know about those cracks?" he asked.

I didn't respond. I'd studied as an engineer but only held a few years of experience, and not in building construction. Even so, the damage sat in plain view and I understood the danger based on classes from freshman year. I hesitated to respond, so Marcus spoke for me.

"He's an engineer."

The man's eyes lit up. "You are? Why didn't you say so? We could use your help too!" He beckoned me to come with him as he parted from Megan's group. He brought me under the main entrance where two older white men stood around cases of equipment that contained equipment I didn't recognize. The older of the two looked up at me as we approached.

"Ken, this guy is an engineer too. Maybe he can help out?"

He looked at me while the other continued to calibrate their tools. "What sort of engineer?"

I shrugged my shoulders. "Chemical. But I've done structural work before."

"Are you a Professional Engineer?"

Again I felt embarrassed and now suddenly upset for saying anything at all. "No. Can I help anyway?" Once again I knew my experience would be useless to help the group or the greater relief effort. I silently wished for a moment that I studied civil engineering instead.

He thought for a minute and looked over his gear. Then he took off his camera and gave it to me. "Go the whole way around the building and take pictures of all the fractures. Hold up this tape measure when you do so we can relate the size. We are doing a full report and need to document everything before we shut this place down."

The translator looked as stunned as I did. "Shut it down?" I asked.

"Yeah, of course. This place could go at any time, but there is all sorts of paperwork required to shut it down and get everyone out of here. We've got the inside of the hospital pretty much evacuated, but I want people off the lawn and out of the lobby too."

I knew the damage to the building looked horrible, but I didn't think about it falling. Almost every building in Port-au-Prince had taken on damage. Suddenly I feared for my teammates inside. "Should I go warn the rest of my group to get out of there? They got pulled inside to help."

He shook his head with slight amusement at my lack of knowledge. "No, its fine. It won't go today unless another quake hits. We want to get it shut down in the next day or so. Then we can start a plan for repairs."

After asking some more questions and learning how to use the camera, I left the patio and walked around the hospital. I finally felt qualified to do something. I'd worked construction for over a decade and knew a lot about concrete. Builders used it to erect most of the city, so I believed in my ability to point out what looked ready to fall.

Around the first corner I ran into Marcus standing near the entrance. Megan and Jared joined with the Red Cross to pass out water and food to victims. So many doctors tried to help that it turned into a hindrance to be there and take up space. Our team often brought water or food to a family only to find out that another group of volunteers had visited them ten minutes earlier.

"Marcus, want to help me take some pictures for the engineer's report?" I wanted to include him in something; he looked terribly bored and probably felt as useless as I did. He smiled and nodded before following me to the back of the building as we talked about the walls and the earthquake. People commonly cut spending on buildings by filling in concrete roofs with cinder blocks and lower grade concrete while using much smaller rebar than required. Sometimes it only takes one major fracture to make the whole thing topple.

Around the back, the thin outer wall had fallen apart in huge chunks that revealed tiny strips of rebar and steel. Dozens of holes bigger than basketballs dotted the wall like chicken pox. All the shattered glass lay in fragments in the grass, and the entire building sagged. My stomach turned while standing so close. Marcus and I took dozens of pictures. Even in the basement the support walls were cracked or broken. Several doorways were split down the middle with half of the wall an inch or so lower than the rest. I wondered if a good punch or kick might topple it over like a Jenga tower.

We returned to Ken in the lobby and gave him the camera. "Get some pictures?" he asked.

"Yeah. It does look ready to fall. I don't really know how it's still standing."

He pulled out a sheet of paper and wrote something on it before giving it to me.

"We are going to be here for a few weeks. If you want to stay and help with engineering efforts call this number and we will give you a place to stay if your team leaves earlier. Okay?"

I looked at the paper. Missionary engineers. These guys went all over the world to work in disaster situations. I wanted to stay and help, so I put the number in my pocket and promised to call. For once it seemed that someone actually needed my help and wanted to use my skills. As much as I desired to switch to their group in that moment I still needed to talk with Jana.

Marcus and I found Faith and Jana near the steps, deep in conversation.

"What were you guys doing?" she asked.

"Sean finally got to be an engineer," Marcus said proudly, putting his hands on my shoulders. I blushed and felt suddenly uneasy with the praise over such little work.

"All I did was take some pictures, but I got a number to call if I want to stay and help."

Jana clasped her hands. "That is wonderful, Sean. Are you going to stay?"

I said yes, even though I didn't know for sure. Then we told them about all the damage to the building and how they planned to evacuate soon. Jana stopped me mid-sentence.

"Is it going to fall any second?"

I told her I didn't know, and I really didn't. Something about how it teetered with all the broken supports under it made me want to get as far away as possible.

She agreed. It felt good to have my opinion mean so much. She told Faith to round up those inside and called Megan over to get everyone outside for the rest of the day.

We treated patients under tents and in the open alongside French and Puerto Rican disaster teams. A few of the Haitian men I met outside worked with the doctors by translating Creole to Spanish and English.

We left at sundown. As we did, we overheard yelling from inside the hospital. Another wall in the basement had collapsed, injuring two people and causing new cracks to form on the first floor. They evacuated the building for a few hours before moving back inside to work again.

We made it back to the orphanage an hour after sunset. The team of doctors we'd picked up earlier was eating dinner in the main hall when we arrived. I grabbed some granola bars out of my pack and made my way inside. Cindy and Cameron put together a simple dinner of rice and beans for the team and we ate together in the hall after prayers.

Afterward, we sat around an old black and white TV used by the orphanage caretakers in one of the common halls. A man entered the hall to see Cindy. He carried something in his arms wrapped in a sheet. As she got up to meet him he pulled back the fabric to reveal a newborn baby girl—the one from the night before. The girl's father had finally made it back to Haiti after spending the whole night in Florida finding a flight. Cindy asked if she could hold her, and she glowed as he handed her over. She rocked back and forth, gently touching her little nose with her finger as she spoke in a nearly incoherent baby talk.

"What's her name?" Cameron asked as he got up and stood next to his mother before gently rubbing the belly of the baby he helped deliver.

"We named her Cindy," the man replied.

Tuesday, January 19th 2010

6:20am

Port Au Prince, Haiti

We set out the next day just before dawn and drove north-west, just south of the docks and bayside markets. The cracked, worn road ran parallel to a tall concrete wall that hugged the curb. Graffiti, flyers, and tattered papers covered it in thick layers with gum, glue, and nails that bound the trash together. People sold goods near the wall and used homemade tables covered with old cloths to display inventory. Others crowded the sidewalk and road as they shopped, shouting at vendors and bartering for food and clothing.

Marcus stopped near a break in the wall where a worn wooden gate sagged on broken brass hinges. The wood was warped and rotted, and someone had tried to fix the hole by nailing pieces of plywood across the face. From the back of the truck I took in the sight of the largest tent city in Port-au-Prince. People had tied tarps and sheets of all colors to trees, light poles, and each other from one end of the field to the other. The area teemed with life and people finishing daily routines in the new village. Jana talked to a man guarding the door for a few minutes. Afterwards, she addressed us from the stairs.

"This is a dangerous spot, everyone, but we found out last night that no medical teams have come here yet. They're letting us in to help, but stick together and don't wander off."

I tried to listen but I didn't want to be in this part of town. When we stopped, people crowded around us and demanded

225

food and water. Men glared at us from a distance in small groups with worn machetes at their sides. They kept close to the wall and grew in number as they neared. I tried to look for an exit if I needed to run. Jana spoke again to the whole group.

"If you don't want to leave the truck I can understand, but it's probably more dangerous for you to stay here alone than come into camp with the entire group."

We unloaded our supplies and filed in one by one through the gate.

The morning sun hit my face as we passed through the entrance and then east into the camp. A small gravel road pushed forward through the tangled web of tents and split into small trails on either side that darted and disappeared behind crowds of people. Smoke and dirt rose into the dry morning air and filled the sky with dust. Particles stuck to my sweat as I walked and left me gritty and oily. It didn't take long before sweat soaked me completely, and I struggled to hold all my supplies under the heat.

Water bottles stuck out of each of my cargo pockets and little kids walked beside me and tried to grab them while I batted their hands away while trying to hold on to everything I carried. Women looked at me and yelled. I didn't know if they wanted us here or not.

I fell to the back of the line while I stopped to give out a bottle of water to a group of kids. After picking up my gear I looked back toward the gate a few hundred feet away. Someone had closed it and several Haitian men stood in front of the door. About twenty feet ahead of us a dozen men stood in the road. They held machetes and sticks.

To my surprise, the leader shook Jana's hand as we approached. They spoke for a few moments as we stood surrounded by a growing throng of desperate people. He pointed to others in his group and directed them around us to create a barrier. I found out later that the Haitian leader knew the owner of the orphanage and had expected our visit.

We moved forward more and more slowly as we pushed deeper into the camp. With each step the men pushed people out of the way and waved their weapons back and forth. Families glared at us from their shelters with frightened looks at the Haitian leader and his followers.

They led us to a clearing in front of the only building on the property, a derelict mansion that sat cracked and condemned in the sun. Huge pillars extended from the ground to support the roof above the third floor as it sagged into the house, and large chunks of rock from the walls lay on the ground. The windows and doors had disappeared long before our arrival and no light came from inside. A fire burned in a pit beside the front deck, and the wind carried the smell of cooked meat to my nose. We stopped at several long benches that sat in a circle near the front of the building. The men stopped and surrounded us before putting their hands up to keep the crowd that trailed us at bay.

"This is our camp," Jana said. "The men have agreed to control the crowd and help us throughout the day." Later she told us the truth about our guards; they were local thugs and gang members. In any other circumstance the same men might rob or even kill us, but in the midst of disaster they stood guard to allow us to treat their families, friends, and community.

The team split into pairs and claimed sections of benches as workspaces. Once situated, the guards allowed people to enter the circle one at a time. First they admitted a young boy with a broken leg. Electrical tape and rope tied a tree branch against it, and a huge purple bruise covered it all. The splint caused me to shudder when I tried to imagine the pain. He stretched his leg outward. Faith and Luke worked on him together to remove the branch, clean an opening near the break, and replace the branch with a proper splint.

Two guards escorted him out as soon as Luke and Faith finished their work and immediately brought a ten-year-old girl to Jared and me. She had shirts wrapped around her foot. Dirt and blood covered her clothes, and white chalk from the initial quake coated her hair. We unwrapped the dressing. Besides her pinky all her toes had been severed clean, and removing the shirts restarted the flow of blood. She cried out. Jared cleaned her foot with bottles of saline and gently wiped with gauze until he applied ointment and slowed the bleeding. She sobbed as she sat limp on the bench and stared at her foot in disbelief under the sun. I wrapped it with gauze and bandage using tape to keep the dressing taut. We gave her a set of crutches as the men helped her off the bench. She nodded in thanks as she left and returned to the mob outside the circle. She'd need to learn how to walk again without her toes, but the crutches helped.

The guards continued to bring in patients one at a time for each set of workers. They maintained strict order and only allowed in a new patient when we finished with another. They even held back parents from accompanying their children. I looked around once in a while and noticed how hard they worked to keep the crowd at bay. They sweated under the sun while constantly pushing back groups of people.

They brought a little girl to me and sat her on the bench. At first I didn't notice her injuries so I asked the guard for help. He pointed to the back of his head, and then at her. I angled her forward and peered along the back of her skull to see a long jagged crack run vertically on her crown. Thick staples covered in dry blood were hammered into her flesh from work done by another doctor days before. Apparently someone did visit the tent city before us. It oozed fluids and smelled rotten. I took a second to adjust to the smell. Using a latex glove I ran my finger over a few of the staples to gauge her reaction to touch. She didn't recoil in pain or start to cry but sat quietly. Touching again, I kept my eyes on her face. Still she did not react. I crouched in front of her and said, *"Est-il blessé?"* pointing to her head, asking her if it hurt.

"Non," she replied while keeping her eyes to the ground.

I waved to Cindy and asked her to look at the injury. She felt the staples as she ran a flashlight over the crack.

"It looks bad, but it doesn't hurt? Well, clean and cover it. There's not much more we can do."

I squirted saline on the crack and lightly brushed away dried blood and dirt with clean gauze. Once clean, I coated it with ointment before wrapping new bandages around her head.

A few hours later an old woman with a thin, frail frame approached the group. Sparse, wiry hair dotted her balding head adorned with a bandana, and a light fitting dress hung from her shoulders. She held a cloth to her breast and looked to be in pain. Dean waved to Jana and she joined them. She moved the cloth from the woman's breast and then held her hand to her mouth. At that moment I didn't have a patient of my own so I walked over to see what had caused the reaction. Most of her breast had been sheared away, and what the quake left behind appeared ragged. The flesh turned green in the light. Others in the group looked as well, and all eyes turned to see the woman with Jana.

"She's got gangrene," Cindy said.

Unable to properly treat her wound, she had allowed the opening to fester for days. We couldn't help her, but we promised to take her to a hospital and let them try. Jana spoke to the woman for a few minutes more and then sat her on the bench. She put the cloth back over her breast and remained quiet for the rest of the afternoon.

The team worked into the evening hours as we rotated victims in and out of the circle. The Haitian men who guarded us worked tirelessly to keep order in an increasingly hostile crowd. As the sun set people realized that time was running out for our stay and they began to push, shove, and yell in desperation. The guards looked around them uneasily, and I no longer felt comfortable there. After one of the men spoke to Jana quietly, she instructed the group to pack up.

The crowd erupted into panic. We moved toward the exit. We helped carry those picked for the hospital as we walked, and the guards now pushed the crowd away as we clawed toward the exit. They held weapons but never used them. We needed to start the drive back to the orphanage before roads closed and the nightly riots resumed.

We packed into the back of the truck and fit a dozen injured Haitians with us in the already impossible space. We raced along the streets in the dark, and with each bump I lifted off the floor momentarily only to return painfully to the steel a second later. I closed my eyes to relax. I listened to the chatter of everyone in the truck over the sounds of the city in the background. Several different conversations in multiple languages took place at the same time and made it hard to concentrate. I instead focused on the rumble of the truck as Marcus navigated our way home. It amazed me how he'd learned and remembered all the routes in the city after only one drive. The man has the ability to draw a map in his mind, and his memory allows him to remember the kind of tiny details that led us back, like breadcrumbs for Hansel and Gretel.

We stopped at the hospital and gave the injured to the staff. We made it back to the orphanage before nine. Sunburned, worn out, and suffering from a terrible headache, I made my way to the tents. By the time I got there, the energy in my legs ran empty and I struggled to walk. I stripped off my sweat soaked clothes, and wearing nothing but my boxers, slipped into my sleeping bag. I slept amazingly well in Port-au-Prince. Most mornings I barely remembered getting into my sleeping bag at all.

Thursday, January 21st 2010
6:15am
Port Au Prince, Haiti

I sat up and listened to children play in the courtyard. Some of the early risers snuck away from their beds and tried to creep around our tents and gear while they waited for us to wake. I saw the silhouette of a boy against the tent as he tried to listen for movement. I snapped my hand against the wall, scaring and surprising him as he jumped and ran away. I brushed my teeth and gargled just outside. Toothpaste, soap, and sunscreen became worth their weight in gold. Several teammates had already run out, and I begrudged giving away any of my precious toothpaste. I felt I deserved a little personal space. Only toilet paper surpassed toothpaste in value. Days of erratic eating and high stress had turned my stomach into a hornet's nest of turmoil. I kept a roll close to lessen the response time when I needed to find a bush nearby.

I walked around the compound by myself until I found Cameron alone by the truck. I looked at my watch. "Five?" The sun already blazed on us as the tilt of the earth made it bright and dark earlier than in Pennsylvania.

"Morning," Cameron said as I stopped nearby and filled my water bottle at the cooler. "How'd you sleep?"

"Like a baby. I've never slept so deeply before. You?"

"Yeah—I don't even remember getting in the tent. I woke up feeling like years went by in one night."

233

We talked for a while about the journey. He wanted to continue to make a difference in Haiti and planned to stay as long as possible. Neither of us had any idea how long the trip would last.

After some small talk we prepared breakfast for the group. Afterward, I ran into Jana while I rummaged for clean clothes. She stood alone by the courtyard tree with the remains of her morning coffee while talking on a cell phone to Bob. She spoke quickly and with energy and when she saw me she waved for me to approach. "Oh no," I thought immediately, "I waited too long to ask. Someone must have leaked it to her." I'd left the proposal ideas in a holding pattern for a few days while consumed with work in the field. She gave me a tight hug while setting her coffee cup on my shoulder when I stood next to her. The warm metal of the cup slightly burned my skin, but I didn't dare push her away.

"Sean, thank you for making breakfast. It was very thoughtful." She put the cell back to her ear and said, "Bob, yes he's here now, I'll talk to you later." After she put the phone away she gave me a long stare. She didn't look upset, but instead bewildered, as if she didn't know what to say next. I decided to fill the gap with an apology before I felt any worse.

"Jana, I'm sorry for not..." She interrupted me mid-sentence. "Do you know what Bob just told me? Amber called, and Gordito learned how to roll over and speak today. She taught him! Isn't that fabulous?"

I tried to smile, but the surprise from her statement just twisted my expression into a confused stare. Gordito? The dog? That's what had excited her? I hadn't thought about him in days.

"That's awesome. Is she doing okay?"

She nodded and smiled while drinking the last of her coffee. "She's fine, but she wanted to tell you she loves you and misses you."

"Oh," was all I could reply. I'd almost ruined it for Jana. Somehow everyone had kept quiet all the way until now.

"What was it you were saying?" she asked.

The question caught me off guard, and I thought of the first lie that came to mind. "Oh, I uh… I heard that the coffee wasn't strong enough. I'm sorry if I didn't make it right." What a perfect lie.

She chuckled before giving me another hug. "Sean, don't worry about that, I'm just happy to have some at all! Now go get ready, we're leaving in a few minutes."

I got my bags and loaded up, feeling a big load off my shoulders that the surprise survived. However, I needed to ask her soon.

We went to another hospital, this one much closer to the orphanage. I moved alone from person to person at a hurried pace. I'd learned a lot since arriving in Haiti almost a week before and felt comfortable completing a wide array of procedures on the fly. I'd begun to feel useful and valuable to the group, and really enjoyed each moment I spent helping the injured.

My teammates worked even better and still seemed unfazed by the trauma around us. I didn't know if they let their emotions loose in private, but they performed perfectly in the field. I wondered if I looked cold sometimes, preventing my feelings from surfacing and looking disconnected and devoid of compassion.

I continued my rounds removing bandages, cleaning, and disinfecting wounds. With several days now passed, most of the work revolved around maximizing the recovery of those we'd treated. The news coverage added an extra layer of complexity as each hospital became swarmed by media crews. I avoided cameras and pulled my cap over my face when they approached. I understood the need for them, but the extent and penetration actually slowed the work. It felt wrong videotaping people in their weakest and most vulnerable state to plaster on the world news. Many Haitians covered their faces when news crews came, and I grew angry if they refused to leave a patient alone who wanted privacy.

I wondered about my friends at home and if they watched the news coverage. I wondered if they even cared. Before I'd made this journey, I'd changed the channel to sports to avoid looking at everything happening in Haiti. While eating at Outback the bartender had turned off the news to watch college basketball and no one, including me, complained. During my work in Port-au-Prince I began to feel protective of the Haitians at the hospital and disregard for everyone at home on comfy couches eating huge dinners. But somewhere deep inside I knew that if I hadn't come on the trip, I'd continue to turn off the news, too. How long would it take me to forget my experiences in Haiti and become complacent with ignoring everything outside my circle?

The hospital seemed to hold more doctors than patients and our presence became more of a nuisance than an asset. Every time I worked on a new case someone breathed down my neck to ask for my name, address, and credentials. A coordination crew arrived with the newest set of doctors and worked tirelessly to institute what seemed like martial law on the hospital grounds. When we arrived that morning we checked in with a registration desk before going to work. The tide of politics had finally caught up to us since departing the outpost in Jimani.

After I finished bandaging an exposed knee, a shorter white woman in her late forties confronted me in the parking lot. She wore a bright green t-shirt and a nametag hung from her necklace.

"What is your name? What were you doing in that tent?"

The answer seemed obvious but I tried to respond without appearing snide. "I was working on someone. Can I help you?"

"Yes you can. I need your name, the type of doctor or nurse you are, and what sort of work you have been doing here today." She put one hand on her side and extended a clipboard with the other inches from my face. Her nose wrinkled into a sarcastic and annoyed expression that made me angry. I tried to keep calm.

"I'm not a doctor. I'm with a group of them though. I'm just trying to help."

"Well, we can't just have anyone walking around here doing whatever they want. I'd appreciate it if you'd find your group and leave," she said.

"Are you serious? There's a ton of people still out here who need help."

"And they'll get it—from someone who's trained properly."

She left me standing at the entrance of a shelter holding the clipboard in my hand. In almost every way I knew she was right; I wasn't a doctor or even a nurse, and I had no business treating people as if I'd been trained as one. However, I still felt she was making a mistake under these circumstances. Up until recently, the injured had overwhelmed us and people begged us to work. In Jimani it had been so bad that a surgeon made me assist in the surgery room. I felt offended by her comments. I felt I had a right to be there helping too. I'd earned it.

I walked to the entrance of the hospital and met most of the group ready to go. We waited for Faith to end her work inside. Marcus stood by a concrete ledge and waved as I approached.

"Hey Sean, I think we're going to leave soon. There's too many volunteers here, and some of the people in charge don't want us getting in the way."

"I think I met one of them a few minutes ago."

"Me too," Dean said. "She asked me to fill out a form."

"It's getting political now. Jana doesn't like to get involved with that stuff."

Jana brought Faith out of the hospital and we left halfway through the day. For the first time we lacked a location to work so Marcus brought the truck to a bakery in the southwest part of town. So far we'd survived on rice, beans, oatmeal, and granola bars. Most of the city sat in ruins, with the new homeless on the streets at night, scratching to survive among the chaos. In this part of town, however, the reality of the extreme class differences appeared plainly on the street.

The bakery stood on a clean street in a quiet part of town, brand new and freshly painted in lavender and maroon. Huge, thick windows covered the walls, and inside ice cold air conditioning kept the store comfortable. An older French man ran the counter. A long glass window displayed perfectly crafted pastries under soft light. Expensive furniture sat on a marble tile floor. All around the bakery high-end clothing stores, coffee shops, and restaurants filled the square. Cop cars sat on almost every corner with officers standing under the sun with guns drawn.

Jana wanted to take a break from the chaos to regroup and breathe, and the majority of the team agreed. We sat inside for a half hour soaking in the air conditioning. Most of the team got coffee and a few, including me, splurged on pastries. It felt odd and honestly quite wrong that such a place existed amongst the chaos that drowned most of the city and its people in despair. This little section of the city felt untouched by and uninterested in the tragic state of the country. But to be honest, my mind eased while in the cocoon provided by the bakery, and for a few moments I too forgot about everything happening just down the street.

My first bite into a fresh chocolate éclair shocked my taste buds. The sensation of the sugar and the texture of the fresh dough wrestled with my tongue. I ate it slowly, taking a few moments between each bite to close my eyes and experience the flavor. My belly groaned before I finished half of it. My stomach had spent the past week learning how to survive on meager meals, and now it seemed opulent food actually hurt it. I wondered what else would feel different once I got home. After the short break we loaded into the truck and left that strangely serene part of the city.

Halfway back to the orphanage we stopped at a collapsed church. At the intersection, rubble from its stone walls poured onto the street to mix with cloth and stained glass. Only the main arch had stood against the quake with a stained glass window under its keystone still intact. Broken benches, tables, and floorboards splintered under the wreckage and jutted into the sky like blades of grass. A granite and wood crucifix sat crooked near the road with piles of rubble against it. The setting sun cast its glow through the glass and blanketed the site with color.

The team spent time taking pictures, praying, and walking around the site as the sun slowly set and the stained glass darkened. Even other Haitians hushed as they walked past the landmark. As I stared at the church, I felt goose bumps form on my arms and legs. The air smelled cleaner, the breeze bit cooler, and the sun cast the perfect amount of light. I sat on a rock and closed my eyes as I cleared my mind and focused on my time in Haiti and home. I even prayed. After the sun completed its journey for the day a much quieter group of volunteers gathered in the back of the truck. Marcus pulled away, and after a few moments the church disappeared as we turned off the street.

After dinner I sat on the front steps of the orphanage. The stars burned brighter than anywhere I'd been before and I watched thousands of them fill the sky. I remained still and let the heat from my body transfer into the dirt as the evening breeze moved slowly over me.

I turned on my phone to call home. I'd racked up over fifty voicemails and a hundred texts. I was surprised my mailbox could hold all of them. I called my parent's house. My mom answered the phone.

"Hey mom…" It's all I got out before she realized it was me.

"Sean! Your father told me you called the other day. Is everything going well? Did you do 'you know what' yet?"

I smiled and let out a short, quiet laugh. "No mom, not yet. The opportunity just hasn't come up. We're pretty busy here."

"Oh. Well, don't let it go for too long."

"I won't. How are things at home?"

She didn't react to small talk the same way my dad did. She almost negated my question all together. "Home? Who cares about home? How are you doing? What are you doing there?"

"Eh, just helping out at the hospitals and stuff." This was the communication problem Amber always complained about. I didn't do so well at talking on the phone, and now I compounded the problem with a general disbelief with what I was doing in Haiti. I truly couldn't articulate it. "It's hard to talk about, but I'm doing fine. I love you."

We spoke for a while longer, and she made me promise to try to call her again. After I hung up the phone I pulled off my hat and looked at it. Stained in dirt, sweat, and blood, it had turned into a stark reminder of the trip. The Raven patch on the front had peeled halfway off the day before, and now the side of it curled into ribbons and left the bare purple underneath it surprisingly clean. Endless streams of sweat had softened the inner band to turn it smooth as silk. I sat it on my knee and ran my hand through my buzzed hair. My scalp itched from grime.

I heard talking and laughing. I turned my head to look, but only saw the dark alley between buildings. The laughter continued. I got up and walked toward it. I reached the end of an alley between buildings and looked right. Jared, and Luke stood in the dark, smoking cigarettes and Dean sat on a nearby ledge as he picked grime from his fingernails with a small knife.

"Hey Sean, what's up man? Want a smoke?" Jared asked.

I thought for a moment. Both my parents smoked religiously, and I spent my entire childhood in back seats of cars smelling their fumes. I didn't just hate the smell; I hated everything about them.

"I don't smoke man, but thanks."

"You sure? It'll calm your nerves."

"Nah. I've never had one before."

Jared looked stunned, "Never?"

"Yeah."

"Well shit, if there was ever a time to have your first, this would be it."

He had a point. Curiosity had always surrounded cigarettes like a forbidden fruit I'd never indulged. The rest of my world had turned upside down when I set foot in Haiti, so why not?

"Sure. I'll take one."

Jared nodded and presented the pack to me as he grinned. I took one and twirled it between my thumb and index finger. For all the things I tried in high school and college, something seemed momentous about it, some checkpoint in life, and some rite of passage. I lit it and put it to my mouth before taking a long, slow drag.

"So?" Luke asked after a few moments.

I paused, inhaling again before answering. "Not bad."

Thursday, January 21st 2010
2:00pm
Port Au Prince, Haiti

After more than a week at the hospital Lucas broke down his shelter and returned with his mother to the remains of their home. She began to walk with the help of crutches and the openings on her chest began to scab and show signs of healing. The hospital crowd grew until even checkups proved impossible to obtain. People stole from each other in the night, and stories of rape and assault grew from hushed whispers to stern warnings told in the open from one person to another. No one collected trash. After a few days the smell saturated every inch of the parking lot. Piles of rotten food, moldy boxes, dirty medical supplies, and heaps of empty plastic bags sat like giant effigies. The gutters filled with refuse. The grass died from traffic and allowed mud and dirt to reign supreme. Eventually Lucas felt safety lay outside the hospital grounds, so he took Tasha home.

The home they once lived in had been reduced to a jagged pile of rubble and twisted metal, with most of their belongings buried beneath the sudden tomb. The few things not trapped by wreckage had disappeared while they'd stayed at the hospital, including the frame of his briefly prized motorbike. Dust covered everything with a sticky film, and the majority of neighbors' tents had disappeared. Most had chosen to join one of the many tent cities that dotted the capital. The first night, he set Tasha up under their tarp from the hospital, and he slept outside on the edge to keep it in place. The nights grew surprisingly cold, and he used whatever fabric he found to cover himself until morning.

The next day he began work on a permanent shelter. The few remaining neighbors helped him pull material from the wreckage. One even gave them a few extra blankets, tarps, and rope from his personal stash. Lucas tied a large tarp to shrapnel that stuck out from his home and draped it across the front yard using two poles near the road. When he finished, he built a small bed for his mother from wood scraps and donated blankets. He made a bench to sleep on from several chairs he took from a wrecked store across the street and hung the remaining blankets around the perimeter for privacy. When he finally finished it, their new abode held rain and wind at bay. The roof kept them cool in the day and warm in the evening.

Each morning before the sun rose he walked to the Red Cross station set up in the middle of his neighborhood. Zac and his brother went as well, and they often saved Lucas a spot in the endless line that formed each morning. The Red Cross provided clean water, food rations, and hygiene supplies that refilled each evening, but never brought enough to help everyone. Some days he got a package; others he didn't.

The neighborhood reached a sense of calm. Living under tarps and eating food rations became the norm. Lucas spent most of the day in the city looking for work. Before the quake he'd worked in a grocery store owned by his mother's friend. Now only rubble and broken glass remained.

Lucas soon realized that no jobs remained. Most people looked alongside him and far fewer places existed to employ than ever before. Highly skilled people took on low-level labor for minimal pay or food. Construction crews hired bankers, lawyers, and engineers to start the clean-up process while leaving normal, unskilled workers with nowhere to turn.

Lucas spent his days tending to Tasha and waiting at the Red Cross. Every day she grew a little stronger, and after another week of practice she moved around with crutches like a seasoned veteran. She visited neighbors and tried to clean up around the tent in the evening. As time passed and they slowly removed the rubble of their collapsed home, they uncovered lost belongings, piece by piece. He found much of their clothing, a working clock, and some intact dishes. He found broken tables, chairs, and cabinets. He sold or repurposed everything for the shelter. He sold dozens of feet of electrical wire pulled from the walls and metal from window trim and doors. They needed money badly.

Lucas woke in the dark. His mother slept on her bed covered in blankets and sheltered by a sheet that shielded her from the wind. He rubbed his arms to warm them. The evenings brought frigid, strong winds that kept him shivering throughout the night. He heard noises outside. The men in the neighborhood woke up earlier each day to beat each other to the aid station, but something seemed different.

Outside, a large crowd walked down the hill toward the Red Cross. Military vehicles sat in front to block the dozens of people trying to enter the building. He joined the crowd. As he walked down, the sound of loudspeakers, angry screaming, and running engines got louder until it overwhelmed him.

Over a thousand people crowded the Red Cross. White UN military vehicles sat on either side of the entrance and pointed lights on the crowd.

"Please go home. The Red Cross is closed," a man shouted over the loud speaker. "There are shelters set up outside of the city."

Anger rose as the mob pushed closer to the entrance. Lucas felt suddenly uneasy and slowly let everyone pass him as he worked his way toward the back. He turned to go back to his mother. They needed to leave.

The next morning he woke to silence. Outside the shelter it seemed as if everyone still slept. He walked back to the town square. The UN vehicles, the Red Cross, and the crowd had disappeared. Another boy his age sat on a ledge near the road, smoking a cigarette. Lucas approached.

"Hey, what happened to the Red Cross?"

"You didn't hear? They left—moving on to another area in the city."

"Where are all the people?"

"Don't know. Probably went home or to look for work. Some are going to the shelters they are setting up outside the city."

"What shelters?"

"They have food and water. We're going today."

Lucas felt a glimmer of hope. "Thanks."

The other boy nodded. "No problem."

Friday, January 22nd 2010
6:20am
Port Au Prince, Haiti

We left the orphanage before dawn. Jana had heard about a few small communities in the area without access to doctors. We learned that some of the groups that lived only a few miles away were taking care of several injured victims on their own and needed help. The mission teams never knew they existed and the city hospital network fell short in the outskirts of the city. It became almost impossible to help at the overstaffed hospitals, so we decided to try and find a few of the stranded victims.

Marcus navigated southeast through destroyed residential neighborhoods as we moved toward the outskirts of the city. The hilly, erratic land turned the roads unreliable. Narrow dirt tracks washed away by rain and worn from use hugged cliffs, ravines, and walls. In many spots the slightest misstep would result in a deep drop to the pits on either side. The truck barely kept all four tires on the road, and with each sharp turn my stomach tightened as I anticipated falling off the edge.

We stopped at an intersection on top of a hill. A collapsed set of homes blocked the road and steep declines too extreme for the truck descended left and right. To the right the road snaked down to a garbage dump and hugged a craggy cliff as it disappeared around a bend. The road to the left ended at a small group of huts covered with tarps. The morning sun cast a strong glare against the gray walls and gravel, and I shielded my eyes to see.

"That's where they are," Jana said to the group.

We slowly made our way down the rocky trail. I tried to walk upright, but with every inch forward a few rocks dislodged under my shoes and pushed me off balance. I carried a stretcher, a pack with water bottles, and crackers. I took another step and lost my footing, my right leg slipping from under me as I plummeted to the ground. I stood with knees bent to fight the slope the rest of the way down.

At the bottom of the hill ten small concrete homes with tin and zinc roofs sat in a semi-circle around a flat expanse that reminded me of a cul-de-sac. Huge tarps had been draped between homes, providing shelters where all of the residents lived after the quake. Sheets hung vertically from twine to create temporary walls separating the living spaces. Each area was packed with belongings, and families sat on their possessions as we entered the shade.

What heat the roof kept out it replaced with a strong, pungent odor that made me nauseous almost immediately. Three children, a woman, and two old men lay on blankets near the entrance covered in dust, blood, and waste. Family members sat on the ground or on small chairs around their loved ones.

A woman greeted us once we put down our supplies.

"Bon Maten. Mèsi pou vini." Good morning, thank you for coming, she said.

"Good morning to you too, we are glad to help," Jana replied in Creole.

They continued to speak, and I looked at those on the ground. The six injured appeared to be in bad shape.

"These people have been here since the quake," Marcus informed us after listening to the woman.

A little girl lay on the ground with a soiled sheet rolled into a ball under her knee. Long, jagged gashes peppered her legs and feet. Infection lined the openings with dried brown and yellow flesh. One of them left a patch of muscle bare to the elements, and dirt had caked it dry. Another child had a broken arm set with a splint that looked flimsy and ready to fall off. Bloodied clothes wrapped around the third child's head and hid a cracked skull. A pregnant woman complained of tightness and pain in her chest, but lacked any surface wounds we could work on in the field. The first older man had a broken hand and a few gashes, but seemed okay otherwise.

A stone wall had fallen on the second elderly man, bruising or breaking many of his ribs. His breathing sounded shallow and erratic. Each inhalation was loud and full of strain, and each exhalation barely audible. Gashes and bruises covered his upper body, but the worst ran from his tailbone to shoulder blade. Metal attached to the wall had sheared down his back when it fell on him and opened the flesh as it filleted through his muscle and tendons. Without any training or supplies, the women had tried to close it but failed. We removed the sheet and inspected the deeply infected wound. White puss lined the lower dermis, and yellow mucus covered the muscle tissue.

Cindy and the Berkley guys worked on the children, but we lacked the equipment and training for the pregnant woman and older man. We needed to get them to a hospital. After cleaning and feeding the children we put the woman on a stretcher.

From the bottom the climb looked impossible. The weight was distributed evenly between the six of us, but our footing and the incline made the ascent dangerous. Every step turned steeper and put more weight on the rear. Those in front compensated by crouching while bringing the stretcher near the ground while those in back held it above their heads. Rubble broke free with each step and sent one or two carriers off balance while forcing sudden weight on someone else. The handle felt slippery as sweat and grime ran down my arm and soaked the wood. I switched hands every few steps to dry my palms on my shirt. Each jolt swung the stretcher from side to side and caused the woman to moan.

I looked up the hill—only halfway there. The others looked exhausted but we needed to push. My legs felt like rubber bands and threatened to give out while my feet burned with each step. The sun beat down on my back and sucked the water from my skin.

I thanked God when we reached the top. Marcus pulled the woman into the truck and laid her on a bench. I sat on the dirt under the shade of the bed. My shirt was soaked with sweat. I pulled it away from my skin to allow air in between, and the hot breeze dried the fabric rapidly. I pulled off my hat and fanned my neck. I stood and looked down the hill. It seemed miles away now. Slowly, the others stood and gathered together at the side of the road. We stared down the hill for a few moments to delay the inevitable.

The second trip nearly broke the team. The older man weighed much less than the woman, but exhaustion overcame us from the first climb. He lay on his side in the stretcher and put most of his weight on his hips, legs, and arm. He tried to sit up to avoid touching the stretcher to his ribs or back. Every time he shifted his weight we stumbled and lost footing.

In the early afternoon the sun glared off the white buildings and road, forcing me to walk with my eyes almost closed. I felt the sun pulsating on my skin as it burned. Eventually I dried off and felt cool. My body had run out of water to release.

At the top of the hill we sat the man on the other bench. I plopped on the ground and drank my last bottle of water in seconds, but my throat stayed dry from exhaustion. The entire team hid under the slim shadow created by the truck and rested. After everyone caught our breath we loaded into the truck. We got back to the orphanage at dusk with the wounded still on board. Most of the team got out, but Marcus, Jana, and Faith drove into the city to deliver the two Haitians to the closest hospital.

At the orphanage I ate a quick meal, took a cold bucket shower, and changed into my last clean pair of boxers. A cool breeze blew from the west over the hilly landscape, and I found a seat on a stone ledge that faced toward the bay in the north. The spot provided a moment of solace, and I used the time to think.

I suddenly felt anxious and sad, like I wanted to cry but just didn't have the tears to do so. I'd watched others break down, write, and even get furious during our journey, but on the surface I felt unaffected. Even here and in this place I couldn't display emotion. I felt as if in some way I didn't deserve to. I replayed sad times in my life: the death of my dog, the loss of my uncle—anything to start the flow.

I felt the others on the team noticed my lack of connection and equated it to apathy. I wanted to show the others I did care, but in that very moment and in the center of all the chaos I just couldn't let go. Instead I sat alone in the dark, watching the stars light the sky as I dreamed about home, Amber, and life back in Pennsylvania. I went to sleep angry and alone.

Clouds blanketed the sky the next morning and kept the air cooler than usual. Morning dew stayed on the grass longer and made the countryside glisten from the sun's glow. After getting dressed and eating breakfast I returned to the west edge of the compound to grab my hat. I had left it out on a pole during the night in hopes that the evening breeze would air it out. It sat drenched in dew, the purple much darker and the brim soggy.

Ink flooded the emblems and blurred it significantly. I held it to my nose and sniffed: fortunately, the smell had dissipated. I pulled it over my head and felt the dew soaked in the fabric cool my head and wet my hair. It finally fit perfectly.

I pulled out my cell phone and dialed home. After a few rings Amber answered, still half asleep when I called.

"Hello?"

"Hey baby, good morning."

Her voice perked up after recognizing me, "Oh my God! Sean, is that you?"

"Yeah, how are you doing?"

"How am I doing? Everyone back here wants to know how *you* are doing. Is everything okay? What is it like?"

I paused, "It's...hard to describe on the phone. But I'm safe."

"Oh, okay, that's good," she paused for a few moments. "So when are you coming home?"

"Not sure yet, that's up to your mom. They need a lot of help, and work said I could stay as long as I want."

"Well come home soon. I miss you. Please be safe."

"I will. Love you."

"Love you too."

I wanted to go home, but at the same time felt drawn to stay. Something about the area, the circumstances, and the group I worked with made it feel like a time capsule, as if the outside world was frozen in place while we worked. Short phone calls home provided a small glimpse of the world outside and made me miss it, so I made them as rarely as possible. I wanted to stay in the bubble of Haiti to help, and thought of home only brought me further from that zone. I found it odd that this place so far from my regular life somehow felt normal after only a week, whereas home seemed like a strange place.

Marcus brought us to another tent city in Port-au-Prince near the northern markets. We worked through the morning redoing bandages and giving out pain medicine. With each passing day the number of new injuries decreased, but the continual care needed for recovery persisted day after day. I got into the rhythm of changing bandages, so much so that it felt routine as my efficiency increased. Remove, clean, saline squirt, apply antibiotic, re-bandage, repeat. Each time I would finish and send someone off, a new person took his or her place. We drained our supplies each day, but every evening restocked at the hospital or at the orphanage for the next outreach with the group.

Every once in a while someone came to us with an untreated wound. With each passing day they grew more dire and gruesome. Gangrene, sepsis, and other diseases started to sprout here and there. Unequipped to treat the worst cases, we either took them to the hospital in the evening or sent them on their way, unsure of their fate. At some point it turned into a numbers game. We chose to treat twenty-five people with a high chance of survival over spending a whole day transporting one or two people with far worse odds. I never made these calls; Jana and Marcus did. I respected their ability to do it, and never questioned the choices they made. I could have done no better.

A man brought his wife to our team that evening at sunset. She used crutches made from tree branches tied with sheets to walk and kept her right foot off the ground with a splint made from plastic scraps and rope. She sat on the bench and removed the splint. Her shinbone had broken through her flesh, and the surrounding skin was black and smelled awful. She'd contracted sepsis. No one wanted to say it, but she'd waited too long to find help. A long line stood behind her, and packing up to take her prevented us from helping many others. We applied antibiotics and new bandages, and gave her the last set of crutches. Her husband helped her sit nearby and she waited in pain for hours while we tended to the others. We took her to the hospital later that night. The doctor at the hospital confirmed our thoughts. She held little chance for survival without amputation. They completed the surgery that night. At least she got anesthetic before they started.

Friday, January 22nd 2010
4:00pm
Port Au Prince, Haiti

The early shipment of patients to the hospital left us with several hours of sunlight before the day ended. The team was slowly breaking down both physically and mentally over each successive day. I found myself entering a zombie-like state during the endless ordeal. My mind often wandered to faraway places while my body completed the work. Jana noticed the mood overtaking the entire team and decided to take us on a small field trip for the rest of the day. We'd be visiting a few sites, though she wouldn't reveal exactly what.

The truck strained as it climbed a mountain face near the southwest edge of town where the buildings suddenly stopped as trees, huts, and steep hills filled the view. Halfway up we stopped at a church built between the narrow road and steep cliffs that dropped hundreds of feet to a forested valley below. A wooden deck extended out and allowed church patrons and tourists alike to take in the panoramic view. Directly below, small, twisted trees clung to the steep face, jutting their branches out over the expanse below and into the sun. Near the bottom the city butted against the mountain. The urban sprawl spilled from the mountain and crammed every inch of ground into the distance, until it seemed to overflow into the sea like lava boiling out of the earth. From the church, the water looked blue against the brown and tan city. Cars and people filled the streets with activity and created a vibrating buzz that swirled between rising smoke and smog.

Just past the church grounds, vendors sold paintings, sculptures, and souvenirs. At first I chose to avoid them; the thought of buying souvenirs seeming a little rude considering the circumstance gripping the country. Yet some of the trinkets beckoned me to come closer, and I convinced myself to look by reasoning that a purchase may help out the vendor and his family.

Upon closer inspection most of the wares proved cheaply made and touristy: shot glasses, bowls, pipes, and flags. As I browsed from shop to shop a goat mask caught my eye. In one of the smallest booths an older man sold wooden sculptures that clung to the wall with rusty, bent nails. The man had black, wrinkled skin that hung loosely from his small frame. White, wiry hair sat in erratic patches on the sides of his head. His eyes were sunk into his skull, and when he spoke his mouth revealed two gum lines devoid of all but a few teeth. He wore simple clothes: a thin, tan t-shirt, ragged, dirty jeans, and Adidas sandals that had fallen apart at the heel.

Behind him a single mask stood out among all the other sculptures. The large, empty eyes pierced right through me.

"It's a *trajos*," he stated in mottled English as he sensed a sale. "It's good luck or bad—depends on the owner."

He grabbed it off the wall and placed it on the table. I picked it up and felt its weight in my hands. It weighed more than I anticipated and was carved from one solid piece of wood. The colors had been formed through careful burning and rubbing dyes. I put it on my face and looked through the eye-holes. It fit the contour of my bones perfectly, and I felt the smooth and oily wood rub up against my skin. It looked strangely mystic, as if something lived inside the wood. I noticed him looking cautiously at my hands as I touched the mask as if holding it the wrong way could cause it to explode into flames.

I looked at the mask again. It represented something important to the man, something intangible I couldn't quite grasp, based on beliefs and traditions he may have practiced his entire life.

I gave him twenty dollars and took the mask.

"Thank you very much sir. Maybe the mask will bring you good luck."

I thought about my impending talk with Jana. "I hope so. Thank you, too."

I returned to the truck. Jana stood near the back and beckoned us to gather around her.

"We are going to the top of the mountain. There are some great views of the city," she looked at me and continued. "The home where Amber was born is at the top. I'd like to show it to Sean as well."

Other people bought souvenirs too. Purchases included paintings, sculptures, flags, postcards, and photos. A few people, including Faith and Luke, didn't buy anything. I took the mask and shoved it into my backpack between a towel and an extra roll of gauze before sliding the pack under my seat.

My eyes were glued to the cliffs as the truck climbed high up the mountain. Every hundred feet the road turned as it grew narrower and steeper to climb the mountain in a zigzag that seemed to hold onto the incline only by the most delicate and crippled connections. I held my breath each time the tires flirted with the edge of the road, silently fearing our fall to the bottom as a huge lump bobbled up and down in my throat. Eventually, Marcus stopped the truck. At this point, the road was reduced to a single lane too narrow for the big Daihatsu, so we went on foot.

Past the short stretch of narrow road we reached a plateau near the top of the mountain where the scenery changed. Homes turned extravagant and well protected. Electric fences, sentry guns, and massive stone walls were the norm. One even sported a helipad on the roof with a brand new copter parked neatly in the center.

Dozens of mountain flowers grew on the side of the road. As I walked I grabbed every kind I found as a small bouquet grew in my arms. Shades of light blue, red, violet, yellow, and orange mixed with petals like bells, domes, triangles, and circles. Bright colors painted the fields with a vibrant glow as tall grasses waved back and forth between patches of ancient stone piled haphazardly among the flora.

We walked over one last hill. Past it sat a sloping valley several hundred meters wide. Mountain peaks surrounded the valley and protected it from the outside world. It felt like looking at a hidden place, something ancient and long guarded. Tall grasses filled the fields and lined the road, which was paved with small stones. It continued to snake back and forth as it came close to driveways for huge mansions that dotted the landscape.

On the far left edge of the valley near the cliffs a short, narrow, one-story home slept behind rusted metal gates overgrown with shrubs and trees. The red roof sagged on top of the tan walls, and the few windows were glossed over with dust and time. Shrubs crowded the corners and crept up above the roof.

"That's our old home," Jana said.

The group picked up its pace as we got closer. A heavy chain bound with a padlock wrapped the front gate and sealed it shut. Planks nailed into the outer wall covered the front door and bars screwed into window wells prevented entry. Several of us hopped over the waist-high stone ledge and walked across the tile patio to look into the largest window. Settling dust muted the scene, but still, the brightly painted walls and kitchen cabinets provided clues to how the place had looked more than twenty years ago. I walked around to the back porch. It sat so close to the drop-off that looking over the edge caused my stomach to knot and my knees to tremble.

Jana and Faith stood in the front yard and stared intently at the home, reminiscing. Jana waved me over and put her arm around me as she spoke.

"This is it," she said as she hugged me. "It's such a blessing you get to see it. We may never see it again." She noticed the flowers. "What are those for?"

"I collected them on the way up. I think I'll give them to Amber as a present so she has something from here."

"What a great idea. Come with me, then."

She brought me to a small patch of blue flowers in the corner of the yard. The petals were small and triangular and formed a tall cone that covered most of the stem. Thorns lined the stalk in a helix that ran to the base and made them extremely hard to pick.

"We planted these when Amber was born. I gave birth to her in this house."

"Wow," was all I could utter, I couldn't think of anything else to say.

"Take one. Amber will love it."

We stood alone for a moment on the front porch of the house where Jana gave birth to Amber with the help of Bob. I looked at the flowers in my hand and then at the surroundings. The rest of the team examined the property out of earshot. Jana's eyes stayed on her house as she relived memories in her mind.

I took a deep breath and thought through my words. I'd had plenty of time to think about what to say and had spent a lot of time working alongside her. I knew she liked me, and Marcus and Bob both reassured me she'd say yes. I looked at her again. It amazed me how much Amber looked like her. They both wore scarves to wrap their hair. They owned airy dresses dyed with brilliant tropical colors. With the flowers in my hand intended for Amber I felt suddenly very nervous. Finally, I knew what to say.

"Jana..." I started, tapping her on the shoulder, "Can I talk to you?"

She turned her body but kept her eyes pinned to her home in the same way Amber did when she only half paid attention to me. She replied without looking. "Yes?"

"Well, I was..." Suddenly Faith interrupted as she yelled from across the gate for us to come. Jana immediately looked over to see what was going on. "Hold on one second, Sean," she replied. I hung my head as she walked away.

At the front of the yard a group of Haitians spoke with Faith and looked bewildered to see foreigners this high in the mountains. As Jana approached, an older man shook her hand and spoke in Creole.

"Good day. What are you doing here?" the man asked.

"I used to live here with my husband a long time ago."

"How long ago?"

"Oh, it's been at least twenty years now. My husband worked in the city." She pointed to Faith. "This is my daughter."

He looked at Jana and then at Faith and nodded slowly as he rubbed his chin with thumb and forefinger. After a few moments he pointed at Faith and spoke. "Luna?"

Her eyes widened and mouth dropped. He'd called her by her birth name, something only family and close friends used. "Yes?" she uttered, shaken.

A wide grin formed across his face. "I remember you as a little girl. You and your sister," he looked at Jana and continued. "You would take the girls for walks through the valley. How could I forget the only white family who lived up here?"

The rest of the team listened in, stunned and quiet at the unfolding scene.

"What else do you remember? Jana asked, her right hand on her chest and the other holding the man's hand.

"I remember your husband too, a doctor and a very friendly man. You were wonderful people. Where do you live now?"

"We moved to Puerto Plata. Luna is going to medical school, and my youngest daughter lives in America." She looked at me briefly. "That's her boyfriend." I gave a shy wave.

Faith pulled out her camera and took several photos with the man. I took a couple shots of the three long-forgotten neighbors, and they held each other shoulder to shoulder as they smiled for the camera. Afterwards Jana and Faith both hugged him, and he waved goodbye as he continued down the road with the rest of his family.

Night settled into the small valley. We needed to get back to the orphanage. I watched the evening transform the city on the walk back down the hill. As the sun retreated into the ocean, streetlights and headlights dotted the shadows until the entire city glowed. The blue sky turned purple and then black as it sucked the heat from the day into the great abyss above.

As we loaded into the transport the night stars illuminated the area. Faith sat with Jana in the front, and she rode with her head resting on her mother's shoulder the entire ride home. I slumped against the bench and leaned out the side as I looked skyward. I'd missed my chance to ask Jana.

The city grew quiet for once, and it allowed me a moment of peace. Instead of screams, sobs, or sirens I listened to the hum of passing cars and the chatter of working merchants. The cool breeze raced over my scalp and coaxed me to sleep as well.

I held the flowers in my hand, and I watched as the lights from buildings and cars rippled over the petals. Each one looked different from any I had bought before from the shops in town at home. Some wore jagged leaves and thin, long petals while others displayed fat, short petals that clung lazily to their stumpy stalks. Each one looked unique, though together they fit to create a diverse bunch that somehow reminded me of my surroundings. They were beautiful in a new way, different from roses or tulips. I'd picked them by hand, each a different step up the cliffs to the place where Amber was born. I couldn't wait to give them to her. I wrapped them in a few bunches of paper on the truck floor before pressing them in my backpack. When I got back to the camp I rolled them into a few of my dirty shirts before placing the package at the bottom of my bag.

I took my first real shower in almost two weeks with the recently fixed water line. Afterward I sat at the edge of the camp watching the stars. Exhausted from the day, I drifted off, sitting against the stone wall.

I awoke in the dark to the sound of drums. I shivered from the night air and dew that had formed on my skin. I stood and looked back toward camp. The power was turned off and the only glow came from bright stars. Looking out I couldn't see any activity in the city—it felt eerily quiet as if a celestial blanket covered the terrain in slumber. Then I heard them again. Beating drums. The sound felt rhythmic and fast, as if trying to recreate the stomping of a herd of buffalo, but screams, yells, and chants mixed with the beat in a hypnotic pattern.

Vodou. I hadn't heard it before but I knew residents practiced it. My stomach froze up, and I suddenly felt like being watched. Just listening to the ritual felt like trespassing. I grew afraid from the noise and paranoid that someone would catch me. I looked at the circle of tents huddled less than fifty yards from where I stood. My feet were frozen to the ground. The drums grew louder. I sprinted toward the tents in utter panic. Every horror movie and scary moment I'd ever experienced appeared in my thoughts and drowned out rationality. I ripped open the front zipper of the tent and hopped inside. Jared woke up.

"What the hell are you doing?"

I felt embarrassed. "Nothing, just had to go out to pee."

Half asleep, he didn't question me. "Okay whatever, just be quiet."

"Sorry."

A few minutes passed. "Hey Sean," Jared asked from inside his sleeping bag, "Do you hear drums?"

"Yeah." I answered, trying to keep calm.

He went back to sleep. I stayed awake listening to them. At least I had my tent.

Saturday, January 23rd, 2010

8:55am

Port Au Prince, Haiti

We reached another tent city just before nine the next morning. We'd stopped visiting the overcrowded hospitals completely. Jana wanted to explore and find people in need that lacked the ability to reach hospitals, so we drove to a new tent city each day.

The inhabitants didn't overwhelm us with requests when we set up camp, so eventually Jana split us into smaller teams to find those in need. Piles of garbage littered the site like artillery craters in a battlefield while rotten, putrid food sat in heaps against tarp and blanket shelters under the sun. Each tent was packed with people and smelled terrible, even when I tried breathing through my mouth. Human refuse sat in gutters and potholes while swill ran from them down the street into other camps. Bloodied mattresses and blankets covered dumpsters filled with wet cardboard, twisted metal, broken glass, used medical supplies, and empty containers of aid packages.

I knew the site had probably started off looking much better in the first few days, but the absence of any law or civic services had turned it into a ghetto full of desperate souls. After the camp learned of our presence, people approached from all sides begging for clothing, food, and water—but not medical attention. Parents dragged their children to me and used them as leverage to persuade me, but I just didn't possess anything to give. At first only eyes followed as I walked through the camp, but eventually people did too. I'd grown accustomed to standing out, but suddenly I felt more like a target. Nerves twisted my stomach as fear crept closer without any real reason to believe it.

I reached an old tree with a dozen small shelters tucked underneath, the entrances facing a central fire pit. I approached an elderly man sitting next to the fire with a young boy and asked if anyone needed medical attention, but he responded by gesturing his hand to his mouth and then pointing at my pack. I gave them two broken granola bars. As I did I noticed the man looking behind me, concerned. I felt my hat suddenly pulled off my head, and then someone turned me around.

Three large, muscular Haitian men blocked my way out. They looked well fed, wore nice clothing and jewelry, and kept long dreadlocks. The man in the middle held my hat and put it on his head to taunt me.

"What you got for me too, brother?"

One of the others nodded in agreement, while the third stood quietly and crossed his arms.

"Nothing. What do you want?" I replied calmly, trying to restrain myself from panic.

"What you got in your pockets? You got more food? I'm hungry too."

I pointed to the elderly man. "I gave him the rest of my food."

He took a small step forward. As he shifted his weight his shirt lifted slightly to reveal a large machete that clung to his waist by a leather belt.

"What's in your wallet then? I'm hungry. Give me money for food."

I pulled out my dummy wallet without any hesitation. I left my passport, credit card, and cash back at the orphanage. I brought one with twenty dollars, an expired credit card, and ID. I considered it enough to satisfy a mugger but not a big deal if stolen. I handed it to him while keeping my eyes on the ground. He opened it and then threw it on the ground with my hat.

"That's it? Where's your money?" he demanded.

Sweat formed down the center of my back as I froze. I tried to act calm as I picked up my hat from the ground. I stood up and spoke softly, feigning confidence.

"It's all I got. I'm just here to help the wounded. I'm just a volunteer, man."

He looked me over and noticed my backpack and cargo shorts.

"Empty your pockets. You'd better not be lying."

I emptied them and pulled the fabric inside out. A pack of gum, a few coins and some receipts fell to the ground. I thanked God I'd left everything at camp. I opened up my pack revealing a towel, a few medical supplies, and a Nalgene bottle. Luckily, I'd left the mask back at the orphanage.

The man grew upset as he looked over my things. I feared the worst. The thought of a machete entering my gut or hacking off a limb quickly replayed a hundred times over in my head. I wanted to cry. I wanted to go home. I looked around as others watched the scene unfold. I believed no one wanted to help me. I felt betrayed. Would they just stand there and let this happen?

As if my thoughts were suddenly heard by the crowd around us, a few men approached the three standing over me. The thugs looked around to look at the others before questioning me again, this time in a worried tone.

"Where's your camp?" he asked.

I decided to lie and pointed in the wrong direction. I waded deep into the settlement and wanted to buy time while they looked. They took off in the opposite direction. Several of the men followed. As soon as they left I sprinted toward the group. Out of breath, I approached Jana as she cleaned staples on a young girl's scalp.

"Jana," I spat. She stopped her work and looked at me.

"What happened?"

"I almost got mugged."

She paused. "What do you mean almost?"

"These guys cornered me and wanted money. I didn't have any, and then they wanted to know where our camp was. I pointed them in the wrong direction, but I'm sure they'll find us soon."

She acted swiftly and announced to everyone around. "Group, pack up. We're out of here right now."

We grabbed the supplies and shoved them into our bags. As we worked, people in the area grew loud and angry. They didn't understand why we suddenly packed to leave. A man asked Jana and she told him my story.

We finished just as the three men reached our group. I pointed them out to Jana who in turn showed the elderly Haitian man that helped us set up camp. He pointed as a few other men that waited with their injured wives and children approached the muggers. The muggers retreated back into the maze of shelters, but a good-sized group followed them. We got to the truck and sped away. My hands shook and I edged to the brink of tears.

Marcus drove through the streets, weaving in and out of traffic and around piles of wreckage. We got back to the orphanage around four, the first time we'd returned with sunlight to spare. I sat with some children in the front courtyard but stayed quiet. Faith approached and sat down next to me.

"How you doing?"

I tried my best to fake a smile, but put my hand out to show it quake. "I'm a bucket of nerves. I'm tired, and I'm ready to go home. You?"

She paused for a moment before replying. "I wish I could stay longer. Today was bad, but it doesn't mean it's always going to be like that. You have to understand just how desperate these people are. If you had a wife or a child starving or dying and you saw someone you figured was rich, would you feel bad stealing from him?"

I tried to reverse the situation as she suggested, but I struggled to think clearly. After a few deep breaths I tried to think about how looked to them.

"No, you're right. I'd definitely steal for my family." I paused. "But I wouldn't beat someone up or kill them."

"You sure? Have you ever been that desperate? And did they actually hurt you, or did they just threaten to?"

She made a point, and in a way I felt bad for reacting the way I did. "They didn't actually hurt me at all."

"They just wanted you to know they would so you'd give them your stuff. To them, you're so rich that they figure you wouldn't miss a couple hundred bucks. I mean let's be honest; you spent a couple thousand in Vegas last year, right? You were upset, but you got over it in a few weeks. If one of them had a thousand dollars, they could feed their family for a very long time. You spent it on blackjack."

She was right. It changed my perspective. It seemed I still lacked the ability to see things from another's point of view, even after all the time spent in Port-au-Prince. To me it felt like a betrayal, but she managed to see the reality of the situation.

"You're right. I'm sorry we packed up early."

"Don't worry about it; there wasn't much for us to do anyway. The medical relief, or at least the first part, is pretty much over."

I nodded and then put my head between my knees as she rubbed my shoulder.

"So when are you going to ask my mom?"

She grinned and I realized she'd successfully changed the subject. I got excited just thinking about it. "I missed my chance at your house when that guy showed up. That would have been perfect. And I've tried a few times at night, but it never feels right. I've got to do it soon."

She agreed, "Yeah, you do. We're leaving tomorrow, or at least trying to. She thinks it's too dangerous now, and we've been here for quite a while. Marcus will take us to the airport, and then he will drive the truck home."

"Guess I'm out of time, then."

She winked at me while she stood and reached out her arms to help me to my feet, "Not yet." She gave me a hug. "I can't wait for you to be my brother! You really are a great guy. Just remember that when you ask her, and you'll be fine."

Sunday, January 24th, 2010
7:30am
Port Au Prince, Haiti

Lucas and his mother tied folded sheets, blankets, clothes, and tarps together using twine and secured the stacks to a pair of wheelbarrows. They'd decided together to move out of the city and into a refugee center located on the outskirts. People spoke of shelters, food, water, and electricity for anyone displaced.

He'd spent the last few days dismantling every part of their temporary home and it surprised him just how much they'd recovered from the wreckage. Between dishes, photographs, toiletries, furniture, food, and building supplies, it took more than a full day to load everything they still owned. After taping the stacks to the top of the pile, he draped a blue tarp over each wheelbarrow. He cut holes using a steak knife and ran rope through them and under the hull as he slowly secured the contents underneath the shell.

When he finished, the carts resembled bloated blueberries ready to pop. He tried to lift the heavier one—it budged, but barely. The other weighed much less, filled with fabrics, photos, and food so that his mother could push it during their ten-mile journey across the city.

He helped Tasha stand with the weight on her back and then put on his own. It sat uneven, and he needed to slouch to

275

the right to keep it from falling over. He looked at his home one last time, and then picked up his load to leave.

They descended the first hill backwards, putting themselves below the wheelbarrows and pulling them slowly to the bottom. When they reached level ground the road stretched northeast. They followed it at a steady pace and swung around potholes, rubble, and parked cars. Sweat formed on Lucas' neck and soaked the shirt under his pack before the sun even breached the mountain range.

After an hour into the journey they'd made it a mile. The road twisted over sharp hills and through steep declines that made moving at more than a crawl impossible. They learned only a few minutes into the trip that Tasha lacked the strength to carry her load, so they took turns moving one cart at a time with Tasha guarding one while Lucas moved another. Each exchange presented a gamble that left at least one of the carts within eyesight but out of reach.

His mother limped past him toward the heavier cart ahead.

"Mom, you're limping again." He'd noticed before but kept silent. It had grown more pronounced, and she seemed on the verge of tears with every step. Even with the brace on her leg and the crutches she could barely move.

"I'm okay, don't worry about me," she retorted, holding her head high and continuing to the cart alone. Frustrated with her pride, Lucas looked away and reached the lighter cart. He picked it up and pushed it quickly across the street and down the alley to the first.

As he turned the corner he saw people crowded around his wheelbarrow. Two men picked through Lucas and Tasha's cart as she cried and pleaded for them to stop. They made a mess of their stuff as they randomly threw things on the ground and pocketed trinkets, silverware, and food. Lucas put down the second cart and approached the older men. One of them stopped rummaging as Lucas approached and turned to face him directly as he closed in.

"Back off kid," he said as he pointed a metal rod. The other pulled food and water out of the wheelbarrow and put it into a trash bag. "You don't want to get hurt."

Lucas' mother stood on the side of the alley in disbelief as the other man stole everything they had. "How can you do this?" she shouted at the man with the pole.

"Shut up," was all he replied, turning his attention back to Lucas. "Get over there," he shouted, pointing at the wall. "Her too."

Lucas felt the blood boil and rise into his neck as sweat flooded his palms. Rage and fear filled his heart. He couldn't believe what he saw. To his left, some rubble covered the alley ground and up against the wall. Most of them looked too big to lift, but several resembled softballs. He did as they said but pushed his body up against the wall with his hands behind him. As they rummaged he pried a chunk from the wall.

Suddenly Lucas took a step forward and brought the rock to his side in an iron grasp. The man turned and laughed.

"What you gonna do with that?" he said, taunting with the pole and waving it in his face. "You throw that and I'll beat you to death, you hear me?"

Lucas acted faster than the man could react. In an instant the chunk left his hand and landed square on the man's forehead. His skin split as blood spewed from the impact and momentarily blinded the thief. He reeled back and held his face with his free hand. He attempted to gain balance after the brutal blow, but before he could recover, Lucas threw another chunk. It hit him in the shoulder, knocking the pole from his hand as he grasped fruitlessly at anything for balance. Lucas leapt forward and grabbed another rock before bringing it down hard on the man's chin. He screamed out in pain and fell back. Lucas looked up to go at the other thief, but he'd already run away with a half-full trash bag slung over his shoulder.

Lucas dropped the rock and looked at the man on the ground. Blood and dirt covered his face from the assault. He wore tattered rags and his skin clung tightly to his bones. He cried profusely while shielding his face with his beaten hands. Moments ago he'd appeared fierce and frightening, a thief that aimed to take everything that belonged to them. Now he just looked pitiful.

Before he could stop her, Tasha pulled out a Red Cross container from the wheelbarrow with a jug of water and carried it to the man. She dropped the supplies at his feet. Suddenly Lucas saw the truth. The man, like them, was just another victim of the earthquake, perhaps trying to steal for his wife and children. The man didn't move from his spot. Instead, he rocked back and forth, quietly sobbing with the gift of supplies now wrapped in his arms and covered with thin trickles of blood. Lucas pulled a rag from his pile and knelt before the man to offer it.

"Here, you're bleeding everywhere. Hold this to your head."

The man looked up at him with a mixture of tears and blood covering his dirt stained face. "Thank you." He balled up the cloth and pressed it against his forehead and immediately turned it a dark red. "Why are you helping me? I wanted to rob you."

Lucas shrugged.

He helped the man to his feet and watched him walk down the alley the way they'd come while holding tightly to the water and food Lucas' mother had given him. He limped into the light at the end before turning left onto the busy street.

"Let's keep moving mom. The outpost is just a few miles past the airport."

Sunday, January 24th 2010
6:30am
Port Au Prince, Haiti

I woke early and helped Marcus pack the truck after we gave our remaining supplies to the orphanage. After a small breakfast the team took pictures of the compound, each other, and the children. We took a group picture, the "Crossroads" sign clearly visible behind us. I said goodbye to the children. It was time to go to the airport.

We left the compound just before nine. The blue, cloudless sky provided a peaceful canopy for the dry, dusty city. We dropped off Luke at the hospital. He'd chosen to stay for a few weeks more to help.

During the trip, workers had cleared the rubble off several of the major streets and allowed the flow of traffic to increase exponentially, but nonetheless we sat still on a main artery. Motorcycles zoomed past and people shouted, but the big truck kept still.

Eager customers swamped several small shops newly opened in front of two collapsed buildings on the side of the road. The sound of bartering and salesmen had replaced screams and cries over a few days' time. The two buildings behind the newly formed market sat covered in dust and rubble like a fish skeleton in a piranha's keep. Like a seed that grows on a stump of a cut tree, this fledgling market thrived on an otherwise decimated street to breathe life and hope into many that survived in the surrounding area.

The truck crept down the avenue toward the airport a foot at a time. Sweltering heat penetrated the metal roof and left me drenched in sweat. Dust and dirt from traffic hung in the dry, stagnant air before sticking to me, covering me with a thin film. I rubbed my arm against my leg and left a faint streak. The rest of the group appeared likewise deflated and beaten by the long trip. We sat quietly and looked out from the bed as we rode.

A crowd of Haitian men yelled on the side of the road. They spilled into the street and blocked a few of the lanes. It grew rapidly into a feverish mob as violent screams and cheers grew in volume. I moved to the other side of the truck with several others from our group. As we passed them they banged their hands on the side and screamed at us.

Suddenly, one of the men tried to jump in the side of the truck along with several others. They held onto the right and rear of the bed, pulled along as we drove forward. Faith stood and yelled at the men in Creole. "Get off the truck, we are missionaries!" Eventually they let go.

A mile away from the airport the traffic completely stopped. As I sat at the very back of the truck I watched hundreds of people file their way down the road. They wore packs, carried luggage, pushed carts, and pulled small wagons full of what looked like everything they could carry. As the situation in the city worsened, we heard that many people had decided to leave in search of aid at one of the many relief camps set up outside the city. The sight of the massive convoy brewed thoughts of what the exodus from Egypt may have looked like. I tried to imagine being forced to leave my home, and what I would take with me if I could only bring what I could carry myself.

After a few minutes in the standstill, Marcus turned off the truck. The stillness of the air and the heat radiated by the metal roof above us tried to cook us if we sat still, so several of us decided to get off the truck for a few minutes to escape the oven of a bed.

As I stood by the truck, my back against the side and my feet in line with the rear tire, I tried to keep my eyes to the ground to avoid eye contact with the many that wanted to escape the city. Just being who I was made it embarrassing to stand there; every Haitian there knew that I was a volunteer and probably had a good home somewhere. When I chose to leave the city it would be on a plane, and not just to another set of tents.

Suddenly someone tapped me on the shoulder as he tried to say hello in very rough English. I looked up, and at first did not recognize the teenager standing in front of me. He pushed a wheelbarrow filled to the brim with things, and he helped a woman who I remembered was his mother. I'd met him at the beginning of the trip at a hospital near the orphanage. His mother suffered from terrible wounds on her chest and a broken leg. Now, less than two weeks since the initial quake, she was walking with crutches.

"Hello," I said, shaking his hand as he stopped.

"Lucas," he said, pointing to his own chest. I remembered him. He was the one that had told me about his journey to the hospital. I'd heard about his motorbike, and knew he planned to go to the refugee centers.

He looked exhausted. Dried blood covered parts of his face and his arms, and large rips reduced his shirt to rags and revealed fresh cuts. I pointed to his chest and the blood, then asked him what happened in very basic French.

"Quoi?" I asked as I pointed at his wounds.

He tightened his fists into balls and got into a defensive stance before falling on the ground. Then he hugged the wheel-barrow before punching the air and going back to hugging the wheelbarrow. His mother wrapped her arms around the supplies and then put one arm in the air as if to deflect a blow. From the increasing tension in the city I didn't need more hints. It was clear that someone had attacked them to take their things. People had grown desperate, just like the three that tried to attack me the day before.

I grabbed a few waters from the back of the truck and gave them to him without letting other Haitians see the gesture. Our group didn't need our vehicle ransacked this close to going home. He hid them quickly and smiled, saying "thank you" a few times before going to pick up the handles of the wheelbar-row. He wiped his forehead with his completely filthy shirt.

I felt my Ravens cap keeping my hair cool. The morning air soaked it with sweat, but it shielded me from the sun. It kept me safe from the weather, helped me hide when I didn't want to be somewhere, and gave me something to fumble with when I didn't know what else to do. I pulled it off and inspected it. It looked like I'd owned it for my entire life. It fit me perfectly, but it looked awful. Part of me wanted to take it home, hang it up somewhere, and point to it whenever I told people about the experience. But then I looked at Lucas and I knew where it belonged.

I put out my arm and offered the hat to him. For a moment he hesitated, looking as if he wondered if I knew what I was doing. I shook it slightly, and looked at it briefly before looking at him again. He took it and twirled it in his hand. When he noticed the Raven on the front, he pointed to it before looking at me and smiling, saying "Ravens good." He pulled it over his brow and instantly looked steadier with the sun out of his face. His mother looked at me and said "Thank you" before limping away next to her son. I could see the purple of the hat until he shuffled around a corner ahead. Then he, and my hat, were both gone.

A few minutes later we heard traffic move ahead of us. Our team got back into the truck to join the slow crawl to the airport.

The truck pulled into the roundabout of Port-au-Prince International Airport. Dozens of U.S. National Guardsmen stood at the entrance with automatic weapons strapped across their chests. Each person jumped out and approached the guards while protected by a flank of soldiers who kept the Haitian crowds away. I gave Jared a big hug before I walked into the airport. He'd fly home to St. Thomas through Santo Domingo. Marcus gave me a hug just before he got in the truck. "Good luck with Jana," he said just before closing the door. After everyone entered the airport, Jared and Marcus got in the truck, turned the first corner of the roundabout, and disappeared into the chaos.

We walked to the guards posted at the entrance. Two lines formed: one for US citizens, and another for everyone else. Megan split with everyone and followed a guard through the other entrance for Canadians a few yards down the outer wall of the building. After flashing our passports we shuffled into a small, dimly lit room. People shoved behind us and pushed us into those stopped in front.

The small, ten-foot-by-ten-foot room was stuffed with over fifty people and their luggage. I didn't have enough room to breathe. When the doors closed behind us it smelled sour. Thick, heavy, and full of sweat, the air choked my throat to create the sensation of drowning amongst the crowd. I took in small breaths and slowed down my lungs to remain calm. My claustrophobia took hold of my sanity for a moment until my eyes adjusted to the light.

We stood in a line that wrapped back and forth on itself like a tightly wound spring. It ran into itself at every turn and confused the waiting crowd while allowing impatient travelers to push and shove past others. On the far side I noted the top of a metal detector and beyond that, sunlight from outdoors. We shuffled inch by inch as we crept around each turn and got closer to the end.

After an hour I reached the security checkpoint. The guard pointed to a bucket where I placed my wallet and phone. Without warning, a bulky Haitian man grabbed my pack and rummaged through my dirty clothing and personal belongings like trash bags. To my embarrassment, a woman pulled out my toiletries in front of the crowd and inspected them. I could feel my face hot with blood as I blushed. Suddenly I remembered the flowers. I hoped to God they wouldn't find them. I packed them deep in a roll of dirty clothes. If they found the bouquet I knew they would take it.

Moments passed in what felt like days why I prayed for them to miss the flowers. That was all I wanted to take home. Just before they got to the bottom of the pack, the man running the line told me to move forward. I crept towards him while keeping my eye on the pack, continually hoping for a break. I wanted to take those flowers home. Finally satisfied, they crammed everything back in the pack and threw it to the other side of the metal detector. Another guard ushered me through it before handing back my wallet and phone. Continually pushed by people behind me, I threw my shoes in front of me as I dragged my bag outside.

The tarmac was filled by the hundreds in a line that extended endlessly. Tents sat every hundred feet or so and provided shelter under the shade of their canopies. We played cards, talked about the trip and dreamed about home while we waited in the standstill. As morning shifted to early afternoon I watched several American C-17 cargo planes come and go, bringing crates of supplies and taking back full loads of people packed in the hold. Their hulls seemed thicker than buildings and the wings wider than a football field. The windows for the pilots were little more than dots against the gigantic blanket of dark grey that painted the hull.

Hours passed as our group crept toward the front of the line. The shadows grew as the sun turned a deep orange against the western mountain range and the air temperature cooled my skin. Twelve hours had passed since we'd arrived and the day drew to a close. Plane traffic dropped significantly in the evening and I feared spending the night on the ground. Rumors spread that anyone not on a plane needed to come back the next day and gamble with a completely new line. One C-17, the *March*, remained at the airport. For several hours its engines idled and filled the air with the stable hum of turbines.

As the sun nestled into the mountains, the soldiers guarding the line received an order to allow people on board. All at once, the crowd found out and pushed forward to make the line compress like an accordion. As quickly as it began the soldiers stopped it, shouting orders while posturing to show us their guns. I doubted they ever wanted to use them, but the visual worked on the crowd.

I scanned the queue that wrapped around the wing of the plane and ended at the cargo hold in the rear. A slow but steady flow of people entered, but I stood too far away to see just how much space remained. As I neared the loading ramp the line slowed to a crawl as men crammed luggage and people inside. Behind me the line stretched to the security room—at least two hundred yards away.

When fewer than thirty people separated us from the back door, a soldier signaled to the others to turn back the rest of the line. My heart dropped. People shouted angrily and moved in and out of the line while pushing those in front to move closer to the plane. The soldiers beckoned us to remain calm.

Minutes stretched endlessly as we stood near the bay door. Soldiers piled luggage from the ground into the plane and filled up the ramp. People sat in long rows on the floor. A pilot walked down and spoke with the soldier at the front who in turn marched along the waiting queue and counted people aloud. Each time he pointed at someone I feared he'd stop, perhaps even one or two people ahead of our group. To my relief he passed us and continued to count.

"We're in, guys," Dean said.

My heart jumped at the thought of going home and seeing Amber. I wanted to hug and kiss her so badly. I wanted to hug my mom again and tell my dad about everything. I wanted to sleep in my mattress and take a shower in my bathroom. I thought about saying goodbye to Amber at the airport and promising to come home. I remembered suddenly the first time she'd returned to Pennsylvania after traveling for a few months. When I met her at the airport, the rush of holding her once again had almost buckled my knees. I wanted to relive that moment again, and knew that I would soon.

The man stopped less than twenty people after us and waved both of his hands at the rest of the line. Soldiers stepped into action and ushered everyone else back to the terminal.

At the top of the ramp I dropped my bags on a tall, unsteady pile of luggage that two soldiers tied down with heavy cords. Only a few seats remained open in front along the walls of the plane. The elderly, handicapped, and pregnant got real seats first. The lion's share of the crowd sat on the steel floor with only cargo straps to hold. Their shoulders touched and their feet brushed up against the people in front of them.

As each of us entered the hold a soldier directed us to a spot to sit. Children slept on their parents' laps to make as much room as possible. I settled between two older Haitian men near the front. One smelled terrible, and the other slept on the ground, pushing into the little space given to me. The man behind me insisted on straightening his legs into my area as well. I tried not to get upset. I'd gotten a free ride home. Soon I'd hold Amber again.

I placed my pack on the ground and sat against it to push against the man's feet. He swore in protest, but I didn't let up. Eventually he pulled his legs back to their proper spot. Every inch of the plane was packed with people in a tangled mess of arms and legs that almost appeared as one giant organism. The cargo hatch closed and the lights inside dimmed. The crew stood at the front of the plane to take pictures of the crowd, and I managed to crack a smile for their cameras and give a thumbs-up.

The engine roared as the plane moved. It jerked everyone on the ground, and the man in front of me fell into my lap. Without any windows and the lights off the sudden movement disoriented me. Most people fell asleep during the ride to Orlando, but I stayed awake and looked around using the dim green lights as I thought about home and Amber.

After the short flight, we unloaded on the tarmac in Orlando in the middle of the night flanked by police, military, and paramedics. We landed well after the airport had finished its last regular flight for the night, but dozens of people stayed late to see us arrive safely and welcome us back. I lost track of the team while submerged in the massive crowd that filed inside, but it didn't take long after entering the terminal that I spotted a few of them. Jana and Faith sat against the wall while Dean stood beside them looking for others. One by one we found each other until the entire team reunited.

We continued into the main entrance and through a Red Cross station set up to receive the flight. They gave out Gatorade, sandwiches, fresh fruit, granola bars, water, and many other types of food as well as toiletries, soap, blankets, and clean shirts for people to use while waiting for the next flight home. I took a giant apple, several sandwiches, and a Gatorade. I swallowed them before my tongue got a chance to enjoy the taste. I nearly choked on a chunk of apple and forced myself to slow down so I could properly digest the intake.

The team made camp by a row of water fountains in the main terminal of the Orlando airport. The Red Cross gave out cots and blankets to spend the night, and the airport staff dimmed the lights in areas to allow weary travelers to sleep. Some stores, including a Starbucks and a McDonalds, stayed open through the night. I downed a few orders of French fries and inhaled a chocolate shake.

After a few hours of restless sleep the sun rose again and flights started to come and go. The Red Cross found us connections home, and several airlines offered free trips to anyone coming back from Haiti.

Jana and Faith found a flight home. They'd slept throughout the night, but I'd stayed up mulling over the final part of my trip—asking Jana. No matter what I did at this point it wouldn't be the perfect and beautiful exchange I planned, but I needed to do it before they left. I couldn't think of a graceful way to pull it off. How could I possibly get her alone, even for a moment? My head hurt from the stress. If I didn't ask her before she left she'd find out I'd asked Bob and not her. I needed to make the time and get it done, even if gracelessly and with sour timing. I looked at my watch. It was four-thirty. They were scheduled to depart on a six o'clock flight. I wanted to wait until she woke up to leave. Then I'd ask and go home too.

I woke suddenly to someone shaking my shoulders. It was Faith.

"Wake up Sean, we're about to leave," she whispered as my eyes slowly opened. I'd drifted off at some point and had fallen deep into a dream when she woke me. I found it hard to focus my vision until she spoke again.

"Sean, get up. We're leaving. You need to ask her now!"

I sat up and looked around. Cindy, Cameron, Dean, and Justin had left while I slept. Later they told me I'd looked so peaceful that it seemed better to let me rest. The picture they sent later showed me flat on my stomach on the bare airport floor, a backpack and dirty t-shirt covering my face as my legs and arms sprawled out in all directions. I didn't look peaceful; I looked dead.

Jana was finishing putting her stuff into a backpack when I stood up. I gave Faith a hug.

"Thanks for waking me up. I would have missed it."

"I wouldn't have let that happen."

The terminal had filled with people. Businessmen, families on vacation in Disney, and airport employees meshed with the hundreds of Haitians to fill the room up and make it loud, even at the early hour. I walked the few feet to Jana and scratched the back of my head to think, waiting for her to see me.

"It was so nice of you to come, Sean," she said in my ear. "I'm so glad Amber found you. You are the right guy for her." She pulled away and looked at me one last time. Faith came up and stood next to her and looked at the big digital clock streaming departures just over our heads.

"Jana…" I interrupted before she could turn and leave, "can I ask you something?"

She turned back and smiled. She scanned me up and down for a moment as if looking at my insides and trying to see something I couldn't. In the airport and out of the mission setting she looked, if only for a few moments, like just Amber's mom again.

"I've wanted to talk for a while, but it just never seemed like the right time." I looked for words while I fumbled with my hands. I felt nervous, terrified, and excited. More than anything I grew upset that none of my plans had gone the way I wanted and I'd forced myself into such an unmemorable place to ask. Bob had his moment in Jimani, Marcus while overlooking a cliff. I didn't get the bonfire with singing and dancing, or a great dinner with everyone gathered around like I pictured before I left. The time had gone by in a flash filled with moments of grief and sadness but also moments of bliss and joy. I tried to think of the words while wasting precious seconds in the busy corridor. I continued to pick at my nails with my fingers as I looked down in my nervous state.

Then I saw her hands. All of a sudden she reached out and put her hands over mine to quell their trembling.

"Yes, Sean," she said with a warm smile on her face and tears forming in her eyes. "We'd really love to have you in our family."

In that moment I felt all the stress I'd carried during the trip suddenly lift from my shoulders and evaporate into the air. I could see the future and my life with Amber. I didn't reply, but just put my arms around her and gave a hug. Faith put her arms around both of us as all three of us stood alone among the huge crowd going about their morning business. In that moment I couldn't see anyone else.

Monday, January 25th 2010

3:50pm

Harrisburg, PA

The plane landed and I shuffled off with the rest of the crowd. Most of the travelers were returning from Disney World or the Florida beaches. No one asked me why I looked dirty or tired, and I thanked the stars for that mercy. I knew I lacked the strength or will to try and explain my journey to anyone. I only wanted one thing: to see Amber.

As I rounded the final corner to the exit I saw her standing in the middle of the terminal. Her blonde, curly hair shone like a candle in a dark room, and her small figure jumped up and down as soon as she saw me. She ran, much faster than I expected, before jumping on me and forcing all my bags to the ground. Everyone looked. All at once I felt embarrassed, overwhelmed, and loved.

"I missed you, I love you, I'm so glad you're home!" she repeated as she dotted my forehead and cheeks with dozens of quick, small kisses. My bones creaked from exhaustion, but I tried my best to hug her back.

"I love you too," I replied as I kissed her on the forehead. "It's been a heck of a trip."

Instantly she knew how to deal with me, something that no one else could have done as effortlessly. She didn't ask me questions about the trip, or about how I felt, or about what I'd done. She only asked me one question before kissing me again.

"Where do you want to go for dinner?"

"Let's go home and make breakfast food. I'd love to just sit on the couch for a while."

She gave a knowing grin and hugged me again before grabbing my bags and helping me through the door to our car. The cold air licked my face like a punch to the stomach as I stepped outside. The shorts and t-shirt I wore suddenly did nothing, and I wished for just a little of the Haitian heat. She'd already heated up the car. She'd already bought a small bottle of Coca-Cola and a candy bar and put it on the passenger's seat. I reclined, closed my eyes, and fell asleep until she got me home. To what, I planned, would eventually be our home.

Tuesday, February 2nd, 2010
5:30am
Stuarts Draft, VA

I woke in my hotel bed in Virginia to a cold January morning. I week had passed since I returned from Haiti. I stayed in bed to keep my skin warm against the plush sheets and comforter. A gray light penetrated the room from outside as the sun slept just under the eastern horizon. I sat up against the headboard and looked around. The huge hotel room felt too big. The full kitchen sat stuffed with stainless steel appliances, blue ceramic bowls and cups, and marble countertops. A dozen pillows sat on a brand new white couch that faced a forty-six-inch flat screen television propped on a desk that spun 360 degrees to face the bed. I lay on a king size mattress covered with thick blankets that smelled clean and felt smooth. I stayed in the same room as always, but somehow it had grown bigger and grander than before.

I turned on the TV. A commercial for a house cleaner blared and a cartoon bald man helped a white housewife make her toilets and sinks shine until they reflected light with a glittery effect. Next a commercial for a diner played and panned over tables covered in pancakes, waffles, eggs, sausage, bacon, and toast—all of it covered in syrup and jelly while steam came off the freshly cooked banquet for $6.99.

When the news turned back on I watched a story about Haiti. The media had already started to pull away the coverage, but a few of the stations ran stories about the aftermath. I listened to a report about outposts that mission groups had set up just outside the borders of Port-au-Prince to take in Haitian refugees. Already it seemed as if they would be disasters. So many injured Haitians fled to the refugee centers that supplies of food, water, and medical supplies ran scarce. I watched interviews with Haitians, looking for anyone I recognized. I remembered a few of the people telling me they'd planned to go to the centers, and I hoped that they'd changed their minds.

I skipped breakfast and reached my car through a side door to avoid running into fellow employees. I'd started work a few days earlier at the plant and had already grown tired of retelling my experience. People either wanted to hear happy news or didn't want to hear about it all. I lacked anything positive to say anyway.

It took over a month for me to finally break down and cry about the experience. For a while I just didn't think about it at all. My mind had undergone a numbing effect, and I just focused on work. When not at the plant I entered a state of pure nothingness where I zoned out and focused into the distance. I caught myself doing it again and again during the day and at work. I tried to play video games, hang out with friends, and work on my house. Only Amber could relate to me, and she tried from the first moment I returned home to make me open up. She understood, unlike anyone else could, the way I felt. She held me the few times I woke with nightmares and always answered the phone when I called depressed from work. I often felt like a ghost floating from spot to spot, not really working or doing anything except watching time tick by.

A few weeks after I returned to work, my boss received complaints about me. I lacked the drive to care about my work. Even lunch with Nathan felt different. He led the conversation for most of our outings after I got back. He spoke about his new girlfriend or work, but he never asked me about Haiti. Much later he told me it didn't seem right, and if I wanted to talk about it I needed to bring it up on my own. I always silently thanked him for that. Being allowed to sit quietly at lunch while he carried on the conversation gave me the opportunity to slowly gel back into the daily beat.

As the weeks went by I grew accustomed to clean water, ample food, and a big home to call my own. I washed my car, spent more time on the computer, and even started to bite my nails again. I forgot about the bumpy rides in the Daihatsu and cold bucket showers. I grew queasy around even minor scrapes and cuts again.

I held onto many things from the experience, though. I remember the look on a man's face as his arm or leg is amputated, with only a rope to clench his teeth upon and several people to hold him down. I remember the smell of water ripe with human waste and refuse being used for drinking or bathing by Haitian children. I remember the sound of screaming, both in emotional pain and in physical agony—often at the same time. I remember the taste of dirt and dust soaking my tongue. I remember the feeling of a sudden grab from a desperate and dying person on my arm—and the realization that there was nothing I could do for her.

I also remember the songs the women sang in Jimani to help their children sleep that first terrible night. I can still see the sun rising on the eastern mountains in the desert as it painted the sky and ground with colors I've never seen since. I can relive the sensation when Amber's parents said yes, and the excitement from seeing her first home and the garden that Jana planted where I took a flower. I remember the faces of the children at the orphanage, their bright smiles breaking the darkness as they played and jumped around us. I can still hear the songs their guardians sang each night to put them to sleep as they lay under the stars.

While my time in Haiti demanded a lot of strength and tears, it also gave back love and peaceful evenings. Where I spent nights helping treat gruesome surgeries that left nightmares, I got back a sense of accomplishment and belonging. Where I wore my body down from stress, malnourishment, dehydration, and heavy lifting I got back dreams with deep sleep and an appreciation for the life I have in America. Where I lost my ignorance of the developing world I also gained a second family and a wife. Haiti gave me a new perspective. That gift keeps me happier longer, content with less, and smiling often.

Haiti owes me nothing. I'm in her debt.

Epilogue

Tuesday, December 25, 2012
7:30pm
Puerto Plata, Dominican Republic

Almost three years have passed since the experience in Haiti during the earthquake in 2010, and yet I still remember vividly the trip, the experiences, and the people. Only a few things have had such a profound impact in my life, but the opportunity to help the Crossroads team during the earthquake forever changed my outlook on my life and the state of the world.

After returning from Haiti I learned that Bob finished out his work at the outreach center in Jimani until the staff stabilized most of the patients. His honey-based burn and infection treatment prevented amputations, and his skills as a doctor saved the lives of many during that first week. After the bulk of the work was finished he returned to Puerto Plata to continue his work with Crossroads and his practice as a veterinarian in the town of Sosua. He continues this work even today, always working to improve the lives of the Haitians and Dominicans that they oversee. His veterinary practice has become one of the most respected in the entire country and is continuing to thrive, allowing him, Jana, and Marcus to financially support Crossroads when the donations of volunteer groups fall short. He still looks like Santa.

Marcus and Jared drove the Diahatsu through Port-au-Prince on that day through rioting and clogged streets and continued until they returned to Santo Domingo. Jared took a flight back to St. Thomas, where he still lives to this day. He works as a dive instructor on the southeast part of the island, and can easily be recognized by his huge smile, jolly personality, and kind heart.

Marcus continued the trip back to Puerto Plata, bringing our courageous driver and his trusty steed back home after a long and trying trek. He lives at the Crossroads facility and acts as the program manager and coordinator for all incoming volunteer groups. On weekends you may find him in Sosua at the local Irish bar watching a football or basketball game when he isn't busy with the mission outreach programs that run almost every day.

Eventually Faith and Luke decided to split paths, Faith pursuing a medical career that kept her in Bonaire and Luke looking for more opportunities to volunteer both abroad and domestically. He is working on a Masters in Public Health and will eventually return to Haiti for a much longer period to continue to work with the mission teams.

Dean went back with Cameron and Cindy to Haiti eight months after the quake and was surprised to see how little changed since our original trip. He continues to study for medical school on his journey to becoming a doctor and still returns to Crossroads when he can to help those in the villages.

Megan eventually decided to move to the Dominican Republic to work as a missionary full time. She volunteers fulltime in Ascension Village where she works to keep children in school, processes documentation for incoming Haitians, and creates programs to help families become self sufficient through education, skills training, and job creation.

Cameron is working on finishing medical school. After the trip to Haiti he returned a couple times each year with new teams that he put together. He officially started a non-profit that brings medical professionals to Crossroads and is planning to return to Haiti for another trip soon.

Cindy continues to work as a labor and delivery nurse in California. She has given several presentations to help raise awareness about Haiti and to raise money for trips related to Cameron's mission groups. She continues to visit Crossroads when her schedule allows it. She says that the experience permanently changed her, and that she spends every day thankful.

Faith eventually finished medical school in Bonaire and moved to the United States to finish her residency. She married Nick, a great man she met while traveling in Scotland, and they live happily together with their two dogs, Ginger and Nutmeg. Nick is an excellent chef, and Faith plans to finish her education in the near future to become a doctor.

Jana returned to Crossroads after the ordeal in Haiti and continues to run Crossroads with Bob and Marcus. They have expanded the reach of the mission both geographically and functionally, now moving farther out in the region to assist poor communities while always working to bring more medical professionals, construction experts, and other helpful trades to the people that need help the most.

But what about me? After returning home and going through an adjustment period, I finally decided to propose to Amber. She left for a few months to do aquatic research in Bonaire, but during her absence I planned the proposal meticulously. The day after she returned I woke her up by playing guitar, singing her a song I wrote, and finally presenting a ring as I knelt before her. The gift I gave her that day? A simple frame with the bouquet of flowers from the trip neatly pressed below the glass. A phrase sits under the assortment of colorful petals that reads "Home is where the heart is." She may never again get to see the place where she was born, but I hoped that bringing a part of her past with us into the future may be a start.

We got married in late 2010 and have continued to build a life together. We visit Crossroads on holidays, with Christmas being my favorite time of year. The Amelingmeier family doesn't give each other presents; instead they make huge gift baskets and give them out to many of the children in local villages. The first time I experienced the "present-less" day I felt a bit disappointed, but after all I went through in Haiti and my continued understanding and appreciation for their missionary way of life, I am starting to love the idea. I must admit I still prefer to get a present or two on Christmas, but I have loved even more the continued joy from bringing happiness to others. It continues to amaze me how much delight a bag of rice, or a stick of butter can bring to an entire family. Those reminders make my life, my fortune, and my path seem easy, and almost effortless in comparison.

Made in the USA
Charleston, SC
06 October 2013